The true story of a dancer from the movie PORKY'S

MOTOR CITY GIRL

How she overcame the world

LitPrime Solutions
21250 Hawthorne Blvd
Suite 500, Torrance, CA 90503
www.litprime.com
Phone: 1 (209) 788-3500

© 2020 Crystal Gellata. All rights reserved.

No part of this book may be reproduced, stored in a retrieval system, or transmitted by any means without the written permission of the author.

Published by LitPrime Solutions   11/17/2020

ISBN: 978-1-953397-35-5(sc)
ISBN: 978-1-953397-36-2(e)

Any people depicted in stock imagery provided by Thinkstock are models, and such images are being used for illustrative purposes only.

Certain stock imagery © Thinkstock.

Because of the dynamic nature of the Internet, any web addresses or links contained in this book may have changed since publication and may no longer be valid. The views expressed in this work are solely those of the author and do not necessarily reflect the views of the publisher, and the publisher hereby disclaims any responsibility for them.

*Dedicated
To my children*

TABLE OF CONTENTS

Chapter 1. Indian Mother and Suzie as a Young Child 1
Chapter 2. Youth from age 9 to 16 and modeling school 16
Chapter 3. Suzie at the age of 16 to 17, Her Assault and Boyfriend Barry 38
Chapter 4. Her First husband, Barry, and Her Girls Wendy and Stacy 53
Chapter 5. Sue Dancing in Detroit and Mike When He was Her Boyfriend 73
Chapter 6. Second Husband Mike, Son Dana 89
Chapter 7. Third Husband Steve 114
Chapter 8. Friend Guy, Grant, and Florida, Granddaughter Mandy 133
Chapter 9. Name Change to Crystal and husband 4 Mike the Devil 158
Chapter 10. Husband #5 Dave, Alaska, and Tragedy with Dana . . 165
Chapter 11. Husband #6 Butch and Family, Grandson Davey . . 181
Chapter 12. Terry #7, Sailboat, Jamaica 207
Chapter 13. Don the 8th husband and Indian Wedding and Indian Dancing 226
Chapter 14. The enlightening of Dons infidelity and 9th marriage with Terry And her new life as a Jehovahs Witness 231
Chapter 15. More tragedy for Crystal and Terry 245
Chapter 16. The meeting of her half-sister Linda and the passing of her dog 248

ABOUT THE BOOK

Book inspired by Wayne Dyer's writings.

This book is about Crystal's life. She feels her life is unbelievable. To this day, people do not believe her when she tells them about things that have happened to her. You name it; it has happened to her. She has had nine marriages in her life. All of them were monsters, except for the last one. All eight husbands beat her, sexually abused her, or abused her children. All of the men were either alcoholics or drug addicts. Also, Crystal tried a lot of different religions. She was also a go-go dancer and quit when she was fifty years young. Crystal was working in the bars, and she got mixed up with the mafia and many bad men. There are things in her book that she has never even revealed to her best friends. Also, Crystal found God and changed her life, but now it is time for the world to know the life story and how she survived it.

INTRODUCTION

A true story about a girl using her intuitive instincts to better herself and to help others: all through her life, from day one, her life has been an evil, vicious, sexual energy. And also the story of how she turned a negative experience into positive spiritual growth. Her Apache Indian mother, Tina, came from Chino Valley, Arizona, which is where she was born and then moved to Michigan. Michigan is where this Apache woman gave birth to a little Apache Indian princess Crystal. The Apache woman needed a name for the princess, so she decided to name her Crystal Ann. This woman, for some evil, selfish reason, did not want little Crystal; she tried everything in her power to get rid of her. But it didn't work, so she gave her away.

Time went on and one day, two charming German people came to the orphanage where they say little Crystal dying. They were looking for a little girl to adopt. The nuns have shown a lot of little girls, but they weren't satisfied. However, when they spotted Crystal, they knew right away that they wanted her. The nuns at the orphanage told them that they should pick out another baby because Crystal was too sickly and not expected to survive. The German people said the nuns didn't care and that with enough love, she would heal. When the German people first got Crystal, they didn't like her name, so they decided to change it to Sue Ann. The German people, at least, kept her second name, which was Ann.

The German people loved little Suzie, which was her nickname, and they spoiled her royally. They bought her everything they could, but there was always something missing; true maternal love. The German people thought they could buy love, but it didn't work. All of Suzie's life, she craved love, and she looked for it in all the wrong places. When Suzie was seventeen, she started her own family. She was fortunate to have three adorable children, and two of them were from a different marriage. Sue (Crystal) ended up being married nine other times in her life. She hoped number eight would be her knight in shining armor, but eight did not work either.

After Crystal's first marriage was over, she became a topless dancer. Later, one of her daughters followed in her footsteps. Also, her son was a dancer for a short time. There were times when Crystal and her daughter were dancing in the same clubs together. One of the clubs was in Florida. At this time in her life, Crystal was a very talented woman and could have gone far if it weren't for her wrong choices when it came to the men in her life. Crystal was still dancing at the age of fifty. She was very proficient in all of the arts; she even had the opportunity to sing with a famous opera singer, and she sang in the Palm Beach Civic Opera, and also, she was in the movie PORKY'S.

Crystal did not know anything about her biological background and wanted to know where she came from, so she started investigating. One day Crystal went to a psychic fortuneteller, and She told her things about her past and other things about the present. All of the pieces started fitting together now. The physic told Crystal stuff about her history that no one ever knew; something that Crystal would never reveal to anyone until now. The psychic told her that she felt uneasy with her sitting there. Crystal wondered why the physic would think like that, so she asked her why. The supernatural proceeded to tell her she felt Crystal was a witch, and she felt uneasy being with her. Crystal told the physic that she thought she was different but didn't understand what it was. The psychic told Crystal that she would meet her birth mother one day and also said she had a half-sister somewhere. A lot of what the psychic told Crystal came true. She did meet her biological relatives; all of this was very strange because her sister had just met her biological mother five years before Crystal. Another unusual thing was that her sister's name was the same name that Crystal had at birth; Crystal Ann was also. That was a strange thing for her mother to do.

After both of her adopted parents passed away, Crystal decided to look for her biological relatives. At the time, she felt terrible luck for the name of a ship to be changed, so it must be the same for a person. Therefore Crystal had her name legally turned back to Crystal from Sue. What clinched the idea of the name change was when she met a man with the last name of Rivers. She thought it would be unique to have the name of "Crystal Rivers," so, later on, this became her stage name. The marriage to this man was one of the worst mistakes of Crystal's life. This man turned out to be the devil himself. This marriage only lasted a total of six months. Thank God for that.

Crystal's life was terrible from day one. It started with her mother not wanting her, a car accident, many surgeries, assaults, beatings, drugs, and even death threats from getting mixed up with the mafia. Though she had so much evil, pain, and suffering in her life, she keeps plugging along. The thing that pulled her out of her depression at that time was her dancing. She remembered the psychic and what she said about her being a witch, so she thought she would try it out.

When Crystal visited her sister for the first time, she found out that her sister was very jealous of her and didn't like that they both had the same name. So Crystal, the sweet person she was, told her sister that it would be all right for her to call her Crisy. So Crystal went by the name of Crisy when she was with her sister. When they got together, Crystal told Crisy all sorts of things about her life. She said that she was only one year older than Crisy, but Crisy did not believe everything her sister told her. Crystal was very jealous of Crisy, but Crisy tried to overlook it. Also, at that time, Crystal stated to Crisy that they had Native American blood from the Apache tribe. Crisy had always thought she had Indian blood. In the future, Crisy became very involved with the Native American culture and changed her dance to Indian powwow dancing.

At the time, there were many mysteries about her past that were unresolved, but she never gave up searching and was determined to solve them one day. The whole story of Crystal and Crisy's history was ironic. Even though someone raised the girls in two separate worlds, their lives were similar; the two sisters lived the same evil, sexual experiences. Crystal and Crisy were both raised by adopted parents. Both girls were in white uniforms; Crystal was a lab technician, and Crisy became a certified nursing assistant, phlebotomist, and Emergency Medical Technician. Both of the girls were dancers; Crystal was a stripper, and Crisy was a go-go dancer. Both of them were involved with the mafia and had lived violent lives. When Crystal was 77 years young, she found out she had another sister, her name was Linda, and she lived in Texas. Also, she found out she has two brothers; she never could find them.

Now we are talking about Crystal (Crisy), the youngest daughter of the Apache woman. As time went on, this Crystal was still having bad luck and didn't know what to do. She was distraught when her son Dana got taken away, and one of her husbands, Dave, got put in prison. Here they were doing so well. They had just moved to Alaska to start a new life and were fine until all hell broke loose. At that time, Crystal just wanted to end it all. She knew she had to change her life and that no one could do it for her; mostly, she had to hang in there for her children's sake. It was still a hard life with numerous ups and downs, but she worked hard to change it.

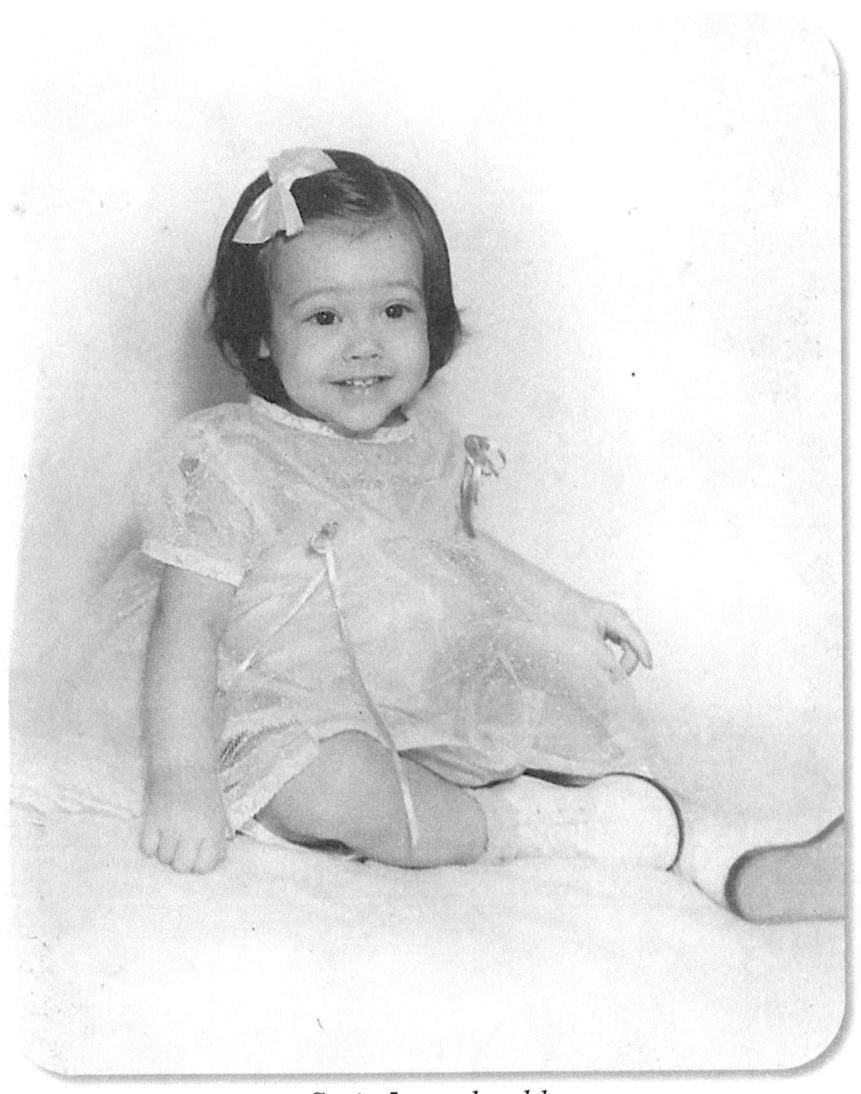

Suzie 5 months old

CHAPTER 1

INDIAN MOTHER AND SUZIE AS A YOUNG CHILD

"Back many, many moons ago;" there was an Indian maiden whose mother had her out of wedlock. It started a chain reaction of unwed mothers in this family. Back in those days, it was taboo for a maiden to have a baby out of wedlock. The maiden Tina became pregnant by a Chiricahua Apache Indian Chief, who lived in Chino Valley, Arizona. At the time of conception, the Chief was drunk and assaulted the young maiden. Luckily for the infant in that error, abortions were not around at that time, and the maiden gave birth to a lovely little Indian girl. Unfortunately, since her bloodline was from an alcoholic father, the child acquired the alcoholic genes from her father. In the future, the gene would probably be passed down/ to other children in the family.

After the girl was born, she was such a tiny baby that her mother gave her the name of Tina. Tina grew up to have a bad life, living as an alcoholic, just like her father. When she was sixteen, her mother moved from Arizona to Michigan, where she started living her evil life. Tina hated Michigan and did not want to live there.

When Tina was sixteen, she was already carousing around. One day Tina was drunk, acting crazy, and decided to hitchhike back to

Arizona. On her way back to Arizona, a truck driver picked her up. Of course, this truck driver liked the little Indian girl and wanted to have sex with her. This truck driver was a redheaded Irishman, and there was such a difference between them that this turned Tina on even more. She was, turned on that she just could not say no, and they had sex in the truck. Tina ended up back in Arizona living with her grandmother, but not for long. A few months went by, and Tina's mother found out she was pregnant by a trucker.

Tina's mother was furious about this pregnancy and went to Arizona to get Tina and made her return to Michigan. Tina's mother was so mad at her because of this pregnancy that she set up a marriage for her with a man that was twenty years older than Tina. Since this man was an older man to her, Tina ended up hating him and her mother for forcing this marriage upon her. Seeing that she hated the man so much, all she wanted to do was drink, run around on this man.

This man Tina had to marry was a tall, dark, handsome Italian man who had his own business, a trucking company. But Tina didn't care. She still hated him because he seemed like an older man to her. Tina's mother set up a lovely little wedding for Tina and her man, but Tina still didn't like it. Since Tina hated her new husband so much, she would never have sex with him, which made him very angry. He knew she hated him, so he would force her to have sex; this way, he could at least get his satisfaction, but she ended up pregnant again. The problem with this pregnancy as she was running around, there was no telling who the father was. Luckily for this infant also, there were no abortions allowed at that time either. So, Tina gave birth to a child with the alcoholic genes; she had a daughter with light-colored hair and skin. Tina still hated the man she was married to and went whoring around even more. By this time, she was about twenty years old and hadn't grown up yet; she was a partyer from the word go.

At this time, Tina got into prostitution with people who were involved with the mafia. Because of this, she was scared of everything and everyone. She certainly did not want another child to cramp her lifestyle and did not want her husband to find out about another pregnancy. So, she gave her first daughter away and tried to abort the second one. With the first child, Tina wanted to abort it, but it didn't work. However, with the second one, she went overboard, trying to terminate the pregnancy. Tina took pills, but that didn't work; next, she tried sticking things up herself; because of this, it damaged the child's head. Even though she tried all of these things, the baby was born anyhow. This one was a girl also, with black hair and olive complexion, and she gave it up for adoption. Tina was turning out to be a devil instead of a sweet little Indian girl. She had stuck things up herself, taken pills, and tried everything imaginable to abort the second child, but nothing worked. Tina will have bad karma to pay for now. When she was about six months pregnant, she ended up in the emergency room giving birth to a five-pound baby girl whose head was severely damaged; the baby turned out to be very weak and sickly. The baby's hed ended up being critically injured and had to have surgery.

The ironic thing about this birth was the name she gave the baby. The name Tina had picked out for the first child she gave to the second child also. Tina figured the second child would not live, so it didn't matter to her what the baby's name was. When the woman gave birth to her first daughter, she called her Crystal Ann and gave her the last name of the Italian man she was married too. Now, she gave birth again, thinking that this child would never survive. But the baby did survive. So, Tina gave her the same name as Crystal Ann and the same last name the Italian man had. Even to this day, the two girls do not know their biological fathers. This evil woman was so awful she tried to slit her wrists because she hated her life so much. Crystal was so afraid that her husband would find her. Even though she slitting her wrists, it didn't work; she had to live on to pay for the awful sins in her life. She hated herself and everyone else in her world, or she would not have tried to end her own life.

After she tried to slit her wrists but was unsuccessful, she ran away again. This time she gave her first daughter to a woman at a boarding house and left the second girl dead in the hospital. Then, thinking her troubles were over, she left town. Since Tina did not have any kids around now, she could quit her husband. Later the Italian man found out about the woman leaving him. He was furious and started looking for them. He put an advertisement in the newspaper trying to find them, without any luck at first. One day, a woman called him and told him that the evil woman left the first Crystal at a boarding house. The woman at the boarding house told Tina's husband that she had another child and left it for dead in the hospital. The Italian man was shocked to find this out. By that time, he had no idea of whether the second Crystal was alive; also, he did not know where Tina was hiding.

The Italian man was delighted to hear about the first Crystal and immediately went to get her. The first Crystal was very fortunate she was found, and the Italian man raised and spoiled her all of her young life. As time went on, the man never found the second Crystal or Tina, but he did hear about Tina turning to prostitution and being an alcoholic. Then the women told him that prostitution was an inherited trait; he hoped the girls would never acquire that trait from their mother. There was a new trait for the two girls; there was the possibility of inheriting the prostitution gene, alcoholism, or maybe both. Even though they lived in separate environments, their lives turned out to be very similar.

The Italian man hated Tina for all of the evil things she had done and would have killed her if he had ever found her. This man had a lot of money and influence and could have done it if he had wanted to. The Italian man raised the first Crystal and bought her everything imaginable, but maternal love was always missing. Crystal grew up to have a chip on her shoulder and never really appreciated what she had. She grew up to be a hard-core, self-centered person. There was a big difference between the two girls; the first Crystal always wanted revenge for what her mother had done to her, and the second Crystal was more cheerful and forgiving.

Later in life, Crystal's Italian stepfather told her that she had a half-sister somewhere with the same name as herself. Immediately she was jealous. The first, Crystal, was jealous because she did not like the idea that they both had the same name.

However, the second Crystal had an altogether different personality and outlook on life. It seemed like the second girl Crystal had more love in her heart, possibly like her unknown father, but so unlike her mother. The first Crystal was more like her mother, Tina, with her hard cold heart.

The second Crystal was more like an Indian princess than her mother or sister ever could have been. This girl was sweet, tiny, dark olive complexion, big dark green eyes, and shiny straight black hair. Crystal had a bad start in life, from day one, her mother trying to abort her and leaving her for dead in the hospital orphanage. She was in the hospital orphanage for six sickly months. Because her mother stuck things up herself and pore, little Crystal's head was so severely damaged when she was born that they had to shave her dark black hair off to do surgery on her head.

Crystal was all alone in a cruel, wicked world, and the only thing her mother ever gave her was a hand-me-down name and a beaded baby bracelet with her mother's name on it. The bracelet was from the hospital anyhow; her mother did not give it to Crystal. The bracelet was pink with black letters on the beads. It wasn't much, but it was all she got from her mother. Several things she did inherit was a lot of talent, courage, and strength to survive, most likely inherited from her father. Crystal's mother was selfish, a weakling, and always tried to take the easy way out. One other thing Crystal did get from her grandfather was her Indian beauty. The Indian genes came through for little Crystal with her Indian features.

One lovely summer day, the little Indian princess had a change of luck. It seemed God was saving her for something special in life. Two German people came to the orphanage looking for a little daughter to adopt. The German people were a lovely couple from Nebraska that moved to Michigan and opened up a dry-cleaning establishment. The German people were well-liked by many people and could easily afford to adopt a little child. The names of the German people were

Hanes and Babe. Hanes and Babe were their nicknames. They were old enough to be Crystal's grandparents, but that was no problem for them. In that era, there was a depression going on, and World War II had just ended. Hanes and Babe were in their fifties at the time and did not have any children of their own. The reason Babe did not have any children of her own was that when she was a young girl, she got pregnant. She had a quack doctor botched up the abortion, and she could never conceive after that.

Hanes and Babe ran a very successful business and could afford to live in a nice neighborhood. They had a cute little white house with a white picket fence around it. The house was a small dream house in St. Clair Shores, Michigan, where the German people wanted to live with their minor child. So they started looking for a child. One day, Hans and Babe went to the Catholic Social Service at the Providence Hospital in Detroit, hunting for a baby. When they arrived at the orphanage department of the hospital, the nuns were happy to have them because there were so many orphans at the time. The nun, Sister Ann, took them around to see all of the infants, and there were all kinds of infants for them to choose.

It was the year 1942, and there were plenty of war babies, so it seemed to be an easy way to find the perfect child for them. As they were looking, they spotted a baby girl that did not look good at all. She had been struggling along for six months now and still only weighed about 10 pounds. She was thin, weak, had a peaked color, and they had shaved her hair off also. Hanes and Babe were very curious about the reason why the baby's condition was so wrong. As the nun proceeded to tell them all about the tragedy of the baby's birth, the nun added, "You better not pick her because they don't think she will live." The German people didn't want to hear any more about it. They had already made up their minds. They told the nun, "Little Princess is the one that we want." The German people said the nun, "With a little love, she will survive." The nuns did not argue with them but decided it would be a good thing for the baby and these lovely people.

SECRETS ARE OUT NOW

One request the German people had as they were filling out the adoption papers; it was to change the baby's name from Crystal Ann to Sue Ann. They didn't like the name of Crystal because of the evil woman that gave it to her. They kept her second name of Ann mostly. After all, it was the nun's name that helped them find the little princess, and the name Ann because it would be her saint name for her christening, also.

Well, it was time to take Suzie home. Suzie was the nickname they decided to call Sue Ann. As they went home, they were very proud and happy. When Suzie arrived home, there were all sorts of surprises waiting for her. Hanes and Babe had bought every toy imaginable for Suzie. She even had her very one dog named Brownie. The main reason Hanes and Babe bought Brownie was that his birthday was on the same day as Suzie's, June 23, 1942. Suzie and Brownie became the best of friends. When Suzie would eat ice cream, she would share it with Brownie; she would take a lick, and then Brownie would make a lick. Brownie became the only living thing that Suzie could relate to at that time. Being the only child and not having many friends or any siblings made it lonely for Suzie. It seemed like later in her childhood, all of her friends were so jealous of her. Suzie didn't have many friends and was the cause of loneliness for her as a child. So Suzie's closeness to Brownie helped her.

Suzie was very fortunate at the time because she had all the material things a child could ever want. But, there was still something missing in her life, parental love. Another reason Suzie was fortunate was that she was a brilliant child. When Suzie got older, she could remember things from her infancy, like being in the baby buggy, crib, and playpen. She must have had some kind of intuitive powers at an early age, but she was unaware of it at the time.

It's a rare thing for an infant to have such a vivid memory early in life, but she had control over people already. Suzie could manipulate people, and she didn't even realize it until she was much older and could look back at her life. She had a very creative mind as a child also. When Suzie would play as a child, she would dress up the kittens like her babies, and she would be their mom. Suzie did not realize what she could do until later in life, when she had discovered it. She was very intuitive at an early age.

Suzie's parents loved her so much that they had special dresses made just for her. The dresses even had little bonnets to match. The colors of the dresses were pretty pink or sky blue and with plenty of lace. Suzie's favorite outfit was her red velvet one with her black patent leather shoes to go with it. The cloth looked beautiful with her ebony hair and olive skin.

At the time, it was hard to get metal because WWII had just ended, but Suzie's father found a tricycle for her. He also purchased a metal swing set and a scooter for her. Since Suzie was so lonely, she loved her toys. One toy in particular that she cherished; it was her real lamb's wool stuffed teddy bear. Suzie used to take her bear everywhere with her. Suzie started relating to her teddy bear. She even had the fantasy that the bear was her boyfriend when she got older. Also though she had no idea what a boyfriend was at that time. Suzie's loneliness put her in her fantasy world. Because of her closeness to the teddy bear, Brownie, her dog, was jealous and decided to tear up Suzie's bear, and so he did. Her teddy was all gone now. Suzie became broken-hearted because of her bear. All through her life, it seemed like the things that she held dear to her were always destroyed.

Now that her bear was gone, Suzie was lonelier than ever. Her parents loved her, but there was always something missing; physical affection and maternal love. The only way her parents knew how to love her was to give her material things. As a child growing up, she could never remember her parents ever hugging or kissing each other, and they never hugged or kissed Suzie, either. It was like they didn't know how to show affection.

When Suzie was in her fantasy world, she could remember listening to the radio. As she stared up at the big brown radio listening to stories, she would fantasize. Some of the stories were Fiber Magee and Molly, The Squeaking Door, and Let's Pretend. They were her favorites. These stories were her way of escaping her lonely world. When she grew up, she felt life has made things too easy for people. These days, people have forgotten how to dream and enjoy the simple things in life. Things like listening to birds, or the smell of newly cut grass, looking up at the clouds in the sky, and imagining they are different animals. Also, listening to the crickets chirp on a warm summer's night. Suzie used to do all of this and didn't want ever to lose it.

Growing up alone was hard for Suzie. Some children can handle it, but she was too sensitive, and she grew up a very lonely child. When Suzie was about four, she had a girlfriend move into the neighborhood, but it didn't turn out too well. The girl that moved in next door was a little redhead from Tennessee. This girl had a brother that was about thirteen, and he was a very mature boy for his age. Suzie's new friend grew up jealous of Suzie because this girl was not as fortunate as Suzie. Suzie was so pretty, well-liked, and had every toy in the world. Everyone was jealous of her, mostly her new little redheaded friend next door. The petite redhead girl was so insecure she would try to get Suzie in trouble all the time.

One day on Suzie's seventh birthday, she was anxiously waiting for her father to come home from work. As Suzie peaked through the white picket fence with Brownie, her dad finally came home. Suzie was so excited because she wondered what her dad was going to bring home for her birthday. Here on the top of his car was a brand new powder blue Schwinn bike with chrome fenders, a bell, and a horn on it. Suzie was so happy now. IT was her first two-wheel bike. Although, there was one bad part about her getting a two-wheeler; her friend was looking out the window, jealously waiting. Her so-called friend was so jealous she didn't come to the party or talk to Suzie for about six months. At the time, Suzie didn't care. She was too excited about her bike. She just loved the blue color of her bike because blue was her favorite color. Suzie had never ridden a two-wheeled bike before and was scared to get on it. So, good old Dad came to the rescue. He told her to get up on the seat and put her feet on the pedals, and he would push her around. He pushed her and forced her around for weeks, trying to get her to learn, but it didn't work. Suzie was so scared she was going to fall. She was too dependent on her dad and didn't have enough confidence in herself to try.

One day, her girlfriend's mother came over to try to help Suzie ride her bike. The lady gave her one push and let her go, and sure enough, off Suzie went. She could ride her bike now. Suzie's girlfriend was jealous now, so bad that she didn't talk to her for another month. Suzie loved her bike. She loved it so much she felt like it was a friend. One day Suzie rode it to school; it was a very cold and frosty day. She felt terrible to leave her bike all alone on the bike stand while Suzie was in school; she was going to miss her bike so much that she kissed it, and guess what? Suzie's lips got stuck on the handlebars because it was such a cold day. Finally, her warm lips melted the frost, and she was free.

It wasn't hilarious at the time, but later in life, when she would think about it, she would laugh. Suzie had to wait until her lips warmed up the handlebars so that she could escape the clenches of the frost. As she was expecting, she finally got free. She was so scared at first; she thought she would be stuck on the bars there forever. Suzie never had a hard time riding her bike to school by herself because of her mother having a traffic light put up at the intersection so that Suzie could cross it. Her mother was a good mom and was always concerned about Suzie's wellbeing. Her mother had to get up a petition signed to have the light put up at the intersection where the kids had to cross the street. Her mother went around for weeks getting people to sign the petition.

Suzie was an excellent student in school. She could have gone far, but when she was in the first grade, she had every childhood disease imaginable. She got whooping cough, mumps, measles, chicken pox, and even rheumatic fever, making her heart weak later in life. Suzie's parents should have held her back in the first grade, but they believed she could make it. For Suzie to continue was detrimental because she missed almost the entire first grade, and she could never make it up. All these diseases was a horrible start for her; she missed all of her necessary skills. Suzie even began to hate school because she was behind and was struggling. She was so embarrassed when she couldn't read out loud in the second grade.

As time went on, things got worse. Suzie hated the thought of school so much that she would get sick on the school bus and throw up. The only peace of mind she got was to gaze out the window at school and get into her fantasy world. At Suzie's young age, she would fantasize about boys, which gave her a lot of relief. She would love the attention that the boys gave her and would think about them. She would dream about having her perfect husband and family someday. Now Suzie was about nine, and her dream world had become more than just fantasy since she had two working parents. Having a lot of babysitters, she lacked the attention and affection from her parents. Suzie liked the attention from the boys since her parents were too busy for her because of their work. In the fourth grade, she loved a little redhead boy that sat next to her. It seemed like she had a thing for redheads. Suzie even had a little boyfriend that lived across the street. Later on, the little boy moved away, and she forgot all about him.

Our little Indian prince was a compassionate and honest girl also. One day, her girlfriend next door wanted her to go to the corner store with her, which she did. Her friend told Suzie she was going to teach her how to steal candy. Suzie went along with her friend's idea because she did not want her friend to quit talking to her for another month. The little redhead proceeded to take the candy. She said, "Come on now; try it; it's fun." So Suzie did it and was scared, but she went along with her friend, stole a pack of gum, and ran out of the store. Luckily for them, the store owner didn't see them, and they both got away with it.

One day passed by, and Suzie's conscience was too much for her. She went back to the store and gave the grocer ten cents; the grocer didn't say anything; maybe they didn't get away with it. The grocer must have known what was going on and didn't say a word. Suzie was ten cents poorer, but she felt more at ease by knowing she made the right decision. Suzie told herself she would never do anything like that again. And she never did. As if shoplifting wasn't enough, her girlfriend wanted to get her into more trouble. She wanted her to start doing nasty things now. Suzie's friend was still so jealous of Suzie and liked to get her into trouble.

One day, her friend asked her to come over and play with her in her brother's tent. Suzie thought this would be all right and a lot of fun. Little did she know what was happening; Suzie was about twelve at the time. The little redhead's brother was about seventeen by then and very tall, skinny, and ugly, with big zits all over his face. Then Suzie proceeded to go into the tent. Her girlfriend was supposed to go in with her, but she stayed behind and let Suzie go in first. She had no idea what was going on. As Suzie walked into the tent, it was dark and scary. The tent was green, had a musty odor, and was cold inside. She will never forget that feeling. As soon as she got into the tent, she was scared; mostly, she was scared after the boy pulled the canopy down. It was dark now. Then, her girlfriend's brother told his sister to leave for a while, and he would call her in after he talked to Suzie.

Here Suzie was all alone in the tent with the big, ugly boy, inside and out. She was growing more anxious since she was all alone with him. Suzie was a very innocent girl. She liked boys, but at that time, she had no idea what boys had on their minds. The lesson that she learned that day was the turning point in her life. As they were in the dark tent, the boy instantly starting grabbing Suzie's crotch and told her he wanted to touch her. She was scared to death now; she didn't know what to do. The boy was grabbing at her, and the boy felt Suzie's body all over. Instantly she knew it was terrible and ran out of the tent. She ran as fast as her little feet could carry her.

After that day, Suzie felt so ashamed. She carried guilt around with her for years, even though it was not her fault. She didn't go back over to her girlfriend's house for a long time. But that did not stop her friend from coming over to Suzie's. At this time, she was only about ten years old and carried her secret around for many years; she never could tell her mom. Then Suzie's friend started coming over to her house even though Suzie didn't want to go over to hers. She was glad to see her friend come over again, anyhow. She missed her. Here was Suzie's friend, coming over to try to get her into more trouble still. Suzie thought for a while, there were no boys around, so what could it hurt? She missed her friend when she would get mad at her and would not come over. So, Suzie decided to go along with her, mostly because of the attention she received from her friend.

As the weeks went on, her friend told Suzie, Let's play in the sandbox. Her friend never let Suzie do anything she wanted to do. It seemed like Suzie's friend had her under her control. Then her friend said, "Let's pee in the box; the cats do it." So Suzie did it because she did not want her friend to stop coming over again. Suzie was a little hesitant to do this, but she did. Weeks went by, and she was getting away with controlling Suzie even more. Suzie's mom thought they were doing bad things and would say, "I knew you nasty girls were up to no good; "Shame on you girls!" Suzie could remember her mom shaking her finger at her, shaming her, and calling her dirty and nasty. She felt awful that her mom blamed the whole thing on her. Here was another sinful thing for Suzie to lock up in her soul. She hated it when her mother shook her finger at her and called her nasty and dirty. Mostly because Suzie did not do anything wrong, but she thought she had. Her friend got her into trouble again.

It was a while before Suzie's friend came over, but she did show up again. Suzie was so sad when she didn't come around, but so glad when she did. Her friend still loved to get Suzie in trouble and kept on doing it. Her friend wanted them to do bad things again, so Suzie went along with her and did. Suzie's friend was always getting her into trouble and getting her mom mad at her. They were tearing up papers and trying to make airplanes one day. They made a mess in the house. Suzie's mom was very mad at her after this.

One day Suzie's friend wanted them to play doctor, and of cores, Suzie was the patient, and her friend was the doctor. Then her friend told her she was giving her an enema, and she would put tinker toys up Suzie's behind. Her friend's brother must have been doing these things to Suzie's friend, and that is where she got the ideas. So Suzie did what her friend wanted. Later Suzie felt awful about this one. That was the start of Suzie's warped mind, thinking that this is the way little girls are supposed to play. Luckily for Suzie, her mom did not see them. Since her mom was always across the street at a friend's house, they never got caught at their little doctor's session. Sexual activities were an awful thing at such an early age for Suzie. Throughout Suzie's life, subjected to many sexual acts, and it got worse a she got older.

Time was moving along, and Suzie had put more secrets in the back of her mind. After a while, Suzie's friend stopped coming over because her friend found another new girl in the neighborhood to explore. Suzie missed her friend, but after a while, she got over it. Despite all the trouble, the two girls got into when they were young, the little redheaded girl grew into a beautiful woman. She got married and had the same man all of her life; she and her husband had children, grandchildren, and she is very dear still to Suzie to this day. However, when they were young, they were in trouble together on more than one occasion.

At least Suzie had some good memories of her childhood. She had many talents. She was born to be a star. Suzie's parents took her for dancing lessons; she took tap, ballet, and Hawaiian dance lessons. The dancing was great for her, and she was in many dance recitals. These lessons helped her to acquire a lot of poise. At the time, she had no idea that she would go into the dancing field in her future. Fortunately, her dancing lessons were the start of her dancing career.

Suzie at 14

CHAPTER 2

YOUTH FROM AGE 9 TO 16 AND MODELING SCHOOL

When Suzie was about nine years old, her parents decided to move to another town closer to her father's dry cleaning business. It was good because it got her away from her friend next door. But this was just the beginning of her bad experiences. Their new house was a large brick house with a big red barn behind it, and it was on an acre of land; it was very nice. Also, there were all sorts of fruit trees like apples, pears, peaches, plums, and much more. The big red barn even came with chickens, roosters, cats, and room for a horse someday. And, there was an excellent spot for Brownie.

Suzie loved the chickens but hated the roosters because they were mean. They would scare her and chase her up the trees, trying to spur her; the roosters had long spurs on their legs. Suzie was so scared of them, so her dad got rid of the mean old roosters and just kept the hens. The hens were nice because they always had plenty of fresh eggs from them. Other than the roosters, she was having a swell time. This move was great for Suzie; she even met a new girlfriend named Diane, who lived across the street. At least this one was not nasty to Suzie like her redheaded friend. Suzie and her new friend were having lots of clean fun. They would climb up the trees, pretending to be cowgirls and Indians, and they would go through apples at each other. Of course, Suzie was the Indian, and her friend was the cowgirl. Her Indian background was coming out again. Suzie was a bit of a tomboy in her early years, but that didn't stop her from growing into a beautiful young lady.

Sometimes the girls would dress up and pretend they were married. They would dress up the cats and place them in their buggies; they were their babies. They would put sheets between the trees and act like they were buildings and taking their babies to the store. One of the sheet houses was their home, where they would cook for their imaginary husbands. It was a beautiful fantasy world for the girls. When they pretended to play house, they would take flour and eggs and pretend they were making a cake for their husbands. There was only one problem; the eggs would get rotten and start stinking up their fantasy house. Luckily, they had a lot of eggs from the chickens that they could waste. The farm atmosphere was a wonderful time for the girls to be living in. Another good thing about her new friend Diane was that she was a good girl. Suzie was able to put her sexual minded friend in the back of her mind, at least for now.

Suzie's father was always giving her surprises. One day, in particular, he came home from work and told her they were going to a riding stable. What was dad up to now? Suzie was so excited she could hardly wait. Her dad told Suzie that she was going to be able to ride a real live horse. Also, he had another surprise for her. Little did she know it, but her dad was going to buy one of the horses. It would be a horse, all of her very own. When Suzie arrived at the stable, she saw so many beautiful horses. Her Indian background started up now. As they were walking through the big barn, her dad asked her, "Would you like to have that big palomino in the pen over there?" Suzie replied, "Of course, dad, I would love it." Suzie was very excited now. So off they went home with the big Palamino.

When they got him home, Suzie could not ride the big Palamino. This horse was too energetic for her to ride. This horse was so crazy that it tried to go out in the street with Suzie on it. She could not control the horse. Suzie's father could not let his little girl get hurt, so he took the horseback to the stable. Suzie's dad still wanted her to have a horse, so he found her a little Welsh pony. She was disappointed about the palomino, but her new horse was sweet, just like Suzie. And guess what the horse's name was? Yep, it was Suzie. Suzie fell in love instantly. Hear little Suzie horse, which was white with cute little freckles all over it. She did not have any trouble riding this one at all.

Also, Suzie had another new friend, her dad had a co-worker with a little girl, and her name was Bonnie. For several years, Suzie and Bonnie were the best of friends. The girls would play dress-up cowboy and Indians and always had a good time together. Bonnie's dad bought a horse and would ride it with Suzie's Dad. She would come over to Bonnie's and put her on the back of her horse, and they would ride all over town. Bonnie wasn't as fortunate as Suzie, so that Suzie would take her everywhere with her. They went to carnivals, movies, roller-skating, and they even got to ride on the floats in parades. Also, they went on her dad's boat. It was terrific for them. Suzie even took Bonnie to Nebraska with her one summer; this was where Suzie's grandmother lived.

When Suzie grew up, she would have parties in her basemen; even boys were there. They would play kissing games, and Bonnie received her first kiss at Suzie's party. When Suzie became a teenager, she lost contact with Bonnie. Suzie was hanging around an altogether different group of girls. She was living too fast when in her teens and did not have time for sweet Bonnie anymore. Suzie had a wonderful time with her horse and rode her for many years. She would ride her horse in parades and even take her to rodeos. Suzie and her horse became inseparable. As the years went on, her horse was growing old. When Suzie would ride her horse, it would stumble and fall, even with Suzie on her back. One day, her horse fell right on Suzie's leg. But, this horse loved her so much that it didn't put its weight on Suzie's leg. It was a miracle that her leg didn't get broken. It's amazing how animals know what's happening. It was like that with all of Suzie's animals. All through her life, they seemed to protect her. Suzie had a way with her animals; they loved her as much as she loved them.

Since Suzie's horse was getting too old and tired, her dad rented a big barn with lots of acreage for Suzie's horse to roam around. Suzie's dad bought her many other horses because he knew her horse Suzie would die one day. Suzie had every kind of horse imaginable; American Saddle breed, Pintos, Morgan, a black stallion, and even a jumper. You name it, Suzie had it! Her horse Suzie was the only one they kept until the day it died. Suzie was very sad for her horse, but that was life. Suzie was always losing things that were dear to her.

Suzie rode her horses in many parades and even got into a competition; she won many blue ribbons in her events. After a while, she got tired of Western riding and took up English riding. Suzie was all decked out with her English saddle and wearing her riding gear. At that time in her life, was the time she got her jet-black American saddle breed jumper. Her horse was as black as Suzie's hair. She was in heaven now. She loved to jump her horse until one day, her dad saw her jump a ditch, and he freaked out. He didn't want his little girl to get hurt, and he made her sell the black jumper. Suzie's dad was a little too protective of her. Here she was, broken-hearted again. No more horse, and this one was the horse she loved the most.

After a while, Suzie's dad bought her a Tennessee walker. Suzie was starting to love this one now. Suzie could do everything with this one. Her dad even bought her a buggy for the horse to pull. From then on, this was her favorite horse. Suzie's new horse's name was Tuck, and he was a bay color. The gate of the walker was so smooth; Suzie thought she was in a rocking chair. Later on, the walking horse became her favorite.

One day Suzie's dad bought a large riding stable a few miles from where they lived. This stable had two large long barns. It had a park for picnics with swings and slides on 60 acres of land, and even a hall that her dad rented out for parties and weddings. They made a lot of money by renting the horses and the building. They also had hayrides. They called the place "Square Acres Ranch." The ranch became a popular place in that area. When Suzie was about sixteen, she was growing fast and getting tired of the horses, so one day, her dad bought a cabin cruiser boat. Suzie's dad was afraid she would be getting tired of the horses, and he didn't want her to get interested in boys. The boat he bought was a twenty-foot Crist Craft cabin cruiser. Suzie was all excited again. This time she got something new in her spoiled, material life.

Their family would go out on the boat all the time, and the way Suzie learned how to swim was from Jeannie, the daughter of one of the men Suzie's dad worked with; she taught Suzie how to swim. To this day, Suzie still keeps in touch with this Jeannie. They would go to a place called Strawberry Island. The bottom of the water was warm and had soft white sand. They would even spend the weekend on the boat. Suzie's mom packed lunches with giant fat hamburgers with onions cooked right in them, and Suzie thought they were sure good.

Suzie's dad took a lot of people out on the boat fishing. Her dad was a well-liked person and had a lot of friends. One of his friends was one woman in particular that he took on the boat a little bit too much, Suzie thought. Suzie had a peculiar feeling about this woman. Her name was Wilma. This woman was very young and pretty, and Suzie's dad liked her a lot. This woman worked for Suzie's dad and was around him all the time. Suzie didn't like Wilma much because she would boss Suzie around and try to act like a mother to her. This woman was always telling Suzie what to do, and her dad would take sides with the woman. At that time was when Suzie rebelled against her dad.

After a while, Suzie's dad would take this woman out to the stables with him all alone. Suzie's dad forgot all about Suzie and her mother and left them behind all the time. That was the start of Suzie's ruination. Suzie did not have much supervision at this time and started doing as she pleased. Becoming a teenager was when Suzie needed guidance the most, and she didn't get it. Her mom was busy with work, and her dad was busy with his girlfriend. Suzie had

SECRETS ARE OUT NOW

some inkling about this woman but didn't realize what was going on at first. She didn't know that this was to be the downfall of her sweet life. When Suzie's father did come home, he would be drunk and beat up Suzie's mom. Suzie can remember one Christmas in particular when her father came back drunk and broke all of the things that he had bought for them. All of her toys and her mother's items that were under the Christmas tree, he had broken them all. Suzie was very sad now and confused at this time in her life. Suzie's dad was drinking and not coming home; he was always with Wilma at the ranch.

Things like this we're going on for years. It became a pattern, her dad being drunk and beating up her mother. Suzie can remember crying so hard and scared to death. Often she was hiding behind the couch, sobbing so profoundly that she could hardly get her breath. She could smell the reek of alcohol in the air; this is when she started hating the smell of alcohol. At this time in her life was the first time Suzie learned all kinds of dirty words. She could not believe her dad would say bad words. She didn't know what it meant at the time, but she knew that it was terrible. Suzie's mother and father fought all the time, usually about money. Suzie's dad was spending more money than they could afford, mostly on that Wilma. He was always beating the crap out of Suzie's mother because of money problems and didn't care about Suzie anymore.

Suzies' dad went on for many years until he moved out to the stable permanently with that evil woman, Wilma. Being at the age of Suzie was now; she put two and two together and knew what was happening. This last incident with her father moving out and arguing with her mother brought back many memories of times that this would occur when Suzie was much younger. There was one time when they were driving; her parents were fighting, and they went into a ditch. The smell of the alcohol and the brake fluid came back into Suzie's mind often. Now she realized what it was all about.

The material world was indeed taking over for Suzie's father now. Wine, women, and song took her dad away from her and her mom;

Suzie lost all respect for her dad soon. His actions became another downfall in her young world. Her little dream world was over for good this time. Now she was in the real world of hell on earth, and there was more to come for Suzie. She had lost all of her fantasy worlds and at a young age. She grew up thinking this is how men are supposed to act toward their families. Suzie put the hateful thoughts of alcohol and violence deep down in her soul.

Much later in life, Suzie realized that children in their youth are so vulnerable and impressionable. Her parents should have been more careful with her fragile life. Her parents did more damage to Suzie's soul than they realized. She was depressed for a long time and used to try to forget by remembering the good things that happened in her past. Back when Suzie was about seven years old, she recalled how her mother would take her to Nebraska, where all of her mom's brothers and sisters lived. They would take a long ride on a train to get there. Suzie would play games on the train to pass the time. One game was getting cards with pictures of cows, barns, horses, and such on them and marking them off when she saw them. It was lots of fun for her. She thought it was great. Nebraska had rolling green hills, lots of farms, and animals of all kinds, which she loved to see.

One of their visits was to Suzie's grandmother. Of course, these relatives were not her biological relatives, but she loved them anyhow. She can remember this visit very distinctly. Suzie got thirsty in the middle of the night, and it was very dark, trying to find the sink for her water. Back when they still used oil lamps. Her grandmother didn't have electricity yet. As Suzie was trying to find the sink, she accidentally stuck her finger in a cup of water. All of a sudden, her grandmother woke up, turned on a lamp, and asked Suzie, "Why do you have your finger stuck in my false teeth cup?" It scared Suzie at first, but later on, she thought it was one of the funniest things that had ever happened to her. There were other times when Suzie would take walks down the hill to the little town called Verdel. There she would go to her uncle's tavern. The tavern was small, and it had an ice cream parlor in it. She would sit in there for hours, swirling around on the stools, and enjoy her ice cream. Suzie loved to go in there.

When she went to Nebraska, her girlfriend, Jeannie, that taught her how to swim, went with her. They had lots of fun. Suzie and her friend went into the phone house, where they could phone their fathers back home. They would lift off the receiver and crank up the handle, where a little bell would ring, and they would tell the operator what number they wanted. She would say, "1197, please." All through Suzie's life, she remembered that number because it was the first phone number she knew. It was her dad's number at work.

There were times when Suzie would go to her Aunt and Uncle's farm and see all of their animals. They had stacks of newly cut hay, and Suzie would love to roll around in it. The only thing wrong with that was she would get jiggers and scratch for months. The Jiggers was so creepy, little red bugs that burrow into your skin and live there. Suzie got the jiggers so bad one year that they wanted to shave her hair off because they were on her head. These jiggers were so bad that they decided to take her to a doctor. He used some new stuff, but that didn't work either. So, her grandma Elsie gave her an old home remedy of using straight rubbing alcohol. Low and behold, it worked.

Another time when Suzie was a little older, they went to her cousin's farm. It was Suzie's birthday, and her aunt and uncle had a cake and presents for her. Suzie had a good time there. Then, her cousin wanted to give her a present he had for her behind the barn. He told her, "Come over here, and I will give you the best present you have ever had." Suzie was excited and wanted to find out what it was. So she went with him. Suzie didn't have a clue as to what was going on. Suzie had known her cousin for years and was very surprised to see what he had for her. When they got behind the barn, her cousin pulled out his weeny and peed behind the barn, "This is your big gift, do you want it?" Suzie just stood there and looked at it while he was holding it. Suzie was subjected to sex again and was worried at first. Then she started remembering all of the things she had put far back into her mind from before. She thought of things

Like the nasty stuff her girlfriend did to her, and it started to seem exciting to her. And she liked the attention the boy was giving her. Her cousin's scared her initially; she had never really looked at a weeny up that close before. Suzie thought for a while and figured she better not fool around with the boy. She has never seen anything like this before, and she did not want her mom to find out call her names again.

Another one of Suzie's trips to Nebraska was her best one. This time, she took her friend Bonnie. They went to Suzie's Uncles dairy bar. They were able to meet boys, and the girls liked that. This time she met a boy named Kenneth that was several years older than she was. Suzie was about twelve at the time. She had started her periods and was developing very early, so boys were really on her mind now. This new fellow told her he had been in love with her for years. He said, "I have been watching you all of these years when you were at your uncle's dairy bar, but you never gave me a glance." This fellow she met was a significant, husky, farmer type. Suzie liked the robust and rugged nature, even at her age. He had long black hair and looked like an Indian, just like Suzie. So this got her excited. One day, they were sitting out on her grandmother's front porch in the warm summer air, and we're listening to the crickets chirp. At this time was Suzie's first feeling of love. They were eating watermelon and spitting out the seeds at each other. They were having a wonderful time.

After they were all finished with their watermelon fight, the fellow told Suzie he loved her, and he wanted to kiss her. This love sure was a different approach than she had ever experienced before. Suzie was in love for the first time. Of course, it was only puppy love, but she thought it was the real thing. Suzie gave him her first kiss. She loved it, and everything was so perfect for them. Not even sweet sixteen yet, and had her first kiss.

It was time for Suzie to go home. They were both heartbroken about her having to leave. For years and years, they wrote each other letters and made plans for their future. They planned for him to come to Michigan and see her and someday get married. One day he wrote

Suzie and told her that he was joining the Marines and would keep writing to her, but she never heard from him anymore. Suzie was heartbroken again. Here another love snatched away from her life. It took her a long time to get over this one. Suzie could remember having many dreams about him. With time, she got over him and moved on with her life.

Back when Suzie was in the first grade, because of being sick with her childhood illnesses, she was unable to catch up in school. She struggled through school. When she got to the sixth grade, the teachers felt that she should be held back and not go into the seventh grade. So, they did not let her into the seventh grade. Here she was, stuck in the evil number six for two years. As people would say, 666 was the devil's number, and it was an evil number for her then. Suzie was humiliated by all of her friends. Now she has to make all new friends. At this time in her life, she felt dumb because of this setback.

Back in the fourth grade, when she was still in Catholic school, she had a nervous breakdown. Her parents pulled her out of Catholic school and put her into a parochial school. Now she was going through a bad trip again. In Catholic school, the nuns were all so mean they would make the kids sit on the floor if they were terrible. Then they would beat them with a paddle. You would never hear of things like that happening these days. And another thing, because the nuns had to wear their hot habits, they would keep the windows open in the winter, and Suzie was always getting sick. Also, she hated wearing those awful uniforms. She felt ugly enough at that time without wearing those uniforms. The Catholic school would cram religion down her throat all the time. They never taught you anything about the Bible. The kids were all made to go to church every morning, and Suzie would get sick and pass out in Church. At this time in her life was when Suzie started hating to go to Church. She felt the Catholic Church was trying to brainwash her. That Church, with all of their statues and gold robes, was a very secular religion. They were mean to the kids also. They never taught anything out of the Bible, just all about the faith.

Suzie started thinking there had to be something better in religion than this. One day, she would start looking for it. Suzie felt that the nuns were jealous. Suzie had a complex now. Being put back into the sixth grade again made her feel even dumber. Suzie didn't have any reason to have a complex. She was smart and still pretty, but she didn't even realize it.

Time went by, and she finally got into the seventh grade. Seven seemed to be a good grade for her. Even though all of the girls were still jealous of her, she got into some enjoyable activities. One of her events was the student council. Also, she was the secretary of the student council. She was a majorette in the band and marched in parades at all of the football games. All of her friends were jealous now.

One day Suzie tried out for cheerleading. She was a natural. Her ballet and dance lessons came through for her. The day before her tryout, she practiced all day with the girls. The next day as she woke up, and she could hardly move. She practiced too much and was too stiff to try out. So, it was tough luck for her. 'No cheerleading for Suzie this year. Suzie figured it was all for the best because all of the other cheerleaders were goodie-goodie-two-shoes and were all "A" students. Suzie could never live up to the expectations of those girls.

When Suzie was about eleven, she started developing in her breasts. She was already wearing a size C-cup brazier. She was an A-cup at eleven and grew to a C-cup by the age of fourteen. Her big boobs were a curse for her at this age. Suzie had started her periods at eleven, and that threw her right into womanhood early. Because of Suzie's big boobs, when she would walk through the halls at school, the boys would bump into her. Of course, they hit her accidentally on purpose. Ha! Ha! The boys were trying to get a feel to find out if Suzie was wearing falsies. All of the girls were jealous of her and would tell all of the boys that Suzie's breasts were false. The boys were amazed when they found out that they were real.

In this era, Suzie felt all of the girls were whores, and all of the boys were hoodlums. The boys would wear leather jackets, chain belts, and pointed black shoes. All of the girls wore tight skirts, sweaters, saddle oxford shoes, and lots of makeup. For Suzie to keep up with the crowd, she had to wear sweaters, skirts, and cosmetics, just like the other girls. Her favorite was her poodle skirt. Since she dressed like this, it made things even worse for her. She was too sexy for her own good. Suzie knew she was a cool cat now, just like the other girls. She was still a virgin, not like all of the rest of the girls. One day, a real close friend of hers named Terry came up to Suzie and told her, "I have had sex with a boy, and I liked it. You should try it." Suzie could not believe her ears. This girl was one of the goodie-goodie-two-shoes in the school. Suzie told her, "I'm still a virgin, and I am staying like that until I have my perfect man." Even though she felt like that, she was still curious, but never did anything about it. She was waiting for her perfect storybook romance.

One day, Suzie went with her parents to their friend's house. Her parent's friends had two daughters for Suzie to play with. To have friends was lovely for her. They were all in about the same age group of twelve to fourteen, and all were very pretty. One bad thing was that the people had their uncle living with them, also. The uncle used to play with the girls all the time. The uncle was a reasonably nice-looking man and only in his twenties. One day the parents all got together and went out to dinner and left the girls and the uncle alone. There was nothing wrong with that; they used to do this all the time, but for some reason, this time was different. Suzie had on one of her sexy pink sweaters on, and the uncle commented, "You have developed a lot in your breasts since the last time I've seen you." Strangely enough, Suzie thought nothing of it. The uncle decided he would play some wrestling games with the girls; no big deal, he always did this with them. He would tackle and tickle the girls just like usual, but this time he grabbed Suzie's breast and crotch; she didn't know if she should tell anyone or keep it a secret. She didn't want to think anything of it, so she went on and put it out of her mind.

Later on, the uncle decided to play a game, hide and seek. The uncle told the girls to hide, and he would find them. So, they all went and hid. Suzie went and hid in the chicken coop, and the uncle found her right away. When he saw Suzie in the chicken coop, he locked the door behind them and told her not to make a sound. The uncle got crazy. The uncle had his hand over her mouth so she wouldn't scream. Then the uncle told Suzie, "You better not ever tell anyone, or I will kill you." Suzie had never experienced anything like this before. The uncle got nasty with her, which brought back the memory of when her redheaded girlfriend's brother had her in the tent. This man had the same evil look in his eyes, like when she was in the tent. Then he tried to take her pants off; Suzie was so worried and started crying even harder. She was sobbing like when her parents would fight, and she would hide behind her the couch. Then he grabbed her boobs and crotch; she was so scared she did not know what to do.

He was just about to make things worse when the parents pulled up in the driveway. They were wondering where everyone was. Instantly, the uncle decided to come out of the chicken coup. Suzie came out after a short while and was still crying. Her parents asked her what the matter was, and she replied. "I fell in the chicken coop and hurt myself while we were playing hide and seek." Luckily for the uncle, Suzie never told anyone about the incident. She knew they probably would not believe her anyhow. She never went back to their friend's house anymore.

Now Suzie had more, gruesome secrets to bury deep down in her soul again. She could never tell her parents because they would never believe it. They have been friends with that family for years. Suzie would always remember the strange look in the uncle's eyes. For the longest time, Suzie would have nightmares about the chicken coop; it turned out to be much worse than the tent. All of these incidents were making her feel dirty and sick. She started feeling like something was wrong with her.

A while back, Suzie could remember asking her mother about sex. Suzie's mother wouldn't tell her anything about sex. She was trying to confide in her mother and wanted to get these things off her chest, but her mother was no help. Susie's mother would say,

"You are a nasty girl to want to talk about that dirty stuff." Her mother would shame her and shake that finger at her like she used to do when she thought Suzie was terrible. Her mom's voice used to haunt her by saying, "Shame on you. You are a dirty, nasty girl." Suzie's mother told her that if a man had oral sex from a woman, he would go crazy or could even go blind. Suzie's mom was the crazy one. Suzie didn't know what oral sex was; she had people trying to do it to her, but she didn't know what it was.

Suzie never told her mother anything after her mother refused to listen to her. She never talked about anything like sex again. Suzie would always bury all of her secrets deep inside her soul again. The way she learned about sex was from watching the animals, like her dogs and cats. When Suzie turned sixteen, her dog Brownie died. She was heart-broken again. Here was that evil six also. Suzie started thinking about these numbers and still couldn't figure it out. Since she had turned sixteen, all kinds of nasty things began happening in her life. She almost wished she could skip the age of sixteen. Whatever happened to "Sweet Sixteen?"

Suzie was fully developed by now and living in her spoiled material world. She had skirts and sweater sets of all different colors; she had a different outfit for every day of the week. Suzie was fortunate that way with her clothing. But the girls in the school were so jealous of her beauty and clothing. It seemed like it was that way all through her life. Suzie was pretty much alone for most of her life because of not having any real friends.

Suzie was walking to school one day, and a bunch of girls jumped out from bushes at her. The girls were making threats at her. They called her names and told her she would be pretty with a bag over her head. Suzie got away from them at that time, but they told her they would get her one day. Every evening, she would get threatening phone calls, telling her they would get her after school. Suzie was in terror. She was so scared she didn't want to even go to school. She told her mother what was happening, but her mom didn't believe her.

The next day as Suzie was walking to school, all of the girls were there again. The girls were harassing her, but this time it was different. They were serious this time. One girl, in particular, stood out. This girl was a redhead named Margery, and she was mean as a snake. This girl started in on Suzie, telling her, "You are an ugly witch, and no one likes you." Suzie started crying, and this got the girl going even more. She knew Suzie was scared, and that redheaded girl loved it.

All of a sudden, the girl lunged at Suzie and started choking her. She fell on the ground and couldn't get up. Then, the girl began pulling out Suzie's pretty black hair. The other girls were egging her on, saying, "Pull her hair and bent back her long nails." Then out of the blue, a girl named Roseanne came along and didn't like what she was seeing. This girl, Roseanne, was big, and she intimidated all of the other girls. Roseanne told the girls to leave Suzie alone, or they would have to account for her. Luckily for Suzie, the girls left her alone; they were afraid of Roseanne.

Suzie was so grateful she couldn't thank Roseanne enough. After the fight, Suzie went on to school, licking her wounds. She tried to comb her hair, but it was coming out in handfuls. She was bruised and scratched from head to toe. Roseanne felt real bad for Suzie. She knew Suzie was a nice person and that she didn't deserve it. After that incident, Roseanne and Suzie became the best of friends. The friendship lasted all through their lives. Suzie finally had a good friend, someone she could relate to, and share all of her secrets.

Then one day, another incident happened. This time, Roseanne came to the rescue with some black kids. One day some of the white girls were picking on Suzie again, and Roseanne and the black kids came to her rescue. It seemed like all of the black kids in the school liked Suzie and Roseanne. Later, Suzie always hung around the black kids and Roseanne. After that, Suzie had a lot of black friends throughout her life. They still had a good time together. Roseanne and Suzie became inseparable; all through life, they were the best of friends. At least at this time, Suzie finally had a friend, and she could trust and rely count on now.

SECRETS ARE OUT NOW

As time went on, Suzie was fully developed and was prettier than ever. The boys loved her, and the girls hated her. Most of the time, Suzie would hang around the boys when Roseanne wasn't available. The boys loved her, probably because she was a perfect 36-19-36. Her hair was black and longer than ever with her beautiful olive complexion and her five-foot-tall, tiny-featured body. Her best feature was her green eyes that shined. When she looked at you, it seemed like she knew what you were thinking. Suzie's intuitive nature was starting to develop even more by now, and she could get anybody that she wanted and wrapped them around her finger.

Even though Suzie had Roseanne, she felt terrible that she didn't have many other girlfriends. One time, she was at a school dance and sitting all alone because none of the girls wanted to talk to her. The reason Suzie was alone at this time was that Roseann was not there at the dance. As she was sitting alone, she just burst out crying. Everyone noticed her, but no one came to her rescue. She hated her life and wanted to die. At that time in her life, Suzie was a lonely girl and didn't know what to do. She was so depressed she even thought about killing herself, but she didn't have enough nerve to do that. So she decided to start hanging around the boys even more. The boys were always too nice to her.

Suzie was excellent in all kinds of sports, and she decided since the girls didn't want to be with her, she would start playing with the boys. Suzie played baseball, cowboys and Indians, and even football. Playing with all the boys, she would win because they would let her. The boys liked playing football with Suzie because they wanted the tackle part of the game. As they would tackle her, they would feel her breast and crotch. Suzie didn't mind when they tackled. She thought it was just how they plaid the game, and she liked the attention.

Even though Suzie was playing with the boys, she was still a lonely girl. She felt bad that the girls didn't want to hang out with her. Suzie felt something was wrong with her and got a deep-seated depression that Suzie told no one about her feelings. She would have thoughts of killing herself again but still didn't have the nerve. Unknown to her at the time, Suzie's biological mother had unsuccessfully attempted suicide. Suzie surely didn't want to be a person like that. Not wanting to feel like this, she put it down deep in her soul and hardened her heart again. It was like she was getting ready for something much worse in her life—what an experience. The girls wanted to kill her, and the boys wanted to feel her up.

Suzie and her friend Roseann were walking down the street one day, and a guy drove by yelling, "I want to get the little one." Him saying that freaked them out. They were so scared they didn't know what to do. As they keep on walking, the guy came around the corner and decided to follow them. The girls instantly ran into a store, and the guy went away. The girls never had anything like this happen to them before. Suzie's friend was more scared than Suzie because she had worse things than that happen to her; she was almost getting used to it.

Time went on, and this happened several times again. One day as they were walking, the same guy came back around a second time, but this time, he got out of his car and started walking towards them. The girls were terrified. As the guy came closer, they could see he was no young boy. He was an older man, and that scared them even more. As he walked by them, he pulled from his penis out of his pants and shook it at them. Suzie had seen one before, but her friend had never seen one. Suzie's friend was freaking-out now. While the man was walking by them with his penis out, they got a good look at him. The girls were shocked when they saw who he was. They came to realize that he was one of the teachers at their school. The girls were going to report him, but they knew the school would never believe them. This man was highly respected in the community and had a family; even one of the man's daughters was in their class. All of this happened in the summer, and when the next school year started, he never showed up at the school. He must have moved and changed schools because they never saw him again.

Finally, some good things started to happen to Suzie. She worked at her father's dry cleaning establishment, trying to save money for a car for herself. Well, she finally made enough money to get her car. Her car was a beautiful, powder blue, '58 Chevy Impala convertible; it had a 348 tri-power engine in it. Suzie thought she was hot now. She had leg pipes put on the car, had it lowered, and she pinstriped it herself. Since she was so talented in the arts, she could do it quickly.

Maybe this car was not something good for her. At this time in her life, all hell broke loose for Suzie. Back when her dad had moved out of the house and Suzie had no supervision, she got into trouble. Suzie's mom was working all the time, and she was alone to do what she wanted to. Here Suzie was sweet sixteen and about to be more than just a kiss. At this time was when most of her real troubles started. Suzie had a lot of friends now. All of the girls wanted to be friends, but just for her car. They forgot about all of the trouble they had caused her in the past. All of her newly found friends loved Suzie only so she could drive them to school. Even the little redhead Margie who had previously beaten her up, they were her friend now. Because Suzie was a forgiving person, she let the redheaded witch into her life again and all of the other girls.

Everyone was using Suzie for her car. She just couldn't say no to anyone. So, Suzie put the past behind her and had a good time. Her friend Roseann thought Suzie was making a mistake by taking in the bad girls, but Suzie didn't care. All of the girls would get together and ride around the streets looking for boys. They had a good time. They went through the drive-ins flirting with all of the cute guys. At the time, that was the "in thing" to do, drive through the drive-ins. Suzie's car was the fastest car on the road, and all the guys were jealous and wanted to race her, so she did. Also, the boys wanted her to join their racing club, but she never did that. Suzie just raced them all on the streets. She would pull up to an intersection, rev up her engine, and off they would go. Suzie loved the power as she ran through the gears.

One night, she was on a road she had never been on before. Some guys wanted to race, so she said to herself, "Why not?" As they were going through the gears, the road split, and Suzie was at a section that was a dead-end road. Luckily for Suzie, she was skilled with her car and was able to pull it out of the traffic and zoomed around the corner on two wheels. Boy, what a close call! Suzie had learned to be a skilled driver from her father, teaching her how to drive on his tractor. The tractor had several gears, not like a car, which led her to drive a stick shift.

Suzie and Roseann were riding along one cold and wintry night, and Suzie slid into a ditch. Suzie was freaking. She didn't know what to do. Her dad would kill her and take her car away if he found out. Well, Roseann came to Suzie's rescue again. She jumped out of the vehicle, told Suzie to put it in reverse, and that she would push Suzie out. Rose was a big girl and knew she could get them out of the ditch, and she did. Suzie was so relieved. What a good friend Roseann was for Suzie, always looking out for her. Roseann was Suzie's friend for life.

One day, a boy came out to Suzie's father riding stable, telling Suzie's dad about how fast Suzie's car was and how he wanted to buy it from Suzie. The boy proceeded to tell Suzie's dad about how he saw Suzie going about 100 miles per hour down the city streets one night. Suzie's dad freaked out and said to the boy, "Sure, you can have the car. You just come out here tomorrow, and it will be here for you to buy." Suzie's dad told her that he would sell her car, but she didn't want to listen. She was so spoiled by her father. Suzie should have listened to him because of the bad things to come. Suzie's car was too expensive for her. She was forever putting clutches in it and having to get the engine tuned-up. Another problem was that the car was much too fast for her.

On one cold wintry night, Roseann and Suzie were driving on a different road in the middle of the night. Suzie was going too fast for the conditions because it was raining on an ice-covered street. Roseann told Suzie she had better slow down, but stubborn Suzie didn't want to listen to her best friend. Suzie told Rose, "No problem, I know this road like the back of my hand." Maybe she did, but not on an icy road. All of a sudden, the road curved, and Suzie didn't.

They went flying down a hill and hit an electrical pole and smashed into it. It would have been better if it had been a tree. This pole was like hitting a brick wall, and they hit so hard that it snapped the electric pole in half. After the sudden impact, they realized what had happened and were in hysterics. Suzie's adrenaline was flowing, and she jumped out of the car into about three feet of snow. Rose got out of the car into the deep cold snow, also. Luckily for the girls, they weren't hurt. Today they build cars cheap, not as they did in 1958. Cars were tough back then. The tow truck came the next day to get the car and couldn't understand how they got out of the vehicle. When they tried to open the door, they couldn't even get the car door open. They had to pry the doors open to be able to tow the car away. They were puzzled and wondered how the girls came out alive. All Suzie had was a broken fingernail and bruised knees. Rose's knees were the same. What adrenaline the girl had, or was it that God was watching over them?

Eventually, Suzie let her dad sell the car. They got it fixed, and Suzie made more money than she had paid for it. The fellow that bought it knew it had been in a crash, but he didn't care because he was going to make a hot rod out of it, anyhow. Suzie was going to miss her car. She used to love the sensation of speeding down the road, stopping at a light, and going through the gears trying to race the boys. Suzie was a good driver, but just a little too crazy. Yes, she missed her car, but she was a survivor and would find something new to occupy her mind.

Now that her car was gone, she got interested in some different kinds of hobbies. Suzie was good at all most everything in the arts. She could oil paint, sing, dance, roller-skate, and even ice-skating. One day, she tried out for the Ice Follies. Her mother took her in the car, and they went to the place where they performed ice follies, and they held tryouts. When they arrived there, they told them to sit down and wait, and someone would be right with them. Finally, it was Suzie's turn to tryout. She was so excited at a chance to become an ice-skating star. The lady told Suzie to do her figure eights and some other moves. Suzie was great. She could do everything the lady had asked. After all of the tryouts were over, the lady came to talk to Suzie and her mother. The lady told them that Suzie made the team and that they wanted her to start right away.

Suzie and her mother were so excited. Then, the lady asked Suzie when she could go on the road with them. Of course, Suzie was ready to go right away. But then her mother told the lady Suzie was not out of school yet. The lady was so surprised. She thought Suzie was at least eighteen and done with school. Suzie always looked old for her age. Suzie's mother threw a wrench in the works and told her, "There is no way Suzie would be able to go because she needs to finish school first." Suzie was disappointed again. The lady told Suzie that when she got out of school to look them up, and she could start then. How many disappointments could Suzie handle in her life, one right after another? Suzie never went back. Too many things came up in her life to be able to be an ice-skater.

Suzie at 16

CHAPTER 3

SUZIE AT THE AGE OF 16 TO 17, HER ASSAULT AND BOYFRIEND BARRY

It was time for Suzie to strive in a different direction, so she decided to attend modeling school. She went down to Detroit and enrolled at the Patricia Stevens Modeling School in Detroit. Suzie was very good at this, and it came very easy for her. She took fencing lessons, poise in walking, and the latest dress, makeup, speech, and how to pose for pictures. She also learned stage makeup and received acting lessons at the school. Suzie went to school for over a year. All of this schooling came in handy for her in the future. The school helped her poise, and she gained more confidence and self-esteem. Because of education, they figured she was good at modeling. Most of the modeling was for photographers. After a while, she quit modeling because they all wanted her to do nude modeling, and she was not ready for that. Suzie had no idea of what she wanted to do now, so she took a break from modeling.

While Suzie was in high school, since she was not very good at her studies, the school didn't want her to waste her time. So, they put her in all of the singing groups and art classes. She was in glee club, girls ensemble, choir, and had the opportunity to sing many solos. One time, there were tryouts for one person to be able to go to Europe and sing. This event was for the foreign exchange students, and Suzie was very excited about this. Many kids tried out for the opportunity to go overseas. As the tryouts were progressing, Suzie and one other girl were the finalists; as they were waiting, they were getting very nervous. It was time for the last audition, guess what? Suzie won it. There was only one catch. The parents had to pay for all of their expenses, and Suzie's parents were broke. One day Suzie's father decided to run away with Wilma.

Because of his extravagant spending on this woman, he was broke. They didn't have the money for Suzie. Suzie suffered another disappointment in life because she had to forfeit her winning to the other girl.

Understandably, Suzie was overwhelmed with the latest disappointment. But, she was still a survivor and handled it by deciding to run away. Her parents could not afford her anymore, and she was so hurt. Suzie felt like she was a burden on her mother and father and thought it would be better for them to leave home. Suzie and Roseann knew of a cottage up North that some of their boyfriends' parent's cottage. The parents had the cabin closed up for the winter, and the boys told them it would be fun for them to go up there and stay with them. Suzie and Roseann thought it would be fun, so they went for it. It seemed like they were driving for hours and hours, then they finally arrived. The cottage was really out in the boonies. As they drove up, Suzie and Roseann thought they were going to get stuck. They had never seen so much snow before, and they had never been that far up North, either. When Suzie got out of the car, the snow was so deep she sunk up past her knees. It must have been twenty degrees below zero because the girls' teeth were chattering. It was such a deserted area that the girls were starting to get worried.

They all finally got into the cottage, and it was frigid inside. The boys proceeded to start a fire in the fireplace. It was kind of nice for a while until two of the boys decided to pull out some of their parent's liquor from the cabinet. As the two boys started drinking, Suzie and Roseann were getting even more scared. All of a sudden, the boys started coming on to the girls. The two boys were getting rough and mean towards the girls. The other boy that was not drinking told the two other boys they better stop, but they didn't want to. Luckily for the girls, one boy brought his car and told the girls that he would take them home. The girls said that would be great. So, the three of them left the cottage and went on home.

When Suzie arrived back home, she felt so relieved that she went right to bed and swore she would never do anything like that again. As Suzie walked into the house and her mom was standing there, instead of her mother being glad to see her, all she would do is call her names and said she was whoring around. Suzie's mother shook that finger at Suzie again and told her she was a dirty, nasty girl. Suzie hated her mother when she shook that finger at her. Fortunate for Suzie, she was still pure as the newly driven snow. Suzie felt the reason her mother didn't trust her was because of having the same deep-seated guilt complex of her own, possibly from the abortion she had when she was young.

Suzie was getting bored with her life again and decided to do something different. Suzie heard about some free classes at Wayne State University to teach singers how to better their music reading abilities. After her lessons at Wayne State Summer Corral, her mother decided to get Suzie a piano. The piano was an old one, but Suzie didn't mind. For a while, Suzie's mother was paying for lessons for Suzie, but later on, her mom's money started running out again, and she had to quit her studies. Suzie felt hurt over that. She loved playing the piano.

At that time, Suzie's mom was so in debt that she tried burning the house down to collect money from the insurance company. Suzie was devastated. Because her mother attempted to burn the house, all of Suzie's clothes burned up, and a lot of her keepsakes that she had saved were all destroyed. All of the ribbons Suzie had won in horse competition, and her yearbooks from school were all gone. Everything she held dear to her was all destroyed.

Years after the fire, Suzie could remember having nightmares about her house burning down. She would dream about being in bed, and her oil paintings on the wall were melting and running down the wall. Another dream Suzie had was about looking under her bed and seeing a scary red spider getting ready to attack her. Instantly she would wake up screaming. It's no wonder she had terrible dreams, with all of the tragedies she had been through so far. Suzie's mom never collected a lot of money from the house burning because it didn't burn down completely. After a while, they repaired the house like brand-new. In Suzie's eyes, the house would never be the same as before. Suzie lost a lot of respect for her mother after that. She couldn't believe her mother was so desperate for money. Since Suzie's mother didn't get much money from the house, her father was still mean to her because he wanted the money that she didn't have. Suzie's father always wanted cash for the whore he was living with up North. He would always come home and beat up Suzie's mother because she didn't have any money for him.

After the fire, Suzie became more independent and not relying as much on her mother. One evening, Suzie and Roseann decided to go on another adventure. They decided to go to Detroit to have a different experience in life. Suzie and Roseann get all dressed up, and they tried to get into a beatnik club in Detroit. Suzie and Roseann could get away with it because they looked old for their age. Suzie was living dangerously now, but she liked the excitement and the challenge of doing new things.

One time on another adventure, they met some black musicians, which asked the girls to come up to their room after the show. So, of course, the girls went for it. The musicians were charming fellows, and everything went well with them. Suzie had acquired a motto at that time. She had to try everything imaginable in life, at least once, to be able to say, "I have tried it all." Suzie was becoming very outgoing and wanted to experience everything she could.

Another time, Suzie and Roseann decided to go to Detroit again. But this time, they tried to get into a strip-show. Since they looked old for their age, it was easy for them still. As they walked up to the ticket counter, little did Suzie know at the time, but the lady selling tickets was Suzie's biological mother. Later in life, she found out all about it. This strip-show was right downtown Detroit on Michigan Avenue, and it was called the Gaiety Show Bar. Them going in the place was one of her best experiences at sixteen years old, getting into a strip-show. Suzie was not even embarrassed. She loved the glamour and beautiful costumes the ladies wore. Her dancing background was coming out now. Little did Suzie know at the time that this was what she would be doing one day?

In Suzie's travels, she met a beautiful black girl who was an accomplished singer. This girl took Suzie under her wing and taught her the ropes about singing. Suzie's friend used to sing in the USO and even had some records cut with Mow Town Record Co. Suzie's black friend told Suzie she needed a stage name, so they changed her name to Sue Bauer. Not much of a catchy name, but it worked for a while. So after that, her new name was Sue Bauer. About this time in her life, people started calling her Sue instead of Suzie. Bauer was part of Sue's adopted last name.

Her new friend did for her that didn't turn out very well was to introduce Sue to the owner of Mo-town Records. Her friend had no idea it would turn out bad for her, but it did. Her friend told Sue to go into the studio and talk to the man at the desk. This knight turned out to be one of the ugliest, biggest black men Sue had ever seen. As Sue went in to talk to the man, she became scared and intimidated. The man had Sue sing a couple of songs for him, and he thought she was great, which she was. Sue was so excited. She was sure this was going to be her big break in the music world. This man had the power to do it for her, but would he? After she had sung, the man said, "You were great, but..." Always that, "but!" word gets thrown into the works.

The man said, "If you go to bed with me, I will make you a star, guaranteed." Sue freaked out. Here, her fairy tale world is tumbling down again; he said he would sign her up and cut all sorts of records for her. There was no way Sue would ever do this. Sue was still a virgin and was saving herself for her perfect man. If Sue had done what he wanted, she would undoubtedly have become a star, but she just was not that way. Sue had one disappointment in life right after another. She was sure that sex was the way most stars made their fame. It seemed like to her that people get famous by sex, money, or they were born into stardom, and this was how they became famous. It was always the same old thing, "Go to bed with me, and I will make you a star." Sue was so disappointed once again. She didn't know what to do, so she put her tail between her legs and left the record company.

Then one day, she met another gruesome guy. But this one seemed to be a charming person, although. Sue never was prejudiced towards black people or any other race. She just found out there were good and evil in all nationalities. This man was an announcer at dances and a group organizer. He helped her out. He introduced her to a lot of people and gave her a lot of opportunities. Now that she had many singing jobs, from this man and also met a lot of celebrities. Sue met and sung with the Fabulous Fabian. He didn't get too far in his career as a singer, but he got a lot further than Sue ever did at that time, and he did appear in some movies.

One night, in particular, Sue was to perform at a place where Fabian was to sing also. Performing there was a crazy night for her. After she had sung her song and of course, she was great at it. She was waiting behind a screen that divided the stage where Fabian was to sing his song. After he sang his song, people started throwing eggs at him. Since there was just a screen between Fabian and Sue, the eggs they were throwing went over the front screen and were striking the wall behind Sue. As they hit the wall, the eggs splashed all over Sue's new white dress. Sue looked a mess. It was sure a good thing she had sung her song all ready. At the time, it wasn't hilarious. But now, when she thinks about it, she laughs. It was very early in

Fabian's career, and no one knew that he would be a famous person one day. At least some people got a break in life, but not too many were happening for Sue.

Sue was still trying to become a singing star. Sue used to sing at a lot of rock-n-roll clubs all around the Detroit area. Finale, Sue, was getting all kinds of exposure. But no breaks yet. Sue was still a little shy, but she belted out her songs. Sue was a very sensuous girl, and all of the men wanted her. Sue was sweet sixteen and still had never been kissed. Well, almost never! It was time for her to go on another gig, but she didn't have a ride to it. Since her dad sold her car, it made it very hard for her to get places. She tried to borrow her dad's car, but he said, "No go." It was not that she was a lousy driver; she just had bad luck with cars. This gig was out in the boonies and not in the Detroit area, and it was hard to get someone to drive her way out there. Sue hated to depend on other people for rides because they weren't very dependable. But, she did this time. She asked one of her so-called "boyfriends" if he would give her a ride. Luckily for her, he said, "yes." But it was not very lucky for her. Sue's boyfriend said he would, but he wanted one of Sue's best girlfriends, Pat, to come along. Sue felt this was fine. It seemed like a great idea at the time. But the more she thought about it, the more she couldn't figure out why. Why did he want her girlfriend along?

So, off they all went to the dance where Sue was to sing. When they arrived, because of a lot of advertising for Sue, the club was packed. Sue was so excited about this evening. There were going to be newspaper reporters there and everything. Sue got a big write-up in the paper about how wonderful she had been at the other dances and how she could be a smash at this dance. But was it worth it because of what she had to go through to get it?

Sue and her friends arrived at the dance place. It was called "Jack Scots Dance Ranch." It was starting to get crowded already. Then it was Sue's time to sing. She looked great; she was wearing a white and silver spaghetti strap dress, and her shoes were clear plastic, with silver straps on them. What a knockout she was. The style of clothing she wore was one like Marlon Monroe used to wear in her movies. Even though she was only sixteen and still a virgin, she looked too mature for her one good. She was such a good singer, also. She had a standing ovation from the crowd, and that's rare at a teenage dance.

After she finished, she was exhausted and went over to sit down. She thought she better find her friends. As she was looking around, she couldn't find her friends that had brought her there. She started asking around, but they were nowhere in sight. Sue was getting worried now. She didn't know what to do. She couldn't call her mother because her mother told her that "If you have trouble getting a ride, don't ask her for help." Her mom said, "If you can't get back and forth from your events, you will just have to quit going." Sue surely didn't want to quit going to her singing gigs.

Sue was so worried and scared now. Sue figured the reason her boyfriend left her there was because she would never have sex with him. Her girlfriend was doing just that. Since Sue didn't have a ride home, she got an idea to ask the manager of the dance hall if he knew what she could do. Sue walked up to the manager to ask him if he could help her. The manager was an older man, huge and scary looking, but Sue thought she would be safe to ask him. Sue said, "I need to know if you know what I can do about a ride home. My friends left me here, and they haven't returned yet." The manager thought for a moment, and his reply was, "Well, well, little lady, I can take you home." As he proceeded to tell her, he would take her home when the entire crowd was gone and when his workers cleaned the place. Sue felt relieved about the ride but still felt funny because of how he was looking at her. He was looking down at her top with scary eyes. It was the same look men had in their eyes before.

Finally, all of the people cleared out of the club, and the men cleaned up the place. It was getting late, and the manager was not coming back for her. Sue was starting to get concerned. Then finally, the man came out of the backroom. Sue asked him, "Are you finished cleaning yet?" His reply was, "Come to the back room. We are just finishing up." So Sue followed him to the back room. When she got to the backroom, it was an awful place, and boxes were lying all around. There was hardly any lighting; just one hanging light bulb over a big dirty table with spoiled food, papers, and cans all over it. The exposed wood rafters were sticking out of the ceiling, and dirty cobwebs were hanging between them. There was an old torn up couch that looked like someone had been sleeping on it. The room stunk like garbage and dirty bodies. Also, in the backroom, she could smell the scent of alcohol. She remembered the alcohol smell of this scent from her father. This alcohol smell brought back many bad memories of her father drinking and being so violent to her mother.

Here in the back room were four men, including the manager, and they were all drinking and sitting around the dirty table. It looked like they had been nipping at the bottle all night. One man was a black man, a young guy, and two old ones like the manager. One of the older men was ugly. As Sue walked into the room, the men said all kinds of nasty remarks to her, and she started to get nervous. The manager told her to sit on the couch, and he would be with her shortly. Sue asked him, "I thought you were going to take me home after you finished cleaning." The manager's reply was, "Come over here and drink with us." Sue got mad and said, "I want you to take me home right now." That was the wrong reply for Sue because the manager got very angry at her. The man told Sue, "Come over here and sing and dance for us. We want to see your boobs and crotch and watch you dance." Sue's reply was, "No way, you jerk." One of the men instantly grabbed Sue and ripped her dress right off of her. Sue was petrified now. She didn't know what to think. Next, one of the men started trying to hold her down, but Sue was an aggressive girl. She was fighting all the way.

Sue was crying and screaming by now, and all this did was excite them even more. Then the manager came back from his car with more alcohol. Sue thought he would stop the men, but he started to sober up a little, and he decided he wanted more. He held Sue down, and while the other guys took turns with her. The two other guys were mean to her and were hitting her. Then the black

SECRETS ARE OUT NOW

guy took his turn with Sue; at least he did not hit her; he was the nicer of them.

They finally finished with her, and they figured they better do something with her now. They couldn't leave her there, so they decided to take her to her home. The manager told the young man and the hideous guy he would take her to her house, but he wanted the young man to drive while he and the repulsive guy would take care of Sue in the back seat. So, they all proceeded to leave. They tried to put Sue's clothing back on her so they could get her to the car. Sue couldn't believe they were finally taking her home; this was because they had more things planned for her in the car. She could hardly walk to the car because she was a messed, all bruised and bleeding.

While they were in the car, the manager and the gruesome guy still didn't leave Sue alone. The manager told her, "You better never tell anyone because we know where you live, and we will come back and kill you and your family or whoever you tell. If you try to hide, we will find you because we have a lot of informative friends. You can't hide from us." Come to find out; they had friends who were in the mafia. The men weren't anxious about it because they didn't believe she would live, anyhow. On her street, they just pushed her out of the car and drove away, leaving her there for dead. Luckily for Sue, it was late at night, and her parents were sleeping. Sue had the bad men take her back to her father's ranch, where Sue and her mom stayed for the weekend. After they pushed Sue was out of the car, she was lying on the side of the road for a few hours. At least it was a warm summer night, and she didn't freeze.

She had passed out, and when she came to, she went right to the outhouse and tried to clean herself up. As she was walking into the outhouse, she was a mess. Sue was experiencing pain as she had never felt before, both mentally and physically. Luckily for her, there was no AIDS at the time, and she didn't get pregnant. As Sue walked into the house and tried to be was very quiet. All she could hear was her mom and dad snoring. That was good for her because they wouldn't hear her come in. She had this ability to be quiet from her Indian background. As she lay down in her bed, she thanked God that she was still alive. Again, the Lord must have been saving her for something, but she had no idea what.

In the morning, Sue's parents went to work, and they didn't even see her. When Sue woke up, she decided she better go over to a friend's house; so Sue wrote them a note that she was going over to a girlfriend's house to stay for a while. Sue didn't want her parents to see her all messed up. Sue stayed at her friend's for a month while she was healing. Since it was summer vacation and there was no school anyhow. All of her outer bruises finally healed, and her parents never found out about it. Her parents didn't pay much attention to her because they were too wrapped up in their problems. Her deep, secret, mental scars never healed; she carried them in her mind forever. She felt so ashamed and blamed herself for what had happened. She ended up hating men for a long time and acquired a terrible attitude about life. Sue thought she wasn' meant to be a singer, so she quit it.

Time went on, and Sue didn't sing for a long time. She hated the smell of alcohol because of her dad and now her rape. At first, Sue thought about killing herself again but still didn't have enough nerve to do it. Sue was a strong-willed person and knew she would survive. At that time, Sue ended up losing all of her morals and didn't care about anything anymore. She felt like a tramp and figured this was what life was all about for her. Sue thought she was not a virgin anymore, so it didn't matter what she did with her life now. She didn't have anything special to save for her perfect man now. She felt her dream world was gone forever.

Her life became a turning point in her life. All of Sue's friends were tramps, so she felt she might as well be one also. Sue decided to have sex with every boy she could find. She thought she should go out with the whole United Nations: Italian, Mexican, Chinese, Japanese, Black and Polish, and others she could find. You name it; she was ready for them all. Sue was looking for love in all the wrong places. It was the way she felt, but she never really did anything like that. Sue did go out with the United Nations over the years. She tried to live her life as if she was still a virgin, but she lived a lie.

One day, she went to the beach with one of her wild friends Terry, the one that had been trying to talk her into having sex for so long. Sue loved the water because she was a Cancer sign. The girls were sunning themselves like crabs in the sand when Sue spotted the most handsome man she had ever seen. The two girls both fell in lust instantly. This guy was a tall, redheaded, Italian man with dark skin and bulging muscles. Here Sue charges into a situation with a redhead again! She sure was attracted to him. They both thought this one was a hunk. Before Sue could get a word in edgewise, her friend threw herself all over him. For some reason, Sue liked this one. At least she found out his name was Tony. She couldn't believe the feelings she had for him already. Then, Sue's friend left her there all alone and took the hunk off. Sue was hurt, but she felt maybe he didn't like her anyway. Perhaps he just wanted sex like all the other men in the world.

It wasn't very long before Tony came back and was looking for Sue and found her again at the beach. They liked each other and started dating. He knew Sue's friend was a wrong move for him. Tony told Sue, "I wanted you, but your friend pulled me away from you so fast; I didn't know what was happening." Sue and Tony started going out. Sue was really in love for the first time. This love made the first love in Nebraska look like puppy love for sure. They got along great and took long rides in his '55 Chevy. The Chevy was powder blue with gold pinstripes, and the name of it was "Stardust."

One warm summer evening, they were cruising around in his Chevy, and he stopped to park at lover's leap where all of the teens parked. He asked Sue to make love. How could she refuse? Everything was perfect, and she tried to imagine she was still a virgin. She wanted to let him, but she just couldn't do it. Sue was so afraid he would hate her if he knew she wasn't a virgin. Here she was in the back seat of a '55 Chevy, and everything was perfect except for her. Sue just couldn't do anything because of the assault; it was still too soon. Sue couldn't bring herself to tell him the truth. Sue's man stated, "It doesn't matter to me. I still love you, and I will wait until you're ready." Sue was happy that Tony didn't mind, and he still kept seeing her.

Tony was about three years older than Sue was, but the age difference didn't matter to her. Tony used to buy her all sorts of things and tell her he wanted to marry her someday. As time went on, Sue was invited to his parents' house and meant his relative's gatherings on special occasions. They both had a favorite song; they called it " their song." The name of the song was Stardust. The song was appropriate because of his car being named Stardust. He even bought Sue a bracelet that had a music box in it, and guess what it played? Yes, Stardust. Sue and her hunk were planning to be together forever until the poop hit the fan. Sue had made the mistake of writing about all of her plans in her diary. In her diary, she plans to have a perfect life with Tony and how they mad love. Sue had it written down. Even though they never did go all the way, Sue wrote it as if they had.

One day her snoopy mother broke open her diary and read it all. Sue's mom freaked out; she found Sue the next day and laid into her. Her mom called her every name in the book and told her she was never to see Tony again. Here Sue's mother was shaking her finger at her and calling her dirty names again. Sue's hunk would try to call Sue, but her mother would tell him, "Sue is not allowed to see a wicked person like you. You are a bad person, and you are never allowed to see her again." Sue was devastated.

Tony was heartbroken also. He was so upset that he joined the Navy and just couldn't live without Sue. He wrote letters to Sue for a long time until Sue's mom found them and destroyed them. Sue couldn't understand what had happened. Then one day, her girlfriend Terry told her she was getting letters from Sue's man. Sue was hurting now; Sue couldn't believe her ears. Sue's boyfriend didn't hear from Sue for such a long time that he thought she didn't want to hear from him anymore. Tony hurt Sue because she didn't understand what the situation was.

Later on, Tony came home and didn't even get in touch with her, so she figured it was over for sure. Sue decided to forget him and move on with her life. Sue hated her mother for ruining, possibly the best thing that had ever happened to her. Eventually, Sue found out that Tony became a preacher, was married and had a beautiful family. After all of her heartbreak, it was time for Sue to start over again.

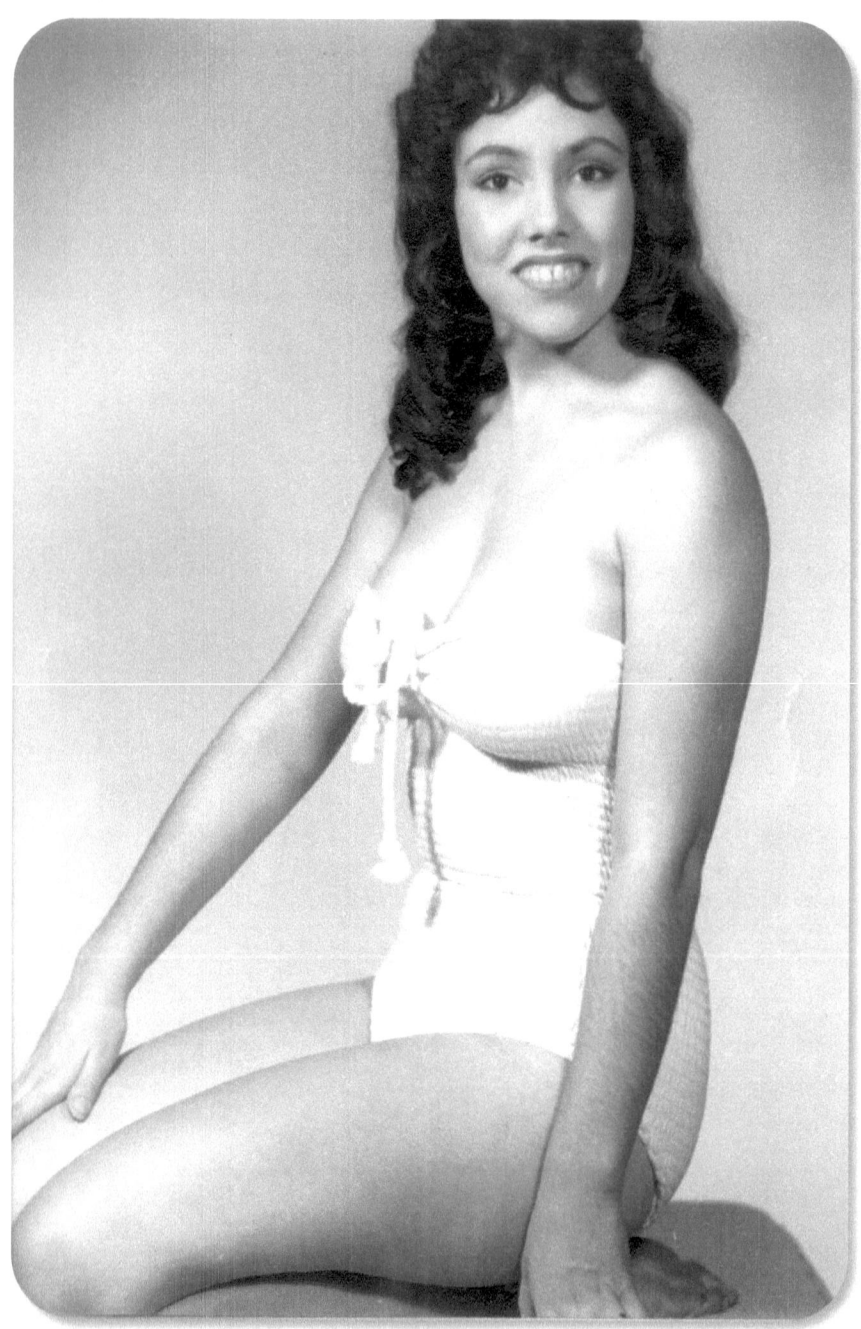

Suzie at 16

CHAPTER 4

HER FIRST HUSBAND, BARRY, AND HER GIRLS WENDY AND STACY

A girlfriend came over one day and asked Sue if she wanted to drive through the drive-ins like they used to. Sue's reply was, "I guess. Why not? Let's go for it." It was a beautiful warm summer night while they were cruising around all of the drive-ins in town. It seemed like a new start in Sue's life, and they were having a lot of fun. The girls were all dolled up and smelling good, too.

As they were driving along, Sue spotted another redhead. This one had straight, dark red hair and looked like he could be Irish. They got a little closer, and Sue was able to look right into his big brown eyes. He was driving a car just like the '58 Chevy Impala convertible she used to have. The only difference was that it was dark blue instead of powder blue like Sues, and he had a floor shift instead of a column shift. Sue just had to meet this one. Sue felt this guy was even cuter than the Italian redhead, Tony. Sue never met him that night, and the girls drove around for weeks before anything started to happen.

Then one evening, Sue finally saw him again and cornered

him. As they pulled into the drive-in, he was stuck behind another car and had to look right at Sue. This guy turned out to be a timid person. Don't let the shy ones fool you. Still, water runs deep. When she cornered him, they were in the old A & W root beer stand. Sue finally got the nerve to talk to him. He admitted he knew they were following him and wanted to speak to Sue, but he didn't know what to say to her. He said, "I'm sure glad you stopped me and talked to me." After their meeting in the driven-in, they started going out. Sue found out his name was Barry; he looked like a Berry with his red hair. They hit it off right away.

One day, he took Sue to meet his family. Sue felt he had a lovely family. Later on, they went on trips to Pennsylvania for his family's reunions. She loved Pennsylvania. She thought it was a beautiful place, with all sorts of mountains and rivers. It was a very romantic place, also. Barry's family went to Church all of the time, and they were strict Southern Baptists. Sue decided to start attending their Church meetings with them. She liked the Church very much and thought it was a lot better than the Catholic Church at the time; they were into the Bible more so than the Catholics.

Her new boyfriend used to take her up on one mountain in Pennsylvania, where this gigantic cross; this made Sue feel so spiritual and a lot closer to God. Sue felt this was a miracle and a significant change in her life. It was a chance to get close to God again. Sue thought she was indeed in love and felt God forgave her for the sin of her rape. Even though it was not her sin, and still felt like it was. Sue's new man would take her up into the mountains and try to make love to her but said no numerous times. She went out with him for a whole year, and he was still bugging her, but she never gave in.

One summer vacation, they were up in the mountains of Pennsylvania again, and he started bugging her even more. He would tell Sue, "If you love me, you'll let me, and we'll get married one day." Sue was so scared. She realized he would know she was not a virgin and probably would not believe her about the rape. One evening they were in the mountains again by a beautiful waterfall. They put a blanket on the ground, and he started bugging her even more about sex. This spot was so romantic she could hardly stand it. She tried to resist, but he overpowered her, and she said, "All right, but I need to tell you something first." Sue didn't want to start her new life out with a lie, so she told him the whole story about the assault.

After she told him, he said, "All of that doesn't matter to me. I love you and want to marry you anyway." So they made love. Sue did not enjoy it because of her assault; she did not enjoy sex; she just did it to make him happy. The fact that Sue told him about the assault was one of the worst mistakes in her life. Even though he said it didn't matter, it ate at his insides for years. They made beautiful love that night. They also did oral sex, which shocked her from this quiet man. They seemed to be very close, like they were perfect for each other. Everything was fine for about two months but guess what? Yes, Sue was pregnant. Sue told him, and they decided to get married. Sue was happy to marry him for two reasons. One reason was that she loved him, and the other was to get away from her mom. When Sue told her mother about getting married, her mother didn't care. Sue's mom was glad she wouldn't have to support Sue any longer. So this worked out okay for the whole bunch of them. Sue thought everything was excellent; this was the storybook romance she had dreamed about since childhood. Or was it? Then her storybook dreams are tumbling down again.

Sue was in the first quarter of the twelfth grade and hated to quit school, but she had no choice. She felt it would be a disgrace to be pregnant and in school. At least this gave her more time to make plans for a little wedding. Her future husband's parents knew they didn't have a place to live, so they put a small down payment on a lovely house for them. The house was a dream house. The house was the little white house she had always dreamed of with a cute white picket fence around it, and the yard was all landscaped beautifully.

At this time, Sue was so happy and in love. She would spend time at the little park across the street from the house, where she could take her new baby one day. Sue's future mother-in-law was a sweetheart. She helped Sue fix up the house and bought the things she needed for it. Sue's mother-in-law-to-be even gave them a beautiful wedding shower. Sue felt her life was perfect now. Sue loved her new man and his mother also.

It was the night before the wedding. Sue was trying to finish painting the house before the wedding; she wanted everything to be perfect before moving into the home. Sue was all alone and six months pregnant by now, and the cupboards still needed to be painted. Here she was, standing on a ladder, trying to finish the painting and was as big as a house. She was waiting for Barry to get there to help her. Barry promised her he would help her. It seemed like hours went by, but he never showed up. Sue was not even married yet, and the crap was starting already. The reason he never showed up was that he was out getting drunk with the boys. Sue couldn't go out with the girls on her pre-wedding night but could go out with the boys. Sue couldn't believe that he would leave her there and not help her finish the house. He didn't help much at all, getting ready for their new life. Here Sue was so sick, trying to go up and down the ladder, smelling the fumes of the paint, and no man there to help her.

Finally, one of Barry's friends came over. He felt terrible for Sue and helped her paint the rest of the cupboards. Sue was so upset and hurt; she just couldn't believe it. What a way to start a new life. Then the bridegroom-to-be finally came home; he was drunk as hell. Sue was so shocked because she thought he was supposed to be such a good Christian boy. It was the evening before her wedding, and Barrys reeking the smell of alcohol on the breath. Sue was so hurt to think that he would do this to her. That familiar stench of alcohol filling the room, and this brought back all of her bad memories. The smell made her feel sick inside and broken-hearted again.

When Barry got into the house and saw his buddy there alone with his wife-to-be, he started in on her and called her names. He said, "I knew you were a slut with all of the lies you told me." Then he started to attack his buddy, shouting, "What are you doing here all alone with my woman?" Sue didn't know what to say. She was

SECRETS ARE OUT NOW

so embarrassed. The buddy ended up going home, and Sue went to her mother's house. Barry stayed there at the house and slept off his drunk.

The next day arrived, and Barry didn't know what had happened. So, he proceeded to get ready for the wedding. Sue got up and decided to go along with her plans; she loved him and didn't have much of choice, anyhow. Sue put her hurt deep down inside again and went on to her wedding. They held the wedding in the Baptist Church that they were attending. Sue had been raised Catholic, but she was giving it up for her new husband. It did not matter to her because of the abuse she took from the nuns when she was a Catholic; she hated the Catholic religion, with their statues and props; mostly, her parents never took her.

The wedding was not very fancy, but it was lovely. Sue wore a cream-colored dress and white shoes with a tiara, which she had worn to Barry's prom dance one year. She fixed the tiara up with some veiling she had bought at the store. It wasn't much of a wedding outfit, but it worked. At Sue's wedding, it broke her heart when her parents never showed up. She knew what they thought of her now, and she suspected her dad wouldn't show up because he was too busy with Wilma. He had her living out at his ranch with him now, and her mom probably didn't show up because she was ashamed of Sue being pregnant. Well, so much for Sue's perfect dream wedding.

After the wedding, there was a small reception in her new mother-in-law's basement. Sue's mom did show up for this; Sue was glad about that, but it hurt that she didn't show up for the wedding. Sue's best friend, Roseann, was there and was also at the wedding. Bonnie was there too. Roseann and Bonnie were the only girlfriends that showed up for Sue's wedding. Sue's new mother-in-law put on a lovely spread, and they received a lot of excellent gifts. They got everything they needed to start their new life. A few months later, Berry's mom had a unique baby shower for her.

It was time for the blessed event. Sue was very sick with all of her pregnancies and as big as a house with all of them. She could hardly walk or tie her shoes because she couldn't bend over. She gained fifty pounds with this pregnancy, and she couldn't do anything after a while. Her skin ripped from one end to the other, and this caused numerous stretch marks. Sue's breasts were gigantic because of having so much milk forming; she even had breast sacks under her arm because there was so much milk. Sue's perfect body was gone forever now. Sue felt losing her ideal body was worth it for her little child. Sue was a natural at being a mother. Sue's husband was not a very compassionate man to Sue or their future child; he would call her fat, and he thought she looked ugly with all of her stretch marks.

Before the baby was born, they went over to her mother-in-law's house. It was a frigid and wintry day, and it had snowed all night. As they were walking into the house, her mother-in-law's floor was very wet with snow. Just as soon as Sue got into the house, she slipped on the floor and fell. She thought for sure that she broke something. Sue was so scared that Sue might have harmed her baby. She was lying on the cold, wet floor; her husband just stepped over her. Also, he didn't even try to help her up or even ask if she was okay. After a few minutes, her mother-in-law came in and helped Sue up from the floor. Sue was ok after a while and wasn't hurt. The only thing that he broke was her heart; to know that her husband didn't attempt to help her. She felt her storybook life would never come true, and she felt so insecure. However, this was not the only time Sue's husband would be uncaring.

Another incident when he didn't show Sue any compassion was when she was on the toilet. Being pregnant, she was always getting constipated, and she would have such a hard time that her rectum would bleed. One particular morning, she was having trouble, and her husband was banging on the bathroom door, telling her, "hurry up because I need to brush my teeth." Sue's husband was a very insensitive person. Sue treated her husband with respect and let him in the bathroom while she went and lay down on the bed. Sue was sad again. She decided she needed to try to harden her heart. Sue's hardening her heart was like telling a bird not to fly, but she did it.

SECRETS ARE OUT NOW

Sue finally went into labor, and her mother took her to the hospital. Sue's husband never showed up; work was more important. Sue was in labor for about twelve hours. As she delivered the baby, its head was face down, and the doctor had to turn it. The doctor got the baby's head corrected, and the baby finally was born, and everyone was okay. Sue had gone through a lot of pain, but she said, "It was all worth it when she saw her little redheaded baby girl." Sue's baby weighed 7 pounds and 12 ounces. That was a big one. The baby had big brown eyes that almost looked black; they were so dark. The baby's eyes were so big that her grandfather called her "Banjo Eyes" for a nickname. Her hair was as red as her Barry's. They gave the baby the name of Wendy Kay. Later on, when the baby grew up, her eyes were still big and brown, but her hair turned straw blond. Since Sue always took good care of her body and took all kinds of vitamins, she had healthy children. Here, little Sue was a mother at eighteen. Being eighteen was a hard start for her so early, but she was a survivor and could handle anything.

Barry and Sue were only married a year, and guess what? Yep, she was pregnant again. Sue was using a diaphragm, and her husband wanted sex so much that she didn't put the device in right, and she got pregnant also. Sue's husband would argue with her and try to make up by having sex with her. During Sue's second pregnancy, she gained another fifty pounds. She was as big as a house again. She was still healthy because of the vitamins she took also. This pregnancy was not as hard on her as the first because of having one baby already. It was time for her to deliver, and her husband was not there again. At least her mom was there for her also. Here Sue had another little girl. This one had very dark hair like Sue's, but it didn't stay dark. Sue thought for sure this one would look like her, but she didn't. The new baby's hair turned a medium blond color, similar to her sister's. The new baby had big brown eyes like the first one, also. Sue decided to call her Stacy. For a while, the girls even looked like twins. The new little one was not as small either; she weighed eight pounds and two ounces. She was a little cutie pie, just like the first one. Sue was glad the second one was a girl because they would have each other as friends to grow up with, not like Sue, who was alone all of her childhood.

After a while, Sue began to get her shape back, but she had a lot of weight to lose. She looked good with clothing on, but she had a lot of stretch marks to hide. She felt ugly after having the girls. It wasn't perfect that she looked pretty anyhow because her husband was a jealous person and took it out on her.

People wouldn't believe how much trouble they were having in their marriage. They looked like the perfect little family. They would go to church twice every Sunday and once every Wednesday evening. Sue loved to go to Church, and she was starting to get closer to the Lord. At first, in their marriage, they were reading the Bible together. Sue could remember hearing people say, "The family that prays together will stay together." Later on, she felt that saying was a bunch of crap. Things were getting worse and worse as time went on. One incident happened when they were riding in the car to get ice cream for the girls. They got ice cream often since they didn't have a lot of money for anything else. All through the five years that they were married, Sue's husband never took her anyplace. Sue was not a selfish person and didn't mind that they never went anywhere. Sue enjoyed being able to get ice cream, though, and the girls loved it also.

The ice cream adventure took place one warm summer day after Church. After they got their ice cream, they were driving along, and Sue turned the radio on. The song that was playing was, "What's New Pussycat?" Instantly, Sue's husband turned it off and told her she was a tramp for listening to that trash. This incident was just the beginning. Sue's husband was obsessed with jealousy, and the thought of her being with another man before they were married just drove him crazy. Sue's past just ate at him, even though it was not Sue's fault. Barry never believed her, and she sure wished she had never told him the truth about her past. Sue was always a loyal wife to her husband, and he didn't have anything to worry about, but he didn't trust her.

SECRETS ARE OUT NOW

At the time, the girls at least had a good life. They never suspected what was going on. Sue would have felt all alone, but the girls were good company for her. Later in life, Sue's girls were more like friends than her children. Sue loved her girls and used to make all of their clothing. She would make matching dresses for the girl because they looked so much alike Sue dressed them like twins. Sue would have given her girls the world if she could have.

Sue's husband didn't make much money, and she wanted her girls to look beautiful, so this was why she made their clothing. Barry was a dairy food manager and only brought home about eighty dollars a week. She used to think that they would be rich if he could get at least one hundred dollars a week! Sue used to be able to buy groceries for her family for only ten dollars a week. Those good old days are gone forever. Although money was never their problem, it was the love and trust that was missing. Sue was a very loyal and honest person and would never do anything to jeopardize her family, but Barry was always mean to her because of his jealousy and distrust.

Since Sue's shape was looking good, her husband grew even more jealous. One day they were driving to go pick up the girls from their grandparent's house. Luckily for the girls, they weren't in the car yet. It seemed like Sue's husband never started anything in front of the girls, so that was good. As they were driving, they pulled up to a traffic light. Sue was sitting there in their car, minding her own business. Then she glanced over; there was a young, good-looking man in the car next to her. All at once, this man started smiling at Sue and winking at her. Barry immediately figured she was flirting with this man and even accused her of knowing this guy. Sue's husband was overly jealous. Her husband is when things started getting wrong in their marriage. Sue began sticking up for herself, and he didn't want to hear it. He called her every name he could think of, and if that was not enough, he punched her in the mouth. After Sue's husband hit her, she had blood running down her lip and all over her blouse. Sue was so shocked to think her dream man would do something like this to her. Many of these incidents happened, and after a while, Sue started turning her love off for Barry.

When they arrived at her mother-in-law's house to pick up the girls, her mother-in-law never said a word about Sue's mouth. She pretended like nothing was wrong. You see, her son could never do any wrong in her eyes. His mother didn't want to get involved in their problems. For many years, Sue felt she had to put up with it because she thought this was how married life was supposed to be. She could remember her mother and father fighting like this and figured she didn't have a choice.

Meanwhile, Sue was trying to keep her mind occupied. She decided to make more money by working at the cleaners her parents owned, and she thought she would go back to school. Sue decided to go to beauty school and become a cosmetologist. She was tired of being a "nobody." Barry would tell her she was a "nothing person," and she didn't want to feel like a "nobody."

One day, Sue's mother told her that she was going to sell the house. The house she lived in, in Roseville. Sue was very upset about her mother selling her childhood home. Sue's mother told her that she would move out to the farm with Sue's dad and make him get rid of that woman that was living there. Sue felt glad about that because she knew her mother had been lonely since he moved out. Sue felt that her mom should have told her something about this a long time ago. Maybe Sue's life would have been better if she would have been with her dad when she was younger. Sue asked her husband if he would buy the house for her and the girls, and he said, "If the price is right, I'll buy the house." Sue's mother said she would sell it for half of what they had paid for it, and they could take over the remaining payments from her. Barry couldn't refuse this; it was such a good deal. Well, they did just that and bought the house. They were all moved into the house, and they liked it. This house was a big red brick house; Sue loved to be back in the place where she grew up in when she was a young girl.

Sue thought since they had moved that things would get better

SECRETS ARE OUT NOW

for them, but this wasn't true. Time went on in the new house, and things were getting worse. Sue worked at the cleaners, going to school, taking care of the house and the girls. But Barry didn't even appreciate the fact that she was working so hard. Once in a while, Sue would try to have Barry take care of the girls when she had to go to her job. But, Barry was not a good father. When Sue would come home from work, the girls would be running around with poopy diapers, and Barry would be out in the garage playing with his cars. He was too busy for his children. Some babysitter he was. Sue was trying to save money by her husband babysitting. Since their father wasn't a perfect babysitter, Sue decided to get her girlfriend Roseann; to sit for the girls. Sue used to pay her friend Roseann to take care of the girls even though she couldn't afford it. Roseann needed the money, and Sue was glad to help her.

Barry continued to neglect his family. There were times when he would arrive home, walk in the front door, and out the back door, never even say "Hi!" or also look at his family. Barry was so into himself that the only time he had sex with Sue was after a fight. He would try to force himself on her. The only time he would talk to her was to yell at her about something. For example, he would yell at her for a cupboard door not being closed or the kid's toys lying on the floor. Sue worked hard to help get beautiful things for their home, but Barry would want money for his six toy cars out in the back yard. But that was not enough; he wanted more cars.

While Sue was working at her parent's cleaners, she was still making the girls' clothing to save money. One of the outfits she made the girls were pale yellow dresses with white flowers on them. Sue bought the girls little white patent leather shoes to go with the ensembles. She even made little yellow coats to match. The girls looked great on Easter. When Sue would go to work, her friend Roseann would watch the girls. One day Roseann decided to bring her little bull terrier over. The girls loved Rose's dog until one day when the oldest girl pulled the dog's ear, and he bit her on the lip. The bite left a scar on her mouth that can be seen still to this day. Everyone laughs about it now, but it wasn't funny at the time.

It was about this time in Sue's life when things started to get even worse. One day when she got home from beauty school, she was fifteen minutes late. She had a long way to drive, and traffic was heavy that day. As Sue walked into the house, Barry tore into her. Sue's man was calling her all sorts of names again and telling her she was out with some other man. He started bringing up Sue's past like he always did. Sue's history was still eating at him, and he never believed Sue was telling the truth. Barry would tell Sue that she let those men screw her and that they didn't rape her.

Another time, late in the evening, Sue and Barry decided to go to bed. Suddenly, as they were sleeping, her husband woke up and started beating the hell out of her. Sue was so shocked. Then he kicked her out of bed and pushed her down the stairs, yelling and calling her names. Barry was pretty crazy for a guy who was supposed to be a Bible-believing Christian that went to Church on Sunday but then would come home and beat up his wife. If that wasn't enough, he still wanted sex from her. Of course, she was not in the mood, so Berry ripped off her nightgown and tried to force himself on her anyhow. He was still struggling with her, getting nowhere, so he decided to stick his weeny into her leg. As he was humping her leg like a dog, he came all over her leg. After that, she thought her husband was nuts. She was so shocked by his actions. Things like this started to turn off her love for him even more.

Sue's storybook love was indeed gone now. As time went on, things got even worse. These incidences were starting to bring back all of Sue's past with men, making her feel insecure and lonely. Even though the love in their hearts was fading, Sue still wanted to salvage the marriage. She was willing to keep working on their marriage for the girl's sake. Sue's in-laws couldn't believe they were having marital trouble. Of course, it could not be their son's fault. There had to be something wrong with Sue. Barry's family thought Sue needed to see a counselor. Sue's mother-in-law told her she should talk to the pastor of their Church, the one who married them. Sue said that she would try anything. However, it shouldn't have been Sue talking to the pastor; it should have been her husband. Sue's mother-in-law set up a time for the pastor to come out to Sue's house to talk. A few weeks passed, and Sue didn't think he was coming over.

Then one afternoon, the pastor showed up. At that particular time, Sue's husband was not at home. As the pastor walked into the house, he had the strangest look on his face. He couldn't imagine what she wanted to tell him. So, Sue proceeded to say to him about all of her problems with her marriage. Sue talked to the pastor of their church, and she told him about her past, also the tole him about men that assaulted her and how her father was an alcoholic; Sue poured out her heart to him. After the pastor listened to Sue's story, he told her, "The problem with you is that you were never taught how to love, because of not having a good father." Then the pastor told her! "Come over and sit on my lap, and I will teach you how to love." Sue was shocked to hear him tell her this. Then the pastor pulled Sue over onto his lap. Sue jumped back immediately and told him her husband would be coming home soon, and she needed to get the house cleaned. The pastor pulled her over to him again and started squeezing her. Then she told him he'd better leave or she was going to tell everyone what he had done to her.

Finally, the pastor left, and Sue broke down into tears. She didn't know what she would do now. Sue knew she couldn't tell her in-laws about this. They would never believe her and would think that she was the one who instigated the scene. Before this incident with the pastor, Sue was close to God and the Church. But after this, Sue didn't want anything to do with the Church or God. After the pastor messed up her head; She started getting books about astrology and witchcraft. One of her friends told her to get these books. She thought she needed some spiritual guidance, and that is where she would look. Sue felt bad; she didn't know where to turn.

The next day, Sue's in-laws wanted to know how things went with the pastor, and Sue told them that it didn't help at all. Sue's in-laws thought Sue was crazy and didn't want help, anyway. One of Barry's uncles got wind of their trouble and decided he could help. Sue felt he might as well try to help and that it couldn't hurt. Sure enough, her husband's uncle came over the next day. When the uncle walked in the door, he walked in and had the same strange look on his face that Sue had seen many times before. As the uncle was coming in, he said, "Since I am a Sunday school teacher, I would like to try to help you." Sue felt, "Why not?" then, uncle proceeded to talk to Sue as she poured out her heart again and told him about all of her past. It seemed like every time she told people about her history; they would take advantage. Next, he said, "Since you kids are getting a divorce, lets we get together? Sue was shocked again. The uncle said, "I have always wanted you since the first day I laid my eyes on you." He also told Sue that his wife never had sex with him, and he needed it. Sue was so shocked she started yelling at him and told him he was sick and perverted. Here he had such a nice wife and children, and he even taught Sunday school. The uncle must have been going nuts. The more Sue yelled at him, the more he started coming after her. He was chasing Sue all around the house, telling her she needed to have sex with him to relieve himself. He said, "My wife doesn't give me any."

Luckily for Sue, her husband came home, and the uncle left the house. Of course, Sue could not repeat a word about this incident because no one would believe her, or they would accuse her of being the one to started things. After that incident, Sue was ashamed to go around the family. Sue could not look at the people in Church, mostly the uncle's wife and children. Sue had not done anything wrong, but she felt guilty about things again. Sue quit going to the Church also. Sue was ready to get out of this family that thought she was crazy. At the time, she started to believe she was going mad; everyone told her that she was, and she started believing it. Sue began to imagining things running around on the floor. She felt that she was losing her mind, and it was time for her to help herself, so she went to a physician who was a psychologist also. He was the gynecologist that had delivered her last child.

The doctor consulted her for months; he told her what her problem was; her father did not teach her how to love. At least what the pastor had told her was true. The doctor found out that Sue had never had a climax with her man, and he felt that she needed to take care of herself instead of relying on her husband. He told her that she didn't trust men because of what they had done to her, and she needed to relax and rely on herself and trust herself. Because she was upset, the doctor said if she didn't take care of herself, she would crack up. Since she thought no one loved her, she had to enjoy herself and not worry about what others thought of her. He said she had to satisfy herself until the right man came along. The right man would have to love her enough to meet all of her needs. The doctor reassured her that she would find the right one someday and not to give up.

Since Sue was so frustrated and needed to get relief, the doctor taught Sue how to masturbate and give herself a climax. He also taught her how to squeeze her muscles to be able to get more out of sex. At least the doctor was very professional with Sue and didn't try anything nasty. Thank God she had one person she could trust. After that, Sue still felt alone. She needed more than just taking care of herself physically. She still needed love and security. Sue eventually did get a divorce, and then Sue and the girls moved in with her mom and dad at the ranch. But she still felt crazy and needed something else in her life. At this time, Sue thought she was lost and didn't have any direction, so she started reading again about different types of philosophies, astrology, religions, and even witchcraft. With the witchcraft, she could manipulate people, and she liked that because she was tired of people running her life and making her feel inferior. Even though Sue tried witchcraft, Sue never really got into it. She did not want to hurt anyone.

Sue and the girls were living at the ranch, which they loved. The girls had all sorts of animals to play with, and they were in heaven. Sue loved it also, but she felt like she was a real burden on her parents again. Sue didn't have money, and her parents didn't have much at that time either. Sue decided to try to move back to the city and get a job as a beautician. One day Sue went over to a friend's house, and the friend told her about a job in a salon where she used to get her hair done. Sue's friend was Phyllis. She was one of her best friends she ever had; they both had many things in common. They were both divorced, both had children, and both had brutal men in their lives. Phyllis was a wonderful, classy lady. Phyllis is still her friend to this day. Later on, they both went to the hospital and had plastic surgery together. They were very close friends. They both got tummy tucks and were both in the same room.

Somehow they lost contact for about thirty years. After all those years, a strange thing happened. They found each other and got very close again. Finally, Sue had her friend back. One day, Phyllis wanted Sue to meet her hairstylist to see if she could get a job there. Sue went for the interview, and she got the job. She was excited about that. Sue became very close to the manager of the salon. He was a tall, dark Italian man named Louis; they started dating and got along very well. Sue always liked classical music, and Louis was into opera. They would go out to her dad's ranch and ride the horses and had a lot of fun. Louis loved Sue's kids and did a lot for all of them. He even refinished her buggy, refinished the seat, painted it black, and made the wheels red. Since Sue had the Tennessee walking horse, the buggy was perfect; they would hook up the horse and had fun riding around in the carriage.

Since Sue was working now, she decided to get an apartment and bring the girls there. The girls didn't like that, but Sue didn't want to be a burden on her parents any longer, and it was a long drive from Sue's work to the ranch. The apartment was a dump, but it was all she could afford at the time. One good thing was that the girls were in school while Sue was working. Sue was working hard to be able to make ends meet and was not doing very well, so she decided to start working evenings, also. Since she was working evenings, she needed a babysitter for the girls. Luckily for Sue, a young girl was living in the same building as they were. Or, maybe it wasn't lucky for Sue. One evening, Sue came home at about ten o'clock, and the girls were scared because when they came home from school, there was no babysitter. She finally found the sitter and confronted her. Later on, Sue found out the reason was not there when the girls came home was because she was drunk in her apartment. She forgot all about the girls.

Time went on, and the babysitter problem kept getting worse, and Sue was getting discouraged with her life again. One day, Sue told Louis about her pain, and of course, Louis helped her. He was a real gentleman and was always buying things for Sue and her girls, and helping them with money. Sue and Louis were falling in love. Even though the Italian man was helping her, she still felt weird. She felt terrible that she needed so much help. There were a lot of times where Sue and the girls would stay the night at Louis's mom's house. It was a good situation for the girls because Louis still lived with his mother. His mother was a real nice person. She would make them all kinds of food; Sue and the girls even started to get fat.

Louis used to cut Sue's hair and used her as a model in hair shows. He even gave her a cut that was called the Sassoon with a batman bang. It was a crazy cut; Sue had always had long hair until she got with Louis. Her hair was really short now, and she missed her long hair. Louis even bleached Sue's hair to blonde one time. Another time he dyed it red, but she didn't look good that way. Later, he changed Sue's hair back to blue-black. Sue felt a lot better in black hair. Louis loved Sue a lot and even took her to Florida for a vacation; it was her first time there. They say, "Get sand in your shoes, and you will return." Later on in life, Sue did return to Florida. On this first trip, Louis and Sue had a wonderful time. They ate and ate and lay in the sun. However, Louis got real burned and didn't feel very well. When he got better, they went to Nassau, where they took a helicopter ride. They went on a boat ride down a river and saw things such as alligators, pink flamingos, and beautiful mansions. They also stopped at a shop where you could open an oyster and find a pearl inside. It was a wonderful trip.

Sue loved Louis, but she knew the relationship was going nowhere fast. All he wanted to do was possess Sue. She didn't like him in the way he wanted her to. At the time, she didn't realize how much Louis really loved her and how much she loved him. Sue was just too young to see what she had. Sue broke up with Louis because she didn't feel he would ever want to get married, and she was too young to be tied down again, anyhow. Later in life, Louis never did marry anyone. He had relations but never married. Sue did not want to live with someone and not be married, so she moved on.

Later in life, Sue felt she had given up the best man she ever had and didn't even realize it. Sue didn't feel good about her life, having to rely on someone she didn't love as much as she should. She decided she wanted to be her own person. Louis's friend was another stylist at the same salon where Sue worked, and she used to talk to him and confided in him about all of her problems. He told her that he hung around many dancers in Detroit, and she should become a dancer. He knew of some places in Detroit that he could take her for a job interview, and she would make a lot of money. That way, she could be her own person and work while her girls were asleep. Plus, she could be with the girls during the day, and she could work at night.

Sue was shocked. She never thought of doing something like that. Sue used to take dancing lessons, but she never dreamed of being that kind of a dancer. Sue's friend told her she could make all kinds of money and still be with her girls. Sue started thinking long and hard about this, and the more she thought about it, the more she felt it might be the right thing for her. Sue decided to go for it. Even though she was terrified, she thought she could do it. Sue couldn't work in Detroit and leave the girls all night alone in the apartment with that unreliable babysitter, so Sue decided it was time to move back home to the ranch with her parents. The girls were ecstatic about getting to move back to the farm. At the farm, they had dogs, cats, goats, sheep, and, most of all, the horses. Sue's dad used to take the girls to all sorts of horse shows. They hoped they could ride in them someday like their mother used to do. Another reason Sue felt this was a good move because she could afford to give her parents a lot of money now to help them, and she could buy the girls anything they wanted.

Sue's friend at the salon told Sue she was beautiful, and she would be an excellent go-go dancer. Back in those days, the dancers worked in fringe costumes in cages. The men never got close to them so that they couldn't grab the dancers. Another good thing was that they wore both tops and bottoms. There were no topless dancers at that time. As Sue was thinking about all of this, she remembered that a while back, she went to a fortuneteller that told her she would be making a lot of money from men one day. Sue didn't think anything about fortunetellers at that time, but maybe there was something about it that made some sense. The more she thought, the more she knew this was the thing to do; to become a go-go dancer. The club she tried out at was the first club, where dancers were in Detroit.

Sue's child support wasn't enough to shake a stick at, so she knew she had made the right decision. At the ranch, her dad used to have hayrides, rent out the horses, and also rented the park where there were swings and slides for the girls to play. Sue's dad even had a big hall he rented out for parties and weddings. Though her dad had all of this income, it still was not enough to pay for all of his bills. Sue's money would help out tremendously. Also, Sue got some modeling jobs. One of her sessions was in her English riding outfit. Her new lifestyle was very glamorous and made her feel better about herself.

Sue Modeling

CHAPTER 5

SUE DANCING IN DETROIT AND MIKE WHEN HE WAS HER BOYFRIEND

It was time to head down to Detroit to get that dancing job. Sue's friend from the beauty shop took her to a place called "Cafe Chablis; it was a turning point in Sue's life. There was one bad thing about her getting a job in Detroit, and that was she would have to drive about sixty miles one way to get to work and sixty miles to get back home. But, she was a survivor, and she could handle it. Sue arrived in Detroit at "Cafe Chablis" and was scared. Her friend from the beauty shop didn't come in; he told her, "You're on your own now." Now she was even more nervous. As she walked into the place, it was huge. They served lunch in the afternoon to businessmen, and Sue had the option to work days if she wanted. Then the owner came up to her and asked her, "May I help you?" Sue replied, "I'm here to apply for a dancing job." The owner asked, "Have you ever danced before?" Sue said, "Oh, yes, I have danced in California." Which was a lie, but Sue didn't know what to say. Sue was a dancer throughout her childhood. All of her experiences were in tap, ballet, and dancing in recitals, she felt she had enough skills to meet the challenge of this job. The owner told Sue to come back that evening when the band was playing, and she could audition for him. Sue was so excited. Sue told him, "I will see you later." Sue instantly went out to buy herself some excellent costumes. The one bad thing about being a dancer was that she was still over-weight, had big saggy boobs, and a lot of stretch marks. When Sue got back into the car and told her friend about her audition, her friend was happy for Sue, and sure it would work. Her friend said to her that she better be careful dancing in a place like that because there were all sorts of hookers, druggies, and crooks. He didn't want Sue to get involved with the wrong people. Sue told him, "Don't worry. I can handle it."

Sue went back that evening and tried out for the job. When she came out on the stage, her knees were knocking, and she was so scared. Even though Sue was afraid, she looked great. She had purchased a black bra with black bottoms, black tights and had sewed the fringe on them. Of course, the costume wouldn't have been complete without the black go-go boots she wore. Sue felt good with her new outfit. Sue was a little stiff, but she did great, and the manager offered her the job after her audition.

Things were going fine with her job; she made seven dollars an hour, and back in those days, that was like making one hundred dollars an hour. Right away, Sue went out and bought her girls all sorts of things, even a new swing and slide set. Also, she gave her parents a lot of money, which made them all very happy. Since Sue's dad was still getting drunk and beating on her mom, this money came in handy for Sue's mom to pay bills. Sue could remember all of the beatings her father did to her mother. It was an awful way for Sue to grow up. One good thing about her situation now was that her dad didn't fight with Sue's mom when the girls were around. Thank God for that. Things were going perfect for Sue for a while. One evening, the owner came up to Sue and said, "All of the clubs in California have been going topless for a long time, and we are going to go topless also." Sue was shocked. She had never thought this would happen. The owner said, "If you want to stay in business, you have to go along with the change." Sue didn't know what to do; she had never done anything like this before.

Sue knew she needed to try to do something because if she were to quit dancing, everyone would suffer for it. Then Sue decided to go to California and try to dance topless there where no one knew her, and she wouldn't feel so embarrassed. It was a long drive for Sue, but it was something she needed to do. The girls were okay at her parent's place, and Sue needed a vacation, anyhow. What an adventurous person Sue was. So, Sue hopped into her' 68 Buick Luxury Sedan and hit the road. The good thing about her car was when she got tired; she could pull over and stretch out in the back seat and sleep. Since Sue was so short, she fits perfectly. Sue could save money this way; she would go into an exclusive neighborhood, lock the doors, and sleep in her car.

Sue's old racing days came back to her on her trip; it was a great feeling for her to be flying down the road again. She didn't have much trouble with the drive except for a speeding ticket of one hundred dollars because; she was going one hundred miles an hour in Arizona. Lucky for Sue, she had enough money with her to pay the fine. Sue always did have a lead foot.

She finally arrived in California after three days and nights of steady driving. She got a motel and decided to get some rest but, she was too excited about being in California that she could hardly sleep. Sue was a little scared, also. Now she was in Hollywood, California, on Sunset strip, looking for a strip job. She could not believe she was there. Sue's motel was right on Sunset and Vine, where there was a whole row of strip bars. The next afternoon, she decided to walk down the strip; then she saw one place called the "Bat Cave." This club was a dump. Sue wanted to pick out a place where there were not very many people. As Sue walked in this place, it did look like a bat's cave. It was all dark, gloomy, and musty smells. Sue was looking around for the owner, and when he came out from a curtain on the stage. The owner said, "Well! Well! What do we have here?" Sue replied, "I'm from Detroit and would like to get a dancing job."

The owner said, "I just happen to have an opening for you." Sue said, "I'll take it." The owner told Sue that she could start right now for his lunch crowd. And that is what she did.

The owner told Sue to go change in the dressing room behind the stage to get ready. As she entered the room, all she could see was a dark, nasty, dirty dressing room. She could see cockroaches running all over the place. Sue was scared to death as she proceeded to get into her costume. Then, it was time for Sue to go up on stage. The place was full of businessmen for their lunch. Before she knew it, it was her turn to go up. The dancers would put quarters in a jute-box and pick out the songs they wanted to dance. The rules were, on the third song, they are to take off their tops. Sue was very shy, but she grinned and bared it literally, bared it. The one reason she was so nervous was because of her hanging boobs and stretch-marked. Sue felt so ashamed to be showing them since the other girls were so firm; the majority of them all had boob jobs. Sue was thinking that maybe she should investigate into getting a boob job, also.

Sue danced at the Bat Cave for a whole week, and then she had enough. She was getting homesick for her family and wanted to go home. Sue told the owner that she wanted her money because she needed to go back home. The owner told Sue, "We only pay every other week, and I cannot pay you until next week." Sue was very disappointed. Sue pleaded with him, but he said, "No." However, he did say that he would send the money to wherever she wanted. So, Sue said, "Ok," and she gave him her address and left. But, Sue never did get paid for her week's work in California. That place got her to humiliate herself, and received nothing for it. Sue felt California was a rip-off and hated it there.

As she was driving back home, she felt awful about getting ripped off, and she felt very lonely. Sue was very tired of driving, and she saw a guy hitchhiking and decided to pick him up. She had never done this before and thought it would be a new experience. Luckily for Sue, this was not in the 2000s when the world became even more corrupt. Sue spotted a young cute, little fellow trying to get a ride, so she picks him up. The fellow got in and was very appreciative that she had picked him up. His name was Bill, and he turned out to be a lovely person, and they had a swell time. As they were driving along, Bill asked Sue if she would like to stop in Las Vegas for some fun. She figured, "Why not?" Her motto was still; "I will try anything once." So, off they went to Las Vegas. Sue and Bill did not have very much money, and they decided to stick with the slot machines. Sue lost twenty-five dollars and decided to quit. Sue's friend Bill decided it was enough for him, also. Sue and Bill were getting pretty close and decided to live it up in exciting Los Vegas, so they got a room and partied together even more. Bill was her first fling since Louis.

The next day, they started driving again and arrived in New Mexico, where Bill knew some people. They stopped there for a while, but Sue was getting anxious to get home. Sue exclaimed, "I need to leave." But Bill didn't want to go, so Sue just left him there and went on home. Sue was glad Bill didn't mind. Sue never saw him again after that. Sue was tired of driving, but she could make it by herself. As she was driving, all she could think about was, she had to go topless back in Detroit. Sue didn't know what to do. Finally, she arrived back home and saw her family; they were all good. The next day, she went to Detroit to talk to her boss. Sue's boss was happy to see her and asked how her trip was. As she proceeded to pour out her heart to him, she explained how she felt about going topless. Her boss, Harry, said he felt terrible for her and he'd see what he could do about it. Sue's boss had become very attached to Sue and wanted to help her, or so she thought. Sue didn't have any money at the time and couldn't afford to pay for a boob job. So, Harry said he would pay for her to get a boob job, and all she had to do was go to the doctor he recommended and pay him back later. Sue was so excited, and of course, she told him that it was okay with her. Sue had no idea what she was getting herself into. Sue was getting into prostitution and not even realizing it. Sue was getting sucked into a bad life now, and there was no getting out of it. Sue was involved with the mafia and did not even know what was going on. So, Sue went into this doctor's office, and he examined her. He told her he would be able to do the surgery in the morning. Sue was excited and surprised that it could so soon. Now, she thought, she would finally feel better about dancing topless.

The next day, she went in for her surgery. All went well, and she thought she would be out of there in a couple of days. While she was in the recovery room, after the surgery, the doctor came in to see her. Of course, Sue was very dizzy and weak. As he came in, he locked the door behind him and proceeded to tell her what she was to do for his services. The doctor said to her that she had to suck his weeny while setting up a camera and took pictures of her. Sue was so shocked; she was a real prostitute now and didn't even realize it. Sue was so dizzy that she had to agree. Sue didn't have any choice, either. Sue's boss lied to her and told her she would be borrowing the money from him, and she could pay it back later. So he lied to her.

The next day she felt a little better, and the doctor came in again and told her, "I am going to have sex with you now." At the time, Sue was not aware of it, but she had been tricked into a prostitution ring. Sue could not believe her life then. Here Sue felt awful about this. She felt dirty and ashamed. Poor Sue felt like crap and looked like it, too. When she got home, she looked at her boobs, and they were a mess. This sick pervert put scars all around her breasts and made them about three times bigger than they should have been. Come to find out; this doctor had never done an operation like this before. This doctor was a surgeon who only removed varicose veins from people's legs. There was nothing Sue could do about it now. Sue just had to live with these freakish boobs forever. Sue had gone through a lot of bad trips in her twenty-two years of life. Always these vicious sex acts. She had experienced more of life than most forty years-olds.

It was time for Sue to go back to work. She still felt even more embarrassed now. But Sue was a great hit with the men. They just loved her big boobs. Luckily for her, at the time, they had to wear pasties and a mesh top that covered most of her scars. It was still different dancing in Detroit because she knew people there. It was more humiliating than dancing in California. One evening, while Sue was dancing, she saw the coolest looking man she had ever seen. She could not believe her eyes. After she got off the stage, this guy came over to her and asked her if she would like to drink with him. At the time, Sue didn't drink and told him, "No." He proceeded to persuade her to at least sit with him. He was so persistent with her. Sue was very leery of him because he was a smooth talker and looked cool also. Sue felt he was up to something. Finally, Sue did give in and sat with him. Then he told Sue that some friends of his were in there previously and saw a beautiful girl with big boobies; that he needed to see. So he was checking out the sexy girl. Sue thought that if her body could get a cool looking guy like this, she must be looking good.

This guy told her all kinds of things; Sue loved all of the attention and praises for being a beautiful dancer. This cool looking guy bugged Sue for weeks to go out with him, and he came to the club every night to see her for weeks. But, Sue was still leery of him and felt he looked too good to be true. This cool guy was tall, dark, and handsome. He dressed like a stud pimp and had muscles that just didn't quit. Sue found out a lot of stuff about him from the other girls like he was Maltese from London, England. Also, his name was Mike. The girls told Sue that he was bad news because he was a pimp, and she should stay away. All of this intrigued her even more.

One night, Sue let herself go. She sat with her Maltese, handsome man and talked to him for hours. He confessed that he was a pimp and claimed that one day, he would have her money and her mind. Sue laughed at him, but inside she was scared it might happen. Sue was frightened, but she didn't think that would ever happen because she had a few powers of her own. Sue's hunk chased her for weeks before he could even get to first base with her. Finally, he did overpower her and broke her down. Sue just could not fight him anymore. Mike started teaching Sue all sorts of things that were bad. Sue was still overweight, and he told her he could get her some speed to help her lose weight. Plus, it would help her energy level at work.

Here comes was a new life-style for Sue. So, Sue did what he wanted, and she did lose a lot of weight. They would go to the Clock restaurant after work, do speed and drink coffee, and sit around talking until the sun came up. Next, he taught her how to smoke marijuana. He even had her selling it. This man would tell her how his girls would make so much money for him and how she could make a lot of money in the streets. Sue thought hard about going to the streets, but she just couldn't do that. He had her under his power, but Sue never turned a trick for him; she had powers of her own.

The friend that got Sue into the dancing profession was indeed right about her getting into all sorts of nasty things. The all-mighty money and man had a hold on Sue now. Mike had told Sue that he loved her and never slept with any of his girls, except for her. Sue loved him and trusted him more than anyone in a long time. Sue was getting sucked in with his good looks and smooth-talking. One day, Sue discovered she had crabs and knew her hunk was lying to her. She decided to quit seeing him. Mike didn't like this, but he had no choice. Sue had powers of her own also.

Sue needed a new man to trust now, and she found one. Sue had all sorts of guys that wanted her that came into the club. Instead of Sue getting a nicer man, she got into an even worse crowd. This crowd was a bunch of dope dealers that screwed her up even more. Now that Sue was one of the devil's daughters, she was fair game for anything, now. The new crowd wanted Sue to take LSD, and Sue said, "No way. My life is ruined enough." So, instead of her going along with them, they slipped it into some hot cocoa she was drinking. Sue loved her hot chocolate and had no idea what they were doing. Sue was still driving home from work every night, and it was a long, hard, sixty-mile drive. That particular night, when they slipped the LSD into her hot chocolate, was right before her long trip home. As Sue was driving along, and suddenly, the lights on the dash started to get brighter, and the lines on the road were fluorescent and wavy.

Sue didn't know what was happening to her. She was so confused. Then she remembered the guys asking her if she wanted some LSD. Sue knew then what they had done. At least Sue kept her head and figured out what was going on. She felt since she was already high, she might as well enjoy it. Being all alone and tripping on LSD was a frightening experience, but Sue handled it. When she arrived at the ranch, she was trying to be quiet, but she was tripping and kind of liking it.

Sue knew she needed to get to sleep, so she tried to drink some milk, but it didn't work. As she lay in bed, she decided to close her eyes, but all she could do was see colors. Finally, Sue did kind of sleep, but it was a bizarre sleep. The next morning when she woke up, she was still high. It was a lousy way to get introduced to a new drug, being all alone and no one to help her. What will happen next to her in life? The next day after work, she tore into the guys that tricked her. They were laughing and teasing her. After a while, Sue started laughing and did admit that she liked the LSD. After that drug trip, Sue went on many other acid trips in her life. These guys introduced her to every drug imaginable, and she tried them all. But, her favorite was LSD and marijuana at that time.

As time went on, these men taught her how to sell drugs such as speed and marijuana. Sue would go into the club to work at night and sell drugs to the other girls. One night, in particular, they searched lockers for drugs, and Sue didn't know what to do. So, she wrapped the drugs in some plastic wrap and stuffed it up into her vagina. She was so scared she would get caught. Luckily for her, she never got caught. After that, she didn't take any more chances and quit selling drugs.

Sue was missing her hunk, Mike. She didn't see him for a couple of weeks. Then, he finally started coming into the club again. He started bugging her, so she broke down and started dating him again. Her hunk would tell her how he loved her and wanted to marry her one-day. He told her he would give up all of his hookers for her— what a liar. Time went on, and Sue decided to start dating him. She just could not refuse anymore. They dated for about a year, and they became inseparable. They went to Mackinaw Island and even went to Florida; they went to lots of places together. They were so much alike, and they also loved the same kind of music, which was jazz. Their favorite singer was by Nina Simone and many other famous jazz artists.

One day, the girls at work told Sue that Mike was married. Sue could not believe her ears. Next, they said to her that he had a son; it broke her heart again. She had been going out with him for a whole year before she found out about his wife. Now it was too late for her because she was so much in love. Heartbreaks were a never-ending thing for Sue. At that time, she should have broken up with her hunk, but she was too much in love with him and just couldn't bring herself to do it. Finally, she did break up with him. It was a struggle, but she did it. Sue was so devastated she started going out with all sorts of men. Sue didn't care about anything anymore. Sue even got mixed up with more Mafia men. Sue thought they were so cool, and it helped to keep her mind off her hunk, Mike.

Sue thought the men she met were cool cats. One man was the coolest she met; he wore black pinstripe suits, a trench coat, a dress hat, and black pointed shoes. He was not very tall like Sue's hunk, Mike, but he was a dark Italian man named Troy. And also, a bad thing about this relationship was that he had power over Sue. Sue still didn't care for this man like she did for Mike, but she just didn't care anymore. This mafia man introduced Sue to more sinister things. One night, he took her over to his uncle's house, where they were all sitting around drinking, doing drugs, and making plans for places they were going to burglarize. Sue was uneasy being at this house. She knew she had better play it cool. Then Troy told her, "You know I trust you, and now that you are in with us, you can never leave our organization." Troy also Sue that she could never tell anyone what she was seeing at his uncle's, or they might make her a nice pair of cement shoes. So, of course, she was hooked now. She didn't have any choice. Sue was petrified to see all of this, but she tried to play it cool.

Then, Troy told her, "Come over here, and I will show you how to shoot up." Sue didn't understand what they were saying. She was learning a whole new language. Here Sue found out the men wanted Sue to try heroin. She had no idea what it was. Sue had thought she had tried it all, but not yet. So, Sue said to herself, "Why not?" Then she could tell she had tried it all. Since she didn't know anything about heroin, they would have to help her. The men said, "Come over here, and we are going to give you some smack." Sue thought they were going to hit her. Then they said, "Sit here." Sue didn't want them to know that she had never done this before, so she tried to be cool. Sue said, "Sure, I will try anything once." First, one of them tied her arms up while; one of the others was melting some stuff in a spoon under a candle. Next, they drew this stuff up into a syringe and told her to hold still. Sue was so scared to have a needle put into her arm, but she pretended to like it was nothing. As they shot her up, they were all laughing.

A few seconds went by, and Sue was feeling awful. She was so dizzy and even threw up. Sue felt like it was in a dungeon and couldn't breathe. She was going into a coma. The guys said that maybe they gave her too much for her first time. One said, "No problem. If she dies, no one knows she's here, anyhow." Sue finally come out of it and didn't die, even though she thought she was going to die. It was the first and last time she ever did heroin. The guys never gave her any more. They didn't want her to die because they had other plans for her.

Sue was still dancing, but she was dancing at many different clubs because she didn't want to run into her Maltese hunk, Mike. One evening after work, she went out to her car and found out that; her portable TV and her tapes; had been stolen. She figured that it was the Mafia guys that set her up, and she couldn't say a word about it. These guys had her under control. They wanted her to know they were always around watching her. One night, one of them said to her, "We are going to set you up with some men, and you're going to be able to make a lot of money." Sue didn't know what they were talking about, but she found out. They wanted her to sell herself and give them most of the money. Sue didn't choose; she had to do what they wanted or get those cement shoes.

They set Sue up with all sorts of men, and Sue hated it. One time, they had Sue work with another girl. There was one man in particular that wanted two girls to work on him and for the girls to play with each other. So, Sue had to do it. She had never done this before and thought it was not right, but she did it. Sue thought it was awful. It was the worst thing she ever had to do, other than being rapped when she was just sixteen. One hot evening, the group set Sue up with a man that they didn't know and come to find out, he was a cop. Sue went into the motel with this man, and he made her do all sorts of things to him. Sue wanted him to quit, but he pulled out a badge and a gun and told her he was a cop, and she had to keep having sex, or he would turn her in. Sue freaked out and was so scared. Sue was crying and exhausted, but she had no choice. She had to do what he wanted.

Time was passing by, and Sue was there for six hours with him screwing the energy out of her. He would talk dirty to her and tell her, "I am going to have sex in every hole you have." Sue was so tired and black and blue from him holding her down. Then he finally said that he had enough and let her go. After that scene, it brought back a lot of bad memories, including memories about her assault. She wanted to run away and hide, but could not do it because they would find her. Sue didn't know how she would get away with quitting because the Mafia men would know. Luckily for her, the Mafia men had a new plan for her. The guys felt they had her sucked into their group now, and she would have to do whatever they wanted, or else they would be getting those new cement shoes for her.

One day, the head of the group told Sue that they had some stolen payroll checks, and they wanted her to circulate them. They called it hanging paper. Sue didn't know what this meant, but they taught her all about it. The next day, they took her over to the head honchos house to tell her what they wanted her to do. As she walked into the place, there was a funny machine on the table with some big, long books. They had two books of payroll checks and a tool to print the names on it. They had several different phony identifications there, too. They matched her up with one that fit Sue's description and gave her the checks. The man told her to take the payroll checks and ID and go out to the store and cash them.

The next day Sue took the checks and ID and went around to the malls and grocery stores and cashed them. Sue looked like a pro. On the second day, she went out again but didn't know how dangerous it was the second day. They gave new checks and a phony ID. It was her worst mistake. The men didn't check to see if the list was out on the payroll checks yet. Sue had purchased a blonde wig to match the phony ID, and off she went into a dry goods store.

Sue gave the clerk the check for some merchandise, and he told her he would be right back because he had to check with the manager. Sue should have quit when she was ahead. Sue was doing well, and she decided to try one more time; so she gave the clerk a check; while waiting, a cop came up and slapped handcuffs on her. Sue freaked out and was shocked. Next, they took her off to the county jail. The next day, they took her to a Detroit jail. Of course, they took mug shots and fingerprints. Sue felt horrible and was so scared.

While she was in there, a big, ugly, fat woman officer came up to her and told her to strip and spread her legs so they could search her. Sue had heard of this kind of stuff, but never thought it would happen to her. Sue felt as embarrassed as the woman stuck her fingers up Sue's privates to see if there was anything up there. All the time, the lesbian officer was laughing as she got her jollies off, playing with Sue's privates. Then, they made her shower in a big room where everyone could see her. After that, they put her in an ugly green dress and locked her into what was called a "bullpen" it had all sorts of weird women. The next day, the FBI came in and questioned her. They told her that if she squealed on the mob, they would let her go. But, Sue couldn't do that because they would kill her and her family. So, she never revealed a thing.

The mob told her that they would get her out if anything ever happened, but they lied to her. Sue was in there for weeks waiting, and she never heard from them. Sue was getting scared and thought she would be in there forever. Sue started doing some praying, which she hadn't done much of in a long time. This prison was such an awful place. There were women in there for all kinds of crimes. One was in there for prostitution, one for trying to kill her boyfriend, and one came dressed up like a man; this one scared Sue. Sue had to play like she was a real tough guy in there, or they would have started hassling her. She would tell them she was in there for a federal offense, which Sue was, but she had to play cool. Then, she said to them how the mob would get them if they messed with her. Luckily for Sue, they would lock each woman in appetite cells at night. Nighttime was creepy in there. Just enough light came into the section for her to see cockroaches crawling on the walls and rats running around on the metal rafters. Sue was so depressed that she was giving up on anyone ever getting her out of there. As she lay there on the metal bed without a pillow, she would cry herself to sleep each night.

When morning came, they fed her some oatmeal without milk or sugar, and she felt like throwing up. Sue was so depressed and knew she had to find a way out of there. Sue was trying to think of something to do, so she called one of her lady friends, Phyllis, and asked her if she could help her. Sue surely did not want to call her mom and get her upset. Sue's mom had enough things on her mind by taking care of Sue's girls. Sue's friend didn't respect her request and called Sue's mom, anyhow. Some friend she was! I guess she was looking out for Sue's welfare. Sue's mom came to her rescue and got her out: she was so grateful but, she was so embarrassed. The next day, Sue hired a lawyer by using a little money she had stashed away from dancing. Since this was Sue's first time being in trouble, the lawyer got her out of it, and all she had to do was pay restitution. Later on, Sue had a lawyer expunge her record. They gave her all of her mug shots, and she burned them. Sue knew she had to lay low now, as she indeed was not going around the mob again.

SECRETS ARE OUT NOW

Several months went by, and Sue was running out of money. She decided to go back to work, but she was always looking over her shoulder, thinking the mob would find her. Sue was feeling uneasy even though she didn't squeal on them. She started a new job at a place called the "Dragon Lady Lounge." This new place was pretty impressive. The owner made Sue a star; he had so many gimmicks for advertising. He gave Sue a whole new identity so the mob wouldn't find her. This owner's name was Ron Knight. He was one of the most helpful people she had ever met, and he became a real friend to Sue. Ron set up a gimmick where Sue would be called on the phone and get people to the club. Sue's boobs were so big from her botched up boob job that Ron used it to her advantage. Ron advertised her as Mrs. Flunger Dunger. Ha! Ha! What a laugh that was. It was silly, but it made her and Ron a lot of money.

At the club, Ron had it set up like a psychedelic cave. He had tinfoil put all over the walls. Then, he had slides made up that he flashed on the screen behind the dancers. Sue's picture was in the newspaper all of the time. Ron would have an all-girl topless band come in, and the other girls would dance to it. At times, Sue would take the cover charge at the door and then go up and dance. It was a wild place, and Sue made a lot of money. Ron had a seamstress come in and made Sue a whole new set of costumes. There were all different colors established in style like a playboy bunny costume, but with a net over her breast. It was excellent for her because it covered up her stretch marks. One time, she even had her skin body painted with all sorts of zodiac signs. It was wild, also. Ron was a comedian and would do skits on the stage with Sue. Ron was a dancer, too, and he was such a cool guy.

Ron was a part of Sue's life for a long time. In Sue's future, Ron would show up out of nowhere. He even came and found her when she was in Florida. Sue was dancing in a club in Florida when he showed up there. They always tried to keep in touch. One beautiful thing was that Ron had respect for Sue and never came on to her. They were just good friends.

Sue Modeling

CHAPTER 6

SECOND HUSBAND MIKE, SON DANA

Since Sue left her job with Ron, she felt she had laid low long enough and decided to go back to her old job at the "Cafe Chablis." Sue was doing very well again at the old place, but she was still scared that the mob would come in. She eventually heard that the guys in the mafia people all got picked up a few years back. Luckily, they never came in, and after a while, she didn't think about it any longer. Then one night, her old Maltese honey, Mike, came in, and it started all over again. This man could talk her into anything. He told Sue all sorts of lies, and she believed them. They were going out for a while; he would say that he was not with his wife anymore. Sue and her man were getting very close again, and she told him about her jail trip and how she would never do anything like that, and she never did.

Time was moving along, but Sue was having a hard time believing her man. Mike would tell her that he was living at his mother's, but when Sue went there after work, he was never there. Sue was going to find out once and for all just what he was doing at night. She got the idea to hire a private detective so she would know what Mike was doing. Sue had to pay the detective a lot of money, but she felt it was worth it.

A couple of days went by, and the detective called he told her to come in; he had some information for her. When she arrived, he told her he had bad news for her. Sue replied, "What now?" He said that her man was going over to his wife's house and staying all night. Sue said, "Wife! He lied and said, "I am divorced!" Well, Sue was so mad that she called up Mike's wife and told her what was going on. His wife could not believe it either and got angry, also. When Sue talked to her, she found out all sorts of lies he had told both of them. Sue also learned that he was still married to her; the entire time, he was seeing Sue. Here he claimed he was not married anymore. Sue felt so hurt and angry. Both women got together and decided to confront him about the lies he was telling the two of them.

Both girls figured they would meet at Mike's mothers' house, where he would go after work. They were going to find out what he wanted once and for all. As they were both waiting anxiously and both very nervous, he came walking into the house. Suppose you could have seen the look on Mike's face, with both of his women meeting at the same time. He was so surprised to see his two women there together; his mouth dropped a mile. The only bad part was that it probably boosted his ego, having two women fighting over him.

As he walked in, Sue was shaking in her go-go boots and asked him, "Well, you lying jerk, which one of us do you want?" At first, he didn't know what to say. Then, he started trying to talk to both of them, but it didn't do any good. All they wanted was for him to make a decision. Then, he finally told them that he desired Sue. Sue was very relieved, but his wife was very hurt. His wife stormed out of the house, telling him she would see him in divorce court, and that she would take everything from him. Well, Sue thought this was the end of his lies, but it wasn't. Sue's hunk promised her the moon now. Sue felt lucky, but in reality, she wasn't. Little did she know that there were more lies to come; in the future. One day, Sue and her hunk decided to take a trip to Florida, and their journey was terrific. He just wanted Sue to quit thinking about all of his lies. Things were quiet for a while with Sue, but what next for this poor girl?

SECRETS ARE OUT NOW

One evening, Sue was driving home from work at about three A.M. It was very dark outside. Sue was still driving sixty miles one way to work and back home. She was exhausted because sometimes she would work sixteen-hour shifts: she was still trying to get out of the hole from her jail episode; money was tight for her then. As she was driving, she saw a car coming down the empty road. Usually, there were no other cars on this road at this time of night. This person seemed to be looking for something. After the driver saw Sue, he instantly turned around and started following her. Then he got right behind her, and then he proceeded to pull up next to her. All of a sudden, he started banging and banging his car into hers, on purpose. It was like he wanted her to crash, or he was just trying to get her off the road or kill her.

Sue was hysterical, but she kept her mind focused, floored her car, and sped away from him. When she got some distance away, Sue could see him in her rearview mirror. He stopped dead in his tracks and was shaking, moving up and down. She thought it looked like he was masturbating; then, he just sat there until Sue drove out of sight. No wonder Sue's hair started to gray early in life! Sue couldn't figure out what it was all about. Sue was thinking about all sorts of things now. She thought that maybe it was her man's ex-wife or maybe the mob trying to kill her. Sue couldn't believe it; she had just purchased a new car. Her new car was a white Cutlass Supreme with a black vinyl top. Sue was so upset. She was an excellent driver and was able to drive out away from him.

The next morning, she went out to see her car. Sue saw it was a mess. When her dad and mom found out, they felt so bad for Sue. She has so much bad luck. Sue didn't keep that car very long because she thought it was jinxed and had too many bad memories. When she told people about the accident, they didn't believe her. They thought Sue was lying, drunk, or something. Another time when she was driving home before she sold the Cutlass, she was going, and some guy looks like a cop waved a badge at her; he was not a cop. He was only pretending to be a cop, but Sue knew better and pulled into a police station. Then the jerk went away with a shocked look on his face. Sue had so many scary incidences with that car; she decided that it was finally time to get rid of it.

Sue was getting tired of her long drive home and the scary incidents, so she asked her boyfriend if he would like to get a place in the Detroit area with her. He said he didn't care, so Sue bought an apartment building in Algonac. It was a little drive from Detroit, but still not as far as Detroit from where her parents lived. The apartment was a four-unit building and was full of tenants.occupied. The place was a little run down, but she thought her boyfriend would help her fix it up. The apartment was in a small town. And it was by the water, and there were many trees around it. Sue was glad about moving there because she wouldn't be a burden on her parents now. The girls liked it there also, but not as well as the ranch.

When they settled in their new place, Sue bought the girls a new bedroom set; it was a white French provincial style, was pretty all trimmed in gold. The best part was the canopy bed because the girls loved that. The girls would try to swing on it and eventually tore down the top and of cores she had it fixed. Sue felt if they wanted to hang on it so much, she better purchase them a new swing set. So, she did, and they loved that also. Another good thing about the place was that there was a young girl that lived in one of the units; Sue would trade rent for babysitting when she had to go to work. The girls also had a charming school there, but they still missed their old school. At first, her boyfriend Mike didn't want to move into the apartment with her but eventually came along. He only stayed there for a couple of weeks before making up excuses that he needed to stay in Detroit because of work.

Time went on, and Sue decided that she should get him to marry her. She figured maybe he might be around more if they were married. Well, she talked him into it; then they went to a justice of the peace, and when Sue arrived there, Mike was drunk. Even though he was drunk, they still got married. Sue loved this man; it was as if Mike possessed her. Sue didn't have any control over Mike and was concerned that he had control of her. But she loved him and put up with it. Sue's hunk was still gone all of the time. Getting married did not help. She got so very bored that she decided to take flying lessons. Sue enjoyed her experiences. Sue's flying lessons were sweet, but she was still tired. One evening Sue decided to check up on her hunk to see where he was and why he never came home. She went over to his mother's house where he was supposed to be, but he wasn't around. Then, she went to a place where he hung out at and sure enough, he was sitting there with a bunch of women. Sue was even more lonely and depressed now, so hurt to see him there with other women.

Then one day, some fellows moved into one of the other apartments in her building. They were cool guys. They would have parties and invite Sue to come over. She had a great time. During this time, Vietnam was going on, and all of the hippies were on a roll. Then Sue heard about Woodstock and how everyone was going and wanted her to go with them. Sue wanted to go, but she couldn't leave her girls; Later on, she found out she could have taken them with her. Later on, she would have kicked herself for not going.

Some of the guys next door decided to have their party, even though most of their friends were at Woodstock. Sue made some marijuana brownies and told the girls that they were for the big people and that she would make a batch just for them. The party was going on, and Sue couldn't figure out why the brownies were disappearing so fast. Suddenly, Sue's littlest girl Stacy was sitting on the kitchen counter and almost fell off. Sue couldn't figure out what was wrong with her. Then, she found out that the girls were eating some of both batches of brownies. The girls got introduced to marijuana early; at least grass was not the worst of all the evils. Sue felt the grass was an herb from God.

One day while Sue was taking her flying lessons, one of her friends told her she should get high when she goes up in the plane. So, Sue decided it might be fun, and she dropped a hit of acid. Sue was flying now and thought it was great. Time went on, but she never got her license to operate because she flunked the written test with flying colors. Ha! Ha! Sue still had her mind on her husband too much. She was tired of working and decided to stay home and get her boobs redone; since that quack messed them up. All of the clubs were going completely topless, and Sue needed to have hers reduced and some scars fixed; Sue hated that doctor because they messed up boobs. Sue knew she couldn't take care of herself or the girls while she had the operation, so she sent them to the ranch with grandma and grandpa for a while. It was summer and no school for the girls at the time. Sue thought her husband would at least help her with this since she was trying to better herself. Since she made more money than him, it seemed like he didn't like it. He didn't want her to be too independent.

Sue went into the hospital again with her friend Phyllis, and she had some other surgery done at the same time. Sue and Phyllis were the best of friends for a long time, and they did a lot of crazy things together. Sue had another breast reduction, both operations went well, but Sue was sick as a dog with this one. She had her husband pick her up and take her home. Sue was so ill; she could not even get herself up off the bed because; of the muscles in her chest having sutures. Her husband dropped her off at the apartment and left her there all alone. That was mean of him for getting her there and not helping her at all.

One day passed, and there was no sign of her husband. Sue was so worried that she thought she was going to die being there all alone. She was mentally and physically depressed and in intense pain, and she didn't know what to do. Sue decided to call one of her other girlfriends, Marline, who she had worked with for years. Her friend Marline was of Indian descent, just like Sue. They were good friends, also. It was good. Marline came to Sue's rescue again, like in the past.

When Sue called Marline, she freaked and thought what Mike had done to Sue was a horrible thing. Marline told her that she was going to bring her gun and kill Sue's husband. Sue said that it would not be necessary. When Marline arrived, Sue was all drugged up and could hardly stand up. Marline said, "You are coming home with me. That man is a jerk to leave you like this." Sue couldn't stand up, so Marline carried Sue out to the car. What a good friend she was for Sue. Sue stayed with Marline for weeks until Sue was all better. Marline even spoon-fed Sue at first because she couldn't move her arms.

Time went on, and Sue was back at home. Sue didn't have much good luck at that apartment since then. One evening, she came home from work to find out someone broken into it, and someone had stolen all jewelry. Things like her baby ring and baby bracelet were gone. Sue had the worst luck in the world. Sue's husband finally came back home and didn't even tell Sue he was sorry. Mike was a cold, vain, self-centered person. Sue was hoping that he would start staying home because of this, but he never did. Sue knew that her husband was still fooling around, so one evening she went to see if she could find him again. She couldn't find him at first, and then come to find out; one of Sue's friends told her that she knew Mike and that he was still going over to his ex-wife's house. Sue confronted him all the time, and his excuse was he was there to see his son. He would always come up with the reason for either his son or his mother. Mike said that they needed him. Well, Sue needed him too, but he was never around. Sue was devastated by finding out Mike was still seeing his ex-wife, so she decided to leave him. Sue wrote him a note and told him he would never see her again. Then she went out and got a different job so he couldn't find her.

When Mike came home and found the note, he went crazy, took a knife, and tore up the whole place. He mostly cut up the girl's bed, and the top canopy were all destroyed. Mike also ripped up all of Sue's clothes and even smashed all the tables in their place. You name it- he tore it up. Funny, but Mike never destroyed any of his stuff. Because of Sue catching him in yet another lie, he couldn't cope with it. So, he went crazy. If that wasn't enough, Mike found out where

Sue's new job was and came in there. Sue thought she was safe and that he wouldn't find her. But, he did.

As soon as he saw her, he immediately began beating the hell out of her. He got her down on the floor and kicked her ribs in; Sue could hear her chest bones breaking. By then, she could hardly breathe. The place was full of people, but no one would help and stop him from attacking her. Then, something came over her. It was the powers that she once had, and her ability started up. A while back, an acquaintance of hers had told her how she could get control over people. At that time, they gave her some books to read about witchcraft. She was thinking about it, and she jumped to her feet and started to punch her husband. It only took one punch, and Sue knocked out his front tooth and bloodied his lip. Mike was shocked as he said, "You ninety-pound little witch. I can't believe you knocked out my tooth." Sue humiliated him. He just stood there in amazement, and then he left the bar. He never hit her again after that. Sue had a bleeding hand, but she felt it was worth it. Sue was amazed at herself. She knew she was into witchcraft now or was it really witchcraft or God helping her again, but she thought it was her powers. Or was it just her adrenalin. People had told her she had skills, but she never practiced anything like that.

She felt she had enough of men's crap, and she was turning over a new leaf and was determined to start a new life. Sue couldn't drive herself home, so she called her girlfriend, Marline, again. Sue was brokenhearted more. Even though he did this to her, she still loved him. Her husband didn't come home for weeks after that. Sue had made up her mind to start a divorce. Also, Sue decided to start putting spells on Mike, and she got out all of the old books that she had in the past, Sue hadn't gotten into witchcraft or read all of the books about it, but she was desperate enough to try now.

Sue got into the black arts, started smoking weed, and taking more acid. Before, she had simply tried it, but she was into it heavy now. At least Sue thought her so. Drugs were a new turning point in her life-style as well, so she started going out with all sorts of hippies and having a good time. Then she said, "forget this crap" It's not right, and she didn't do anything. At this point, Sue decided it was time for her to get a divorce. She got the papers started and made a step in that direction by calling a legal separation. Mike pushed her crazy, and Sue was off on a terror trip now. Sue figured she was not going to be married anymore, so she was going to live how she wanted. She was going to live for herself and not worry about any man.

One afternoon, Mike came back home. Sue was so glad to see him that she forgot all about why she was mad at him. It looked like all of her spells worked, so she thought since he came back and she forgave him again, she never did start the new life-style she was planning. When her husband came back to her, he was crying and begging her to let him return. But, he was still telling her a bunch of lies. Little did he know; that she would have taken him back anyway. Sue stopped doing spells; in a way, she felt terrible for doing it. Sue put the divorce on hold, and they tried once again. Sue loved this man too much to end it. She was somehow under his power, and she did not have any control of herself. Sue did not want to give up on Mike yet; she just loved him too much.

Sue decided it would be a good idea if they got a house in Detroit. Maybe if they were closer to his family, then he wouldn't be able to make excuses about having to stay in Detroit. It was time for Sue to look for a lovely house, and she found one. This house was a beautiful red brick with a fireplace and an attached garage. It was a charming house. Sue got the girls to come back to Detroit with her. At first, they didn't like it, but it was a good experience for them. They went to school with all black kids, and that was good for them also because it made them feel unique and different.

Sue's husband was around a little bit more but was still making excuses about reasons not to come home. Now, he explained that he was going fishing with the guys. He would get up at six in the morning, on his days off from work and not come back until late at night. Sue knew he was fooling around on her again. One day Sue was washing her husband's clothes and found crabs in his underwear.

He was still trying to tell her he was not going out with other women. He also told her it was from his brother's clothing. Because of the crabs, Sue ended up getting them, too. Sue loved him and didn't think about it anymore. She always forgave him for something.

One day, Sue got deathly sick. She had excruciating pain on the right side of her lower abdomen. Sue begged her husband not to leave her that day, but he didn't believe her. He thought she was lying to keep him home. But, Sue wasn't lying. She was so sick that she ended up passing out on the bathroom floor. This incident scared the girls so much that they didn't know what to do. Luckily for Sue, her girls were smart enough to call Sue's friend, Phyllis. Phyllis called an ambulance, and they picked Sue up. Come to find out; Sue had the clap from her husband. Sue knew it was from him because she was never with anyone else the entire time she was with him. If that disease wasn't enough, she discovered she was pregnant and lost the child because of the infection. Here Sue was trying to have a good life and be a nice person, and this was the thanks Sue got for it; a lying, cheating husband. All of Mike's abuse to her was enough to put her into the nuthouse, but she was a survivor and worked it out. Sue was determined to make her husband love her and make the marriage work.

Sue was devastated again, but the more she tried, the worse things got between them. She didn't know what to do, so she decided to run away. She took the girls out to the ranch again. Thank God for her parents. Sue got a plane ticket and flew to New York. Sue got a job there dancing. It sure was different for her. It was a little scary, but she handled it. Sue thought Mike would never find her in New York. She was only there for a week, and her husband showed up. Sue made the mistake of telling her mother exactly where she was. Sue's mother liked Mike and ruined Sue's plans. Sue's mother didn't know all of the crap this man put her through, or she wouldn't have told him. When he arrived, he cried his alligator tears again and told her he would never do anything terrible to her again. Of course, Sue wanted her marriage to work, so she let the lies be the "truth" and went back home with him. Sue was so weak when it came to Mike.

In the past, Sue had tried to go out with other guys in an attempt to forget him, but she loved him so much that it just didn't work. She just could not cut out on him. While they were in New York, they did have a good time. Her husband had relatives there, and he introduced her to them. Sue could not believe that he took her over to meet his family. Since Sue was the second wife, Mikes' mother never wanted anything to do with her. Finally, they decided it was time to go back home, and he drove Sue home in his big, tan, Cadillac. Sue called it his big "pimpmobile."

When Sue and her man were together, they had some good times, but her man was still trying to burn the candle at both ends. Sue was still not enough for him; he needed the attention of a lot of women to boost his ego. Despite this, Sue was just not ready to give him up. Later on, Sue sold the apartment house; she took a significant loss on it. Sue could never find anyone to help her fix it. Her husband was too busy doing his thing to help her, so she had to sell it.

Meanwhile, they arrived back in Detroit from New York, and in less than two days, he was up to his same old tricks. He would tell her he was going on a fishing trip, and instead, he would be with other women. He really could come up with some excuses. He would even swear on his mother's life that he was telling the truth. By this time, Sue was getting desperate. She was ready to try anything to win his love. Sue found out about some people in Detroit that were really into witchcraft and could do a lot for her. So, she thought she would try again. These people were all new people, and Sue needed some new spells. When she arrived at this place, it was quite a dump. But, Sue was not afraid. She met one guy that told her she could get her man to love her deeply. There was only one catch; she had to go to California with him. Well, Sue thought for a while and decided not to do it. Sue left that place and went over to a girlfriend's house. Her girlfriend came running up to her and told her she saw her husband with his ex-wife again. Well, Sue was devastated. She felt so bad that she took off her wedding rings and threw them into the weeds. Sue told her friend about the place Sue had just come from and that she knew for sure she was going to go for it. Sue's friend told her not to because she didn't know these people. But, Sue didn't listen, and off she went.

Sue went back to the creepy old house again and told the guy she had changed her mind. She would go with him to California. He told her he knew she'd be back and would change her mind. It was like they had already put a spell on her. The guy told her there were a few things she needed to do before they left. She needed to buy some books that he was selling and some props she needed to get to do certain spells. They wanted her to do creepy things, but she thought this was gross and didn't do it. She told the guy she did it, but she never did.

Well, the next day, Sue did all of what the guy told her to do, except for the creepy things. Then, he said they would be leaving tomorrow. Then Sue took her girls out to her dad's again. It was summer vacation, and the girls would have fun there. Then Sue and this guy took off to California. After they were in the mountains of California, he told her that they would be where the Manson family lived. Sue was getting excited now. As they drove along and Sue was trying to make conversation, she told the guy about all of the terrible things her husband used to do to her. The guy said, "Don't worry; everything will be all right now."

They finally arrived in California; it was in the middle of the desert. It was a little one-room cabin where there were no other people in sight. The guy told her they would be staying until tomorrow when they met the Manson's. The place he took her to seem very small; there was a little stove, a sink, and a water mattress lying in the middle of a cement floor. It was a creepy placet, and it was cold and dingy inside.

As soon as they arrived, the guy wanted her to smoke some weed. She thought that was all right, but little did she know that the marijuana was laced with angel dust, which sent her on a trip. Sue

SECRETS ARE OUT NOW

was starting to get afraid now. She was so high she thought the room was spinning. Sue told the guys, "stop, didn't want anymore," and he got mad at her. So, she did what he asked and keeps smoking. Sue got so sick that she couldn't move, and she threw up in her hair.

By now, it was night, and the guy told her they were going to start doing some spells on Sue's husband. Sue was ready for that. As he was doing evil things, he said to Sue that they would do some THC. Sue had never done this before and was scared. Sue said to the guy she was high enough and didn't want to do anything else. Then the guy got the worst look in his eyes and told her Sue was doing what he wanted with her. So, Sue did what the guy said because she didn't want him to get mad at her again. She was not in the right spot to be refusing what he said.

All of these drugs were a first for Sue. As time went on, Sue was getting even sicker. She was so high she imagined all sorts of stuff. Sue could not also move. Then the guy jumped on top of her and forced himself on her. He had an evil look in his eyes, just like the time when she got raped at the age of sweet-sixteen. But this time, this guy was even creepier. This man's gaze was worse than her assault, in the chicken coop, and the tent. After that, Sue felt sick, and she puked all over her hair again because she couldn't move her head. After she got sick, she felt a lot better. Sue was tired after all that and didn't even know what kind of spells the guy had done while Sue had passed out. Since Sue was so tired, she decided to try to sleep. She tried to lie down next to the guy on his water mattress. It was frigid in the desert at night, especially with a water mattress on a cold cement floor.

It was about three A.M., and it was getting even colder. Sue was freezing and restless, being in a strange place with an unknown person. Without even realizing it, Sue pulled the covers off of the guy. All at once, he got up, cursing at Sue, then started beating the hell out of her and told her, "What was the big idea taking the covers off of me?" Sue was shocked and even more scared now. What did she get herself into this time? Finally, the guy calmed down and fell asleep. Sue tried to wake him to see how deep he was sleeping. He was out like a light. It was Sue's opportunity to sneak out of place. Sue picked up her little suitcases and left. Being the Indian that she was, she could be really quiet when necessary.

Outside, it was as cold and so dark she couldn't even see her feet in front of her. Then, her green cat eyes adjusted, and she could see well. Sue was scared again; she had heard that there were scorpions, snakes, and even hila monsters in the Arizona desert. She was so afraid she thought she would pee her pants. Sue walked and walked for miles and finally came up to a road. She didn't see it but felt it when she stepped on it. Sue was glad to find it and decided to walk along it to see if a car would come along. As she was walking, it seemed like hours had gone by; she was hoping for daylight, so if someone came along, they could see her better. But no one came along, and it was still dark. Then finally, it was getting lighter, and a car came along. Thank God, maybe. Sue was going to try hitchhiking. So, Sue put out her thumb and decided to try. She had never done this before, either. Sue was having all kinds of new experiences in her life. Then the car finally slowed down and seen her; then the car stopped, and an old, ugly, creepy guy asked her, "Do you want a ride, missy?"

Sue was desperate and didn't have a choice, so she said, "OK." The guy said he was only going ten miles, which would be a more significant paved road. Sue said, "That would be fine." The man only drove about a mile, and he pulled off the main road and drove nearly a half a mile and stopped. Then he told her she had to lick his privates till he came, or he would not take her any further. Of course, Sue said no, so he got mad and raped her, anyhow. Sue was a mess now. The man drove her to a more significant road and shoved her out of the car.

By this time, she looked like hell. But, it was finally getting light out. Sue tried to flag down another car, but that one passed by without stopping. She looked so bad that they just kept going. Then a few hours later, another car came by and stooped. There was another man in it. Sue was wondering if she would be alive after this one.

Well, God was with Sue again. He was a very nice, older gentleman that picked her up. Sue told him about all of her bad luck she was having. Since it was a long ride to the town, they had time to talk. The gentleman felt so bad for her that he took her to Palm Springs. It took several hours for them to arrive there. The gentleman was a very kind person and took her to a bus station, and then he repurchased her ticket to Detroit. Sue was so relieved. Finally, there was a break for her. She could not thank the man enough.

Sue was on the bus for four days and thought she would never arrive home. Eventually, she got back to where she had left her car and was scared that she might run into the creep from the desert. Instead of him, there was another creep. Sue's husband was standing by the car. He proceeded to tell her how worried he was about her and all kinds of lies again. When Sue confronted him about where he had been, he was lying his way out of it, and Sue fell for it all again. The stupid lovesick girl ended up going back with him. Sue hoped that maybe some of the spells might have worked. Since she had gone through all of that hell for it, but time would tell.

Sue was thinking maybe if she should get out of Detroit and the fast life, it might settle her husband down. She was ready to try anything. So, Sue found another charming house in a good neighborhood on the Northside of Detroit, so she put a down payment on it. It was another cute little place. All of the houses they bought, it was always Sue's money that went for the down payment, never Mike's cash. This house was a ranch style with a brick exterior and had a beautiful backyard. They had it fully carpeted in a light gold color and purchased all new French provincial furniture. Their new place was twenty miles away from Mike's work, so that should be good. At this time, she decided to quit her job and stay home and be a wife. Sue was willing to try anything possible to make her marriage work. Things were good for a while. Mike was getting into fixing up the house and working around the yard. Sue was the perfect little housewife and had the house spotless and supper ready for Mike when he came home every evening. Their new home was great for them. It had a beautiful yard. They got the girl's new bikes and all sorts of new toys; also, they made a lot of new friends.

Everything seemed fine for a while, but months went by, where Sue's husband never had sex with her. His excuse was that he was too tired and busy. Sue felt something was going on again. Mike would get up at six in the morning, get ready and leave the house, and not return until eleven at night. Sue was getting very suspicious and worried again. Her man would even do this on Saturdays and Sundays. His excuse was that he was going fishing or over to see his mother. Since Sue was intuitive, every time she felt something was wrong, it was true. She almost hated to have that feeling. Well, sure enough. It was the same old crap again. Since Sue felt this awful feeling still, she started investigating. She would check his pockets and even smelled his clothing. Every morning after he went to work, the clothes he had on the night before he smelled like perfume. Sue felt that whoever this woman was, she might have done this on purpose so that Sue would notice.

At this time, Sue's hair was shoulder length and black. She would always check his clothing, and one day, she found a three-foot-long, red hair on Mike's clothing. Sue became a very suspicious woman, and she had good reason to be. Sue was obsessed with the thought of him being with another woman. Sue had powers that always helped her know when things were wrong. Combined with intuition, it gave her proof of her suspicions.

Back when Sue was dancing and was into witchcraft, she did something at work that confirmed she had the powers. There was this girl that no one liked at her work. This girl would mess with the other girls, make them lose their jobs, and all sorts of nasty things. Sue can remember one evening; in particular, she told her friends that she would get even with this girl. This bad girl used to dance by hanging from the rafters and swinging down onto the stage. Well, Sue cast a spell that would make the girl hurt herself, and sure enough, the girl burned her leg real bad on one of the lights. This girl was out of commission for weeks. After this, Sue felt terrible about doing this. She feared her powers and swore that she would never use them to hurt anyone again. All of her friends wanted her to do more things to the mean girl, but Sue never did. Sue felt it is wrong for a person to dive into black magic with evil attentions. She thought at the time, love spells weren't harmful, but she felt that evils to hurt would people come back to you. Also, whatever you put out would come back to you one day. It is called karma, and she was never doing it again.

A couple of weeks passed by, and one of Sue's friends was telling her about this cousin that was very sick. This girl's cousin was in a coma for weeks and not expected to live. Sue thought to herself that if she had powers to hurt people, why not heal people. So, she started praying for this girl. Every night when Sue came into work, she would ask her friend how the girl was doing. Sue asked for three days. Then the next evening, Sue asked her how the girl was doing. Sue was surprised; her friend said that her cousin came out of the coma, and she would be all right. Sue was pleased with the news. Sue was into praying to God now, instead of black witchcraft. Sue thought that when you are doing good things, it must take a little longer. Sue never tried any harmful spells again. Even though she had her intuitive powers, her thoughts always went back to Mike. Sue was still obsessed with Mike, and all Sue wanted was for him to love her and be a good husband to her. So, she just went about her own business and tried not to let his lies bother her anymore.

One day, Sue and a friend were riding around in a junky old T-bird, and a bad thing happened. At the time, she felt like karma got her for all the bad things she had unconsciously put on people. Some guy made an improper left-hand turn in front of the girls, and they hit him. There was nothing they could do. It happened so fast. Once they hit the other car, Sue flew through the window and was unconscious. When she woke up, after only a few minutes, she could remember the ambulance coming and putting her into traction. While they were carrying her out of the car, she could see a big hole in the windshield where her head hit, and she saw a piece of skin hanging on the glass. Later, Sue found out that the part of her skin was the top of her ear.

Luckily for Sue, when she arrived at the hospital, they had a plastic surgeon there. Sue's face was all cut up. The doctor said she had a list of cuts all over her face. She was a mess. Sue was lucky because she almost lost her sight, but it didn't go that deep. Her eyelid was just hanging on.

The lucky thing for her was a plastic surgeon there, and he was a real swell person. The surgeon fixed her up like brand-new. For weeks after she got out of the hospital, she could still visualize the piece of her ear hanging on the windshield. Sue lost a lot of blood, and at the time of the accident, she was wearing a black leather jacket with a long fringe that she had made, it was full of blood. It was all stiff, and no one could get the blood out of it. Later on, someone has stolen the jacket, and Sue figured the thieves got a real surprise seeing that it was all covered with blood. Later on in life, she made another black leather jacket for herself.

While Sue was in the hospital, Mike finally came to see how she was. All he had to say was, "I will kill that guy if he messed up my wife's beautiful face." He wasn't worried about her health, only her beauty. What a guy! Sue decided to Sue the person that drove in front of them. Come to find out, he was drunk at the time of the accident and got in all kinds of trouble. Sue's friend didn't Sue because she didn't even get a scratch on her. At the court hearing, Sue received twenty-six thousand dollars. She was happy about that also though she would have to live with some scarring forever. The money wasn't enough to go through all of that. Later on in life, that side of Sue's face was drooping, and she was hoping to get it fixed one day.

Mike wasn't worried about Sue's health, only about how much money he could get. He went right out and bought a brand new blue Harley Davison motorcycle; During Sue's reck, her legs were jammed up under the steering wheel and injured her hips. Sue couldn't walk for weeks, and they had to carry around. She had whiplash, which resulted in trouble with her spine forever. Finally, she got well enough to walk by herself, but she still had a problem with her back.

Sue had to go to court again. This time, the drunk got a ticket, and his hand slapped. Without Sue's bad luck, she would have no chance at all. Her insurance company fixed her car, but it was never the same again. Also, Sue had to go to the doctor for a long time. It seemed like Sue was having trouble in all areas of her life and was so depressed that she couldn't figure out what to do. Sue's doctor was the same one that fixed her face, and he told her that she should have a baby. A baby would give her someone to love and have forever. Sue thought about this and figured that her girls were her love, but they didn't want hugs and kisses anymore. They felt they were too grown-up for that stuff. Also, she didn't have a boy, just the two girls. Sue had always wanted a boy, and she thought she would try for one. Sue told the doctor that she would think about it.

Sue was trying hard to make an excellent family for her husband and girls, but nothing ever seemed to work for her. Mike was never a good father to the girls. He would take rides on his bike, but never offer to give the girls a ride. Mike was always yelling at the girls. He never even took them for a ride on the boat. All her husband wanted to do was take his son out (the son from his first marriage) and be with him. Also, Sue's husband bought the giant dog he could find, a St. Bernard, and put it in a small pen in the back of the house. Then Mike makes the girls go out there and clean up the giant piles of poop. Mike was very mean to the girls.

One day, Wendy wanted to keep a dog that had followed her home. It was a collie, just the kind she had always wanted. It was allowed to stay, but then one day, when the girls came home, Mike told her girls that the dog ran away. He took it off somewhere, and the girls never saw the dog again. Wendy was so hurt she cried in her room for weeks. Mike would make the girls stay in their bedrooms most of the time and pointed to his watch when he wanted them to go to bed. He had no feelings for these girls at all. Since Sue divorced, the girls' needed a father figure. Well, it indeed was not Mike.

Sue's husband was so mean to the girls and Sue, also. Mike would not be home and always made up lies that he was fishing. She figured half of the time; she found he was with his X wife and son. Sue didn't know for sure where he was since he lied all of the time to her. Sue did not mind that he wanted to see his son, but he lied all of the time where he was going. Sue started thinking that maybe it would be a good idea for her to have a baby. Maybe having a child would keep him home, and he would pay more attention to Sue and the girls. So, Sue went back to her doctor and started to make plans. Getting pregnant would be a task because Sue's husband never had much sex with her. But, she would find away. Sue went to her doctor and told him she wanted him to take her IUD out, so he did. Now she had to find out when the right day would be and get her man to make love to her. Sue knew that he would never do anything at night because he was never home and the excuse of being tired.

One morning, Sue seduced her husband when he was half-awake, and it worked. Sue planned it perfectly. Sue tried it two times so that she could have her baby on her husband's birthday. She had it set in her mind that this baby would be a boy and would be tall, dark, and handsome when he grew up. Well, that worked also. Sue was pregnant. Finally, her powers were working for the good. Sue started eating even better than usual; she took many vitamins and always tried to have good thoughts. Sue usually did this with all of her babies, but she was thirty years old now and had to be extra careful; at this time, Sue was thinking of becoming a vegetarian, and she started cutting out red meat. Sue did a lot of reading about nutrition and being fit. As Sue was developing, she was getting big as a house, and she gained fifty pounds with her son. She could hardly walk. Sue thought that having a baby would keep her man home, but it didn't work. Her husband was still never around and paid even less attention to her now. Well, Sue was hanging in there and didn't want to get depressed, so she tried not to let it bother her. Then Sue started to get a lot of hang-up calls and knew what was going on. She began to get even more suspicious. One time, she decided to go through her husband's pants to see what she could find. Sure enough, there was someone's phone number in his pocket. The next day, Sue called the number, and a girl answered. Sue started asking the girl all sorts of questions, and the girl lied.

Sue didn't give up but called her repeatedly until finally, she admitted to Sue that she was seeing her husband. Sue wasn't satisfied; Sue wanted to meet this girl in person. The next day, Sue went over to the girl's house. When the girl saw Sue, she was shocked to see Sue was pregnant. The girl started pouring out her heart to Sue. She told Sue that she didn't know the man was married and never dreamed that he had a pregnant wife. Sue was devastated with all the crap the girl told her. Sue didn't know what she would do now. Sue thought maybe her man would feel better and want to make a good life for them after the baby was born. She didn't want to give up yet. This man almost drove Sue to the nuthouse. She was a nervous wreck.

One evening, Sue was sitting in her rocker, trying to think positively, and she started to get hang-up phone calls again. It was Halloween, and it was a scary night anyhow, and all of the kids had finally finished trick-or-treating and were in bed. As she sat back down in her rocker, the door opened up slowly. A person with a ski mask on with a blanket wrapped around them and barefooted entered the house. This person came in with a knife in their hand, and Sue thought this was it: she was a goner now. It scared her so bad she thought she was going into labor. Come to find out; it was the neighbor lady; what a rotten trick to pull on Sue, especially since she was expecting. The neighbor thought it was funny, but it wasn't to Sue. At least Sue was ok and lived through the Halloween prank and didn't go into labor.

Sue was nine months along and was anxious for the baby to be born. Her doctor told her that the baby would come when it was ready. Sue didn't think this was right and went to a different doctor. The new doctor freaked when he saw Sue. He told her she probably had at least a nine to a ten-pound baby in there. By this time, Sue was a month over-due, and the doctor decided to induce her labor.

Sue's pregnancy went way past her husband's birthday, even though she wanted to have her baby on her husband's birthday. So, it didn't matter to her now when she had her baby.

Sue went to the hospital where they induced labor, she wanted to have her baby without any drugs, but the doctor told her not to. Finally, the baby came. Sue watched the whole thing. It kind of scared her because the baby was so dark when he was born. She thought she had a black baby. The baby turned out to be an eleven-pound, black-haired, dark-skinned, twenty-seven-inch long baby boy, just like she planned it. Sue was so happy she cried. This baby would grow up to be the best man in her life. Oh yes, Mike finally showed up at the hospital after the baby was born. The name Sue picked out for her son was Peter, after Mike's father. His second name was Dana so that he would have his own name

During the five years of their marriage, Sue's mother-in-law had never come over to their house. Now that there was a new baby, the woman suddenly came over. Probably the only reason was to see if it was her son's baby. There was no mistake; the baby looked just like Sue's husband. Now the mother-in-law had a good reason to come over. At least she told her son that Sue was a clean person: she meant Sue was clean about her house and the baby. Sue could not believe that she finally came over. Sue's mother-in-law was a lovely person, but she was from the old country and didn't accept second marriages. Sue's baby was Maltese, just like her mother-in-law and Mike.

Sue knew that this would be her last baby and wanted everything to be perfect. Sue fixed up her new son's room very cute. The nursery had all new oak furniture, a bassinet, and even a modern rocker to rock her son to sleep. Sue wallpapered the walls with a carnival print paper. It had all sorts of colors and circus animals, drums, and clowns. This room was fit for a little king. Sue was so happy because, finally, she had a little one for her to love. Sue tried to breastfeed her baby, but she couldn't do it too long because her son was too big.

Time went on, and Mike was still never at home. Sue's son was about three months old now, and Sue's husband still was not around.

SECRETS ARE OUT NOW

Sue has tried everything with this man, but nothing ever worked between them. Sue knew he was again seeing other women; he never made love to Sue, either. She figured Mike was getting it someplace else. At least Sue had a nice son; he couldn't take the place of her man. Sue couldn't stand the lies, late nights, and the smell of perfume on his clothing. She thought she would just die. Sue decided it was time for a divorce. She has tried everything, and nothing had worked. She needed to do this for her sanity.

So, Sue decided to kick Mike out of the house; it was one of the hardest things she had ever done. Even though she still loved her man and would always love him. Since he was seeing other women, Sue just had not to let it bother her. One day, her husband came to the house, snatched up her son, and told Sue that she would never see her son again unless she signed the car over to him. Well, Sue didn't care about the car, even though it was rightfully hers. So, she signed the car over to him. Now Sue was without a car. She loved her car but loved her son more. When her husband brought her son back, he told her he would get him again one day no matter what he had to do. Now her husband had the boat, the bike, the lawnmower, and now her car. Oh well, that's how Sue's luck went. Even though Sue got the house, it still wasn't paid for, and she had to make the payments.

One night, Sue's husband came to the house drunk and raging. He told her he was going to kill her. He said, "If I cannot have you, no one is going to have you." Sue had seen him in rages before, but this time he was scary looking. Sue was screaming as her husband came after her with a sharp kitchen knife. He proceeded to push the blade into Sue's chest. Then Sue reminded him that her girls were in the next room. All at once, after he had the knife into Sue's chest about an inch, he decided that maybe he better quit. By now, the girls were screaming, and the baby was crying. Finally, her husband left the house. Later, Wendy and Stacy said they would jump out of the window and get the police, but they were too scared.

Finally, Mike put his tail between his legs and left the house.

As he was leaving, Mike ran over the mailbox. The next day, Sue didn't know what to do. She told all of her friends, and they said she should press charges against him, but Sue was too kind of a person to do anything to him. Sue still loved him and didn't want to hurt him. Sue finally got her divorce, but she was even lonelier now. Sue needed to get on with her life. At least she had her son and the girls, she still loved Mike, but she had to think of her kids now. So she moved on with her life.

Sue Modeling

CHAPTER 7

THIRD HUSBAND STEVE

By now, Sue was getting lonely again. She was like this for months, and then one day, she walked into a gas station and saw a man that she knew when he was a baby. This man's mother and father were friends of Sue's family and had been for years. Sue used to babysit this guy when he was an infant and even changed his diapers. Now he was a man. Sue couldn't believe her eyes; she was so surprised to see him. It was Steve from the old days. He used to be a kid; now, he is a man. In the past, their families would go out to their cottage and stay for weeks. Sue used to have a great time out there. At this time, Sue's dad had his boat, and everyone would go out on it. Sue could remember the weekends at the lake, mainly when after swimming, they come out of the water and had leeches all over their legs. Sue's dad had to pull them off for her. They scared her at first. But after that, she didn't like going into those small lakes any longer.

There were other times when her parents used to babysit Steve also. Another thing he would go upstairs to Sue's room, and get into her stuff; he broke her toys, filled his pockets with her pennies. He would put on Sue's cowboy boots and run the sides of the cowboy boots down to the point where she couldn't even wear them anymore. This kid used to be a "Dennis the Menace." Now he was a sexy,

SECRETS ARE OUT NOW

tall, blonde, handsome man. Sue remembered his name was Steve. Steve was surprised to see Sue also. He told Sue to come over to his apartment, and they could talk about the good old days. So, she did, and they talked for hours and hours. As the tall, handsome man and Sue raked over all the coals, he told her that he was a Vietnam Vet. And He was injured in the war. He told her he owned a boat and still got out on the lake and went fishing. At this time, Steve was about sixteen years younger than Sue, but you couldn't tell the age difference. Steve said, Sue, you looked great and that I had a secret to tell you. He told her that he has been in love with her ever since he was a boy. His words were great for Sue's ego since, at the time, she was trying hard to get over her husband, Mike. This guy came around just at the right time for Sue.

Steve was tall like Mike, but he was blonde because he was of Polish descent. Sue took him over to her house, and he met Wendy, Stacy, and Dana. Steve was right because he liked her children. Steve started coming over to Sue's a lot. He started paying more attention to the kids than he did to Sue. Steve bought things for the kids and Sue; also, Mike would take them all to the movies. He was a great friend to Sue's children, and it was just what they all needed at the time. They all had great fun with Sue's new man. Sue was looking for a father figure for the kids, and she thought she had found it.

After Sue's divorce was final, her ex-husband would sneak around, trying to spy on her. Sue's ex got jealous because of her new man getting very close to the girls and his son, Dana. Mike was having a hard time letting go. Eventually, he did quit coming around. But Mike never forgot what Mie told Sue. Mike told sue he would get their son away from her one day, no matter what he has to do. Sue never loved Steve; at that time, she just needed someone, and Steve seemed to be a great person to her and the kids. He was trying to get close to Sue by being kind to her children. His strategy did work; Sue's kids loved him. For some reason, Steve was trying to make Sue jealous by standing her up; this didn't make her jealous; it just made her mad. Sue didn't like the games he started playing, and she played the game right back on him. One day, he tried it again and didn't show up for about two hours. Sue was upset and said she was going to fix him and his games. Sue liked him, and he didn't need to be playing games with her. Sue decided this was not the way he should be treating her. So, Sue decided to put a little spell on him, just a little one.

One day, Steve was out on his boat when he was supposed to be picking up Sue. Well, Sue waited this time for another three hours, and he never showed up. As she was waiting for him to come to get her, she said, "I wish his boat would blow up." and guess what? He called her the next day and told her that the engine blew up in his boat. Sue was glad. Sue thought to herself, "Teach him to fool around with Mother Nature." Sometimes Sue would even scare herself with the outcome of her spells. Sue needed to try not to get so mad at people. Sue's power sure was getting stronger now, more than she ever knew it could be. Sue's friend didn't realize that she was the one that did this to his boat, and she never told him.

Time went on, and he started being more considerate to Sue and her family. He was still buying those things and taking them places. Then, he asked Sue to marry him. He didn't ask; he just wormed his way into her heart by saying things like, "We should get married." He told her they would have a new life up North. Steve said he would buy them a farm, and they would have horses and all sorts of animals. At the time, Sue needed a change in her life. He said that up North was called "God's Country," and it was beautiful. He told her he would buy her a farm. The only problem with that was that it would be Sue's money, buying the farm. Steve didn't have a penny. But, it still sounded right to Sue.

Steve promised Sue and the girls all sorts of things, but he didn't have any money to do the things he promised. Sue was lucky that she did have some money left over from her car accident. Sue said to herself that she might as well go for it. What did Sue have to lose? She needed to get away from her X, anyhow. Her X was still sneaking around the house, and Sue would never be able to forget him that way.

SECRETS ARE OUT NOW

Sue still loved Mike and probably always would, mostly because he was the father of her son. It seemed like it was time for Sue to get married, but it was still her money to be put down on the houses. She also ended up paying for the wedding and everything. No man ever really supported Sue, yet.

Despite this fact, they decided to get married up North. It was in February and very cold, but it would be a lovely winter wedding, anyhow. This time Sue put the money on the house, but her new mother-in-law paid for the wedding. Her mother-in-law had a bridal shop in her basement and got all of the dresses for the wedding. All Sues marriages; this was the first time Sue was ever married in a Catholic Church, and it was adorable. Sue's father and mother came to this wedding since they were friends of Sue's new in-laws. Sue's girls stood up for her at the wedding party also. The girls liked being at the marriage, but they hated the hats Sue's mother-in-law picked out for them. They called the caps "monkey hats." They did like their dresses; they were yellow, and Sue's gown was a long and lacy eggshell white color; also, it had a medium length train. The veil was a short net with a baby's breath on it. Sue's husband's brother and sister-in-law stood up for them; they were the best man and maid of honor. Her wedding was Sue's first beautiful wedding.

On the day of the wedding, one funny thing happened. Sue was so nervous she forgot to carry her expensive bouquet down the aisle. Other than that, everything went as planned. Sue had a lot of beautiful flowers and even had a photographer take pictures. Finally, Sue was happy, but she was mostly pleased for the kids because it looked like she could give them a sweet life, with someone that paid attention to them. Sue's last husband didn't pay any attention to Wendy or Stacy at all. At least, she thought things were going to be good. It seems like men are so nice before you marry them, they change after a while. At the time of the wedding, Sue was not feeling very well. She was having sharp pains in her stomach. She didn't know what it was, and at the time, she just overlooked it. Then it was time for the reception. It was a small one in her mother-in-law's basement. It was nice because she got a lot of gifts. One of her mother-in-law's friends made a cake, and it was a two tiers high white cake. Sue felt everything was so perfect because she never had a sweet wedding like this before. As the evening progressed, Sue was still having intense pains in her stomach. She was starting to get weak, but Sue just kept going as if nothing was wrong. Sue could not be pregnant because she just received a new IUD. Then, Sue had an IUD put in after Sue had her son, Dana. This IUD was a Delcon Shield, which later on, she had trouble with the device.

As the party was rolling along, Steve was getting drunk. What a way to start a new life! Sue was getting upset because they were supposed to be going to a fancy hotel and have their honeymoon. Sue surely didn't want him drunk. In a way, Sue was surprised at him, but now they were married, and drunks ran in his family. Sue should have known better, but she was still vulnerable and wanted a good life for her children. Sue figured the reason why Steve was drinking was that Steve's father owned a bar and his grandfather before him. Sue's husband was all most weaned behind a bar. His family's living quarters were in the back of the bar, and her husband was around alcohol all of his life. But, Sue was hoping his drinking would not continue. Other than Steve's drinking, her new family and in-laws were pretty nice. Her mother-in-law turned out to be a little bossy, but she was always like that. However, Sue felt that her in-laws didn't like her. She thought that they didn't want her because she was so much older than their son was. Time went on, and Sue didn't pay any attention to Steve's family or their opinion of her.

Sue was getting tired at the reception and wanted to leave. She almost had to drag Steve out of the house because he was so smashed. They finally left the house and went to the hotel. Sue was expecting a lovely night, but it turned out to be hell. She found out that her man was not as nice as she thought. They were trying to make love, and all Steve could do was bang the hell out of her. He couldn't have a climax because he was so drunk. Sue still didn't feel very well, and Steve was so rough with her. Sue's pain was starting to get worse now. It was to the point where she felt like she was going to pass out. Thank God that Steve finally fell asleep and left her alone.

The next morning arrived, and Sue was relieved; she felt a little better now. They had to go back downstate and tie up some loose ends with her house. They needed to get her furniture and find someone who wanted to rent out the house. While they were there, Sue's neighbors had a reception for them. It was beneficial because all of her old friends came to it; Denice, Doris, Betty, Nancy, and Marline, everyone that was close to Sue. They had a swell time. Sue was having a good time there until her husband got drunk again. It seemed like it was becoming a habit with him now. As the evening went on, Sue wasn't feeling very well still. After everyone left, Steve screwed the hell out of her again and couldn't climax. What an animal. He even got mad at her because he couldn't get off and accused her of faking her pain. Sue tried to get to sleep, but she couldn't because the problem was terrible. Then, she just couldn't stand it anymore and asked Steve to take her to the hospital. It was a good thing that she did go to the hospital.

It was about six A.M. as she lay in the stupid hospital. It was a foolish hospital because they didn't want to do anything for her. Sue was in excruciating pain, throwing up, and kept going in and out of consciousness for hours. The doctors didn't know what to do for her; they didn't know what was wrong. They let her lay there until six-o-clock the next evening. Sue begged them to help her because she felt like she was dying. Then finally, they said they would take her to surgery. By this time, Sue's pain was going up into her chest. Then she had her surgery, the doctor cut into her, and he said that the blood just poured out. Sue had been bleeding internally for a long time. They gave her three pints of blood; luckily for her, AIDS was not going around then. They also found out that Sue was pregnant. It had lodged in her fallopian tube, and the ovary had ruptured.

Sue was in the hospital for about a week. At that time, they didn't know what caused it, but later on, she found out her inter-uterine device created it. Sue had never used this kind of Delcon device before and had all sorts of problems after the insertion. Sue had a lawsuit against the manufacturers of the Delcon Shield, which went on for years. She never received anything out of it but that pain and suffering without compensation. While Sue was in the hospital, Steve would come in and visit her. The only reason he came to see her was to try to have sex with her in the hospital. This man was a pig. Here she almost died, and all he could think of was sex. Since she was not in good shape to have sex, he insisted that she jack him off. So, Sue would do it. Sue was so sweet and smooth going, and she couldn't say no to her man because she didn't want to hurt his feelings. Sue was always the perfect little wife. Sue finally got out of the hospital, and her stomach looked like a road map now. But time went on, and she forgot all about it.

It was time for them to move up North to their new farmhouse. Sue and the kids were excited about the farm. When they arrived at the farm, it was beautiful; it was on five acres and had a lovely, little white three bedrooms, which were a two-story house. There was a large basement with a fruit cellar so that Sue could do a lot of canning. Sue was good at growing all her veggies and was really into growing things organically. She was still a vegetarian and wanted everything as pure as possible. She ended up being a vegetarian for the rest of her life. Also, Sue could make her bread, catsup, mayonnaise, and relishes, and much more.

Another thing she made was some beer and wine for her husband, which was a mistake. When it was time to bottle the beer, Sue and the girls had to siphon it out of the crock, and they all had a great time at that. The girls and two of their friends were in shorts, and they had beer all over the floor. They were all slipping and sliding in the beer. It was funny to see them all sliding and laughing. Sue figured the girls got crocked out of the crock since the crock is where they made the beer. The girls were about thirteen at the time, and later on, she found out that this was not the first time they had consumed beer. Later on, Sue found out that Steve had been giving the girls beer for a long time.

SECRETS ARE OUT NOW

At the farm, there was a large barn where the kids could have the animals they wanted. Sue's father gave the girls some horses that he had at his ranch. At that time, they had twelve horses, a mule, and ponies. Animals made the girls very happy. Sue's son, Dana, even had his very own pony. There were a lot of outbuildings and a lot of fruit trees on the "mini-farm." There were peaches, pears, apples, plums, walnuts, and raspberries. Sue was domestic, and there wasn't anything that she couldn't do where cooking and canning were concerned. Sue and her family were in heaven, finally. Sue was really into antiques, and luckily, she still had some money left from her car accident. They would pack up her old truck and go off to the local auctions. When they were at the auction, they bought all sorts of antiques. Their vehicle was packed full of stuff. They got many great deals for only a thousand dollars; Sue was in heaven for sure, now. She bought the antiques to redo so she could sell them, and of course, she keeps some of them.

As Sue was driving back from the auction, she ran into a deer. Sue was so upset. Everyone was worried about the antiques, but Sue was concerned about the deer. Sue felt awful that she had killed the deer; she just cried and cried over it. It introduced Sue into the Northern country now. The kids felt bad about the deer also. There were six of them in the front of the old truck: Sue, Steve, Wendy, Stacy, Dana, and their friend Kathleen. Luckily for them, none of them got hurt. It was a crazy thing for all of them to be riding in the front seat of that old truck. The good Lord was watching out for Sue and her family again.

Now that Sue and her family had their dream farm, they were all happier than they had ever been before. Steve was still kind to her kids, and they were all pleased. Sue was into all of the things she loved: gardening, canning, and even restoring furniture. They set up the old house on the property as an antique shop, and Sue tried to sell antiques that Sue had restored. She didn't have excellent luck with selling them, but she had a good time anyhow. Sue would load up the kids and some antiques into the old truck, and off they would go to the flea market, trying to sell her antiques, although not much luck there either, but they still had a good time. All through Sue's life, she never had much success with her enterprises.

Time was moving along, and they were all pleased as far as the material world, but there was still something missing in Sue's life; it was what she needed from her husband. Even though Sue and the kids had everything they dreamed of materially, the thing that was missing was love. It was the real love that was missing, and Sue's husband started to act like he didn't truly love her either. Sue tried to love Steve, but he was so mean to her that it would never have worked.

As time passed by, Sue started to run out of money, and her husband still didn't have a job. He was drinking more and acting even crazier. Then, Steve finally got a job and lost it as quickly as he got it. When Steve would get drunk and steal things from his work, and then they would fire him. Sue didn't want to go back to work, but she had to make ends meet. Sue tried to open up a beauty shop in her basement; Sue bought all of the equipment and fixed the downstairs. She spent all of what she had left on equipment for her beauty shop. Now all of her money was gone. Sue wanted the business to be legal, so she had to go to the zoning commission and get a shop license. Well, the neighbors put a stop to that; they didn't want one in the neighborhood. Sue thought the neighbors liked her, but obviously, they didn't. It seemed like if you weren't a born and conceived Pollock in this town, you weren't anybody. It was hard up North to get ahead, and it was hard to be accepted. Sue didn't want to be away from the kids, but she had to do something for an income. Sue tried to open up a shop in the town of Cedar. The North worked out for a while until the newness wore off, and the nosey people were satisfied snooping. Her business started dropping, and she couldn't pay the shop's bills. If that wasn't bad enough, the landlord of her shop upped the rent, and at that point, she had to give up the shop.

One day while Sue was at the shop, she found out she had more bad luck. Steve was supposed to be with the kids on Saturdays because of Sue's work. It was a cold day, and her stupid husband put a piece of coal in the wood burner. He wanted to clean out the chimney that day, so he opened up the stove door, thinking the coal would burn out and cool off. Little did he know that it gave off toxic gasses, and the kids were all asphyxiated. They had two of their friends over, and they all were in the living room next to the stove. Sue's son was upstairs in his crib, luckily. The kids didn't know what was happening to them. Steve went to the beauty shop to pick Sue up. When they got back home, all of the kids acted like they were drunk or on drugs. None of them had a clue what was going on. Steve and Sue were yelling at the kids, trying to wake them up, but nothing helped. Finally, one of the girl's friends, Lori, said she felt sick, so Sue's husband carried her to the bathroom. This girl was so out of it, she threw up all over Steve and peed all over him. Sue and Steve together carried all of the kids out to the car and took them to the hospital, where they gave them oxygen to bring them around. Thank God they were all right. Years later, the parents of one of the boys, who were sick from the woodstove, thought he had brain damage, and they sued Steve over the incident. But, time went on, and it was all forgotten. Now everyone laughs about Lori peed on Steve; he deserved it. At that time, everyone was concerned, and it wasn't funny at all.

Things were looking up when Steve finally got another job. Sue closed up the shop because there were hardly any customers anymore. Her closing was fair, but Steve thought because he was the only one working, he could do anything he wanted. Steve was still drinking a lot and would come home drunk even more often now. One evening, he came back drunk and screwed the hell out of Sue as he always did. The next day, Sue was having excruciating pain and had to have him rush her to the hospital once again. Come to find out, this time, her appendix was ready to rupture. The doctor said that Sue's appendix burst in his hand as soon as he got it out. As Sue was recuperating in the hospital, her husband Steve would come in and want sex again. Here she was dying of pain in the hospital, and he wanted her to jack him off, so she did what he wanted, but little did she know that this still was not enough for him. What an animal! What would happen next?

Yep, more bad things coming! Things were going on at home while she was in the hospital. Years later, after Sue had divorced this animal, she found out that; since Sue couldn't give him any sex, he was trying to seduce her youngest daughter Stacy; She was only about ten at the time and didn't tell her mom until she was sixteen years old. This man would tell Stacy, "Your mother is supposed to be taking care of me." Also, he said, "She can't take care of me because she is in the hospital, and my dick hurts, and I need you to take care of it for me." He would get Stacy drunk and make her vulnerable and force her to have sex with him. Later on, is when Stacy went into detail about everything that happened? At least she told her mother a little bit about it, but Sue felt it should have come out a lot earlier. Sue felt this was the ruination of Stacy's life; because Steve was such a pig. All through Stacy's life, she has been an alcoholic, just like her stepfather, grandmother, and her Indian great grandfather. It seemed like Stacy was the one that carried the alcoholic gene over into her generation. Steve didn't help by teaching her how to drink at such a young age. Stacy was the vulnerable one, but not Wendy; she was too smart for him.

Stacy has been an alcoholic ever since her experiences with Steve. Sue prays for her Stacy and hopes she will be okay someday. Sue has felt awful about this for the longest time and still blames herself for the mistake of marrying this animal. There are even times when Sue cries herself to sleep because of what Steve had done to Stacy. Now Sue feels guilty for her daughter Stacy's lousy life. If Sue had only known about this, she would not have ever married Steve and wouldn't have been with him for three years. But this was only the beginning of the crap Steve put Sue through. It was in the dead of winter one evening when they were driving home from Sue's mom and dad's house.

On this journey home, there was snow knee-deep, and they had an ice storm also. It was right after Christmas, and they were coming home with all of the gifts from Sue's mom and dad's house that was downstate. They were almost back; Sue was driving because her husband was too drunk as usual. She was proceeding up the last hill before the house, and the car was sliding all over the road. It slid off to the side of the road, and they got stuck in a snowbank. Since they were almost home, Sue and the kids started walking, while Steve tried to get the car unstuck. Because he was so drunk, all he could do was gun the engine of the vehicle. He revved up the motor so hard that it caught fire. Yes, it all burned up, and so did all of the kid's gifts and all of their clothing. "Some trip that was! The family didn't have any insurance on the car, so all of their things that got burnt up could not be replaced, Wendy's flute, all their clothing. Sue was devastated again. The girls felt awful. Also, they had money in the car that the girls had worked for by selling candy for the school band. At least the school told them they wouldn't have to pay back the money. They were poor, and Sue decided to go to the big town of Traverse City, which was twenty miles away, and get a job. That did not last long. In the winter, their long driveway was always drifting over with snow, and she had a hard time getting out in the morning. The winters up there were so awful that she could hardly stand it. They were very depressing winters but were beautiful but hard to take.

One time, Sue got stuck in the driveway, and she got the neighbor to pull her out of the snow with his tractor, and he ended up getting his tractor stuck in the snow along with her car. It was so funny; the poor man was trying to help, and he ended up having his disaster. Sue felt terrible for her neighbor. If that wasn't enough, he started trying again to help her get unstuck, and this time, the whole front end of Sue's car came off. Sue felt awful for her neighbor because he felt even worse about Sue's car. It wasn't funny at the time, but later on, they all laughed about that one.

One evening, Sue was waiting for her husband to come home from another new job he had gotten. Sue was so proud of him for getting this job. He was working at a marina; he was always interested in boats, and this would be good for him; then, here he comes home drunk again. If this wasn't enough, he showed Sue all of the stuff he had stolen from the marina. Sue was as mad as a wet hen. She started arguing with him and told him to take all of the stuff back. But of course, he got mad at her. He told her, "No way in hell would I ever take the stuff back." Then he told her if she didn't like it, she could get out of the house. Sue wasn't leaving since she was in her nightgown, and it was her house anyhow. Steve felt she should go, so he pushed her out of the house and down the front porch steps. Sue thought she had broken her back as she lay out in the freezing snow in her nightgown.

Then, Steve locked the doors, and Sue couldn't get into the house. She was yelling at him to let her back in the house, but he had gone to bed. So, Sue couldn't stay out there and started to walk over to the neighbor's house. Once she got there, she tried to call him; of course, he had taken the phone off the hook so she couldn't phone him. Sue ended up spending the night on her neighbor's couch. Sue's neighbor noticed Steve her shoved out the door, Sue's legs and arms were scuffed, and falling down the steps got her nightgown torn up, luckily nothing was broke. The next day, Steve was gone, and Sue got back into the house. She felt so ashamed that she had to impose on her neighbors. Sue found out that he not only stole things from work but also he went to a bar after work and took a sludge hammer to people's car windows and robed their cars. What a crazy person! He used to be a Vietnam Vet and would tell Sue not to make him mad because he was a trained killer and would kill her if necessary. What did Sue get herself into this time? She was thinking she should find a way out of this mess and was getting worried now; to be with him was dangerous for her.

One night, when Steve was drinking again and Sue while she was taking a bath, he came into the bathroom and said, "This is for you, witch." This disgusting pig peed on her and poured beer all over her head while she was in the tub. Steve peeing on her made Sue lose all respect for the jerk, and she lost all feelings for him, which wasn't much, to begin with; he didn't even give her a chance to love him. He got her into what she thought would be a sweet life, and then he peed all over her. Steve was drinking all the time and would get so drunk that he would get out of bed, thinking he was in the bathroom, and he would pee all over the shoes in the closet. Sue was starting to hate this man even more. Things would have changed sooner if she would only have known what he had done to her daughter Stacy, at that time. She would have divorced him long before she did.

One evening they took out the snowmobile and went for a moonlight ride. Of course, Steve had a bottle of vodka hidden in the back of the machine, not a bottle, mind you, but a whole jug. They decided to ride over to their friend's house and visit them. As they were flying along on the machine, Sue fell off the back of the snowmobile. Her husband didn't even know she was gone until he finally realized it and returned for her. At least the snow was soft, and she didn't get hurt. When they arrived at the friend's house, Steve was very smashed and was getting belligerent. Sue didn't want to stay because of his attitude. She started pleading with him to take her back home. Of course, he told her no, and they began to argue about it. Then he called her a bitch and told her to shut up, and then he took his fist and punched her in the chest. He struck Sue that she fell over the chair and onto the floor. By this time, their friends were getting upset with Steve, also. They told him he better settle down or leave. Of course, he didn't want to hear this from them either, but they finally did leave.

The friend's house they were at was a man that Steve worked with, and he never forgot how Steve treated Sue. One evening, quite a few years after this incident, the friend saw Steve in a bar. Steve was drunk as usual and was very belligerent again, and the friend remembered how he treated Sue back a few years ago. Steve started fighting with his friend, and the friend told him this was the wrong thing to do to him. They started tussling in the bar, and the friend laid Steve out. While he was fighting with him, he punched him and said, "This is for Sue." Steve almost lost his eye over this one, although he was lucky and did not lose his sight. Hopefully, this taught him a lesson.

Well, back to the snowmobile ride. Steve finally started to take Sue home, but he decided he had to stop off at the local bar. Sue didn't want any part of that, so she told him she wanted him to take her home first. Of course, he said no; by now, Sue was getting frantic with him. She didn't want to end up dead on the snowmobile ride, so she decided to walk home. The house was over a five-mile walk, but she knew she could make it. It was a frigid night, and the moon was shining brightly on the snow. Sue was in her snowmobile suit and knew she wouldn't freeze. She was walking so fast that she was even sweating. It was kind of nice for her because the moon was shining on the snow, and it made the snow sparkle like diamonds. Sue was always fond of diamonds and loved nature. As Sue was walking along, she thought she heard something. Sue was starting to get frightened now. She began imagining all sorts of things like maybe there were bears and monsters out there. Sue was starting to feel this walk was never going to end. She sure got into some crazy situations because of Steve's unpredictable actions when he drank. Finally, Sue arrived home, and by the time she got there, her husband was there; already passed out in bed. Sue was so glad she didn't have to put up with him anymore that night.

Sue was always trying to make a lovely home for her kids, but it just never seemed to work. At least the kids were happy, as far as she knew. Sometimes things were good, like when they would go smelt fishing. They would have to stay up until two 2 A.M., and then go to a stream and wait until the smelt came in. They would get right out into the stream and wait and wait. It would be frigid at that time of the year, in the early spring. One time, Sue's girls were in the stream waiting for the smelt, and all of a sudden, they came in. Sue's girls got so excited that they fell on their but's in the middle of the stream. Here they were sitting in the middle of the stream, freezing they're but's off, but didn't care; they were having a good time. Wendy and Stacy had a wonderful time up

North. Wendy, the oldest girl, still lives up North to this day in Sue's farmhouse.

Sue had some other sweet times up North. She had some lovely friends that would go to garage sales and the flea market with her. Sue was really into her garden and being a vegetarian; she was on a roll. Sue loved growing her veggies and getting her hands into the soft, warm earth. Sue needed to eat right so she could keep up her strength. Sue raised all of her veggies organically, and even all the fruit trees were organic also. Sue would trade her organic fruit for some natural honey and Sue also made her maple syrup. She was about thirty or so at the time and was still looking good because she tried to eat right and take care of herself. It was a wonder that she was healthy at all with the crap she had to go through, and still, more to come.

One evening, Sue made the mistake of inviting the town whore over. Sue was not a prejudiced person toward anyone, so she thought it would be all right. Well, the whore friend came over, and everything was fine until Steve decided to get a party going. There was Sue's so-called girlfriend, Steve, and a couple of his friends that came over also. It was not too bad for a while; until the slut girl was so drunk that she tried to get one of the guys to let her suck his dick. Sue couldn't believe it. This girl was crazy. This guy she was trying to seduce was a virgin, and this whore knew it. She wanted to be his first. At least Sue's son, Dana, was in bed. The bad part was, Sue's girls were still up, and Sue's husband started running around without any clothes on. Then he was trying to pull Sue's clothing off of her. Sue told the girls it was time for them to go to bed, and thank God; they went upstairs.

Sue went into the living room where the whore and this virgin were going at it; Sue couldn't believe it. Sue told them all that she had enough, and she was going to bed. The two boys left, and Sue went to bed. While Sue was sleeping, all of a sudden, the whole bed was shaking. At first, she thought Steve had just come to bed and was bouncing around. Then, the next thing she knew, that the bed was really vibrating now. Sue woke up and found Steve and this whore in bed with her; this so-called girlfriend and Steve were going at it. If that wasn't enough, they asked Sue to join in. Sue freaked; she was shocked. Sue told the whore off and told her to get out of her house; finally, the whore left. Then, Steve passed out and left Sue alone.

The next day, Sue felt that this was the last straw, the one that broke the camel's back. Sue was so upset. She thought this was the end of happiness for her and the kids, being up North on their farm. Sue immediately went to town the next day to hire a lawyer and started divorce proceedings. Steve didn't fight her; he knew he was in the wrong and felt it was best. This marriage only lasted three years. One evening after the divorce, Steve broke into the house by the back door. He told her not to leave him, or he would kill her; of course, he was drunk. Steve started choking her and wouldn't let up. Finally, Sue talked him out of that, and he left her alone. What was it with the men she picked out? They were all crazy! Sue must have done something terrible in her past to have to live out this bad karma. She never did anything wrong to anyone; it was just Satin throwing a wrench in her life.

Here she has divorced again and couldn't get married in the Catholic Church ever again. Not that this was bad; she didn't like the Catholic Church, anyhow. Not long after her divorce, she found out that she needed to have a hysterectomy because she had some kind of cancer. Later, she found out that all of her pain was caused by her Delcon Shield, which they had put in after her son was born. Sue went to have the operation and afterward found out that she was pregnant again. Sue was hurt to know that they had to take everything out, including the unborn baby. Sue would never be able to have children also.

After the operation, Sue was having cold sweats and headaches. They said she needed hormone replacement and that she would be on them for the rest of her life. Besides this operation, Sue never had any physical problems in life again, except for a gallbladder operation. Sue had about 60 gall stones, and it affected her liver. It must have been from all of her impure foods; in the past, before she became a vegetarian. Sue was worried about her kids and what they were going to do in life. She was always striving to have a good family life for them, but it didn't seem like it would ever happen. Sue was concerned about their moral attitude, also. She would lie awake at night thinking and praying for her kids to have a good life. Sue couldn't give up; Sue kept searching for a better experience for them. But, she was still looking for love in all the wrong places.

Later on, about three years after Sue divorced Steve, Stacy told her mom what Steve had done to her. Stacy was only about twelve at the time this abuse took place. Sue was in the hospital recovering from her appendix operation when Steve did the sex act to Stacy. Steve was home with only Stacy there. Sue wished she had known all of this long before; she wouldn't have been with Steve that long. Sue keep prayed that things would get better for her and her kids in their life.

Crystal singing at her piano in Florida

CHAPTER 8

FRIEND GUY, GRANT, AND FLORIDA, GRANDDAUGHTER MANDY

Sue's oldest girl Wendy managed reasonably well in life, although Sue's last husband was such a jerk. The first time she got married, she also married an alcoholic. This guy was not only a drunk, but he was sniffing transmission fluid and beating the hell out of Wendy even. The good thing was that she had two adorable children, a boy, Davey, and a girl, Mandy. These children made Sue a grandmother, and she was pleased about that. Sue's daughter stuck with this man for about twelve years. Wendy was a strong woman, more so than Sue ever was. Sue wouldn't have been able to last that long with a man beating her and abusing her like he did Wendy. Wendy's first husband ended up dying at an early age because of his choices in life. Later on, she married Kevin, and they are living in her mother's farmhouse. They are doing great and are very happy so far.

Meanwhile, back at the ranch, Sue was very lonely again and depressed about her divorce still. She didn't know how she would be able to pay her bills now, especially with three kids to support and no job. Sue never did like the idea of living on welfare, but Sue knew that she needed to do something for a while, so she got it. She wasn't on government welfare very long, but it was okay for the time. One day, one of Sue's daughters' friends came over and started showing Sue all sorts of attention; his name was Guy. Guy was a very nice looking fellow. He had long hair, a beard, and looked like Jesus; this made Sue feel safe with him. They would confide in each other, and Sue needed that at the time. Sue didn't think anything of it initially; she just thought he was kind to her; she felt safe and liked the attention. Sue wanted him hanging around because she was still afraid of Steve coming around and bugging her, which he was again doing. Sue thought that Guy was about 22 at the time, but come to find out later, he was only fifteen and a runaway from home and a boarding school he was supposed to be at too. At the time, she had no idea.

Sue never knew about Guy's past until one day; they were all going to town; Sue had all the kids in the car and Guy. As they were coming back from town, an awful thing happened. Just before they turned into the driveway, a police car pulled them over, and all of a sudden, Guy jumped out of the car and ran like a deer across the field. Sue didn't know what was going on with Guy running like that. The next thing Sue knew, the cop was hauling her off to jail, and they put her kids in a foster home. Then She was hauled off to jail, and she didn't know why. After they got her in jail, and they told her that Sue that they would be booking her for aiding to a delinquent minor. She still had no idea what was going on.

Sue was surprised that by having this boy over for lunch a couple of times, she was doing anything wrong. Sue didn't know what to do now. She didn't want to bother her mother and father, so she called up one of her neighbors. Her action ended up being a bad mistake. This person didn't want to help at first but figured she had better. She called up Sue's mother and told her what was going on. Later, this lady became one of Sue's best friends; her name was Josephine, and they became friends for a long time until; Josephine ended up

SECRETS ARE OUT NOW

dying at a young age. Her friend smoked too much. Sue felt real bad about that. Sue cried for weeks over her friend dying.

Meanwhile, returning to jail. While Sue was in this jail cell, she was bored and was reading the writing on the wall. She read a piece that said, "I love Wendy." Come to find out; she was in the same cell as a fellow that was dating her oldest daughter, Wendy, when she was in high school. Later on, they all thought that was funny; Sue is in the same cell as Wendy's old boyfriend. The next day, Sue's mother and father picked up the kids and came and got Sue out of jail. She was thrilled to get out but humiliated about all of this. Even though it wasn't her fault, it was difficult again to have her parents bail her out of jail again. Sue didn't want her parents involved; they still had enough troubles of their own.

Sue's whole life felt like a joke, one crazy thing after another. She was discouraged with being in the North Country now. Since they accused her of aiding to this kid's delinquency, she decided she might as well do what they were accusing her of. This incident just made Sue and Guy even closer. Sue needed someone to confide in, and it was Guy. Guy was very mature for his age. Guy protected Sue when her X was coming around. Guy and Sue started sneaking around to see each other out in the woods. There were times when Guy would set up a tent in the woods, and Sue would go to see him and take him food. By Sue doing this, it was an exciting thing for her. Sue loved the outdoors and the woods. Sue and Guy became very close after all of this.

Sue was still getting sick of the North Country, and how people treated her up there, so she decided to leave. Sue asked her Indian friend, Marline, if she would like to move her family into Sue's house and rent her home for a while. Marline and her family could live in "God's Country" and get out of Detroit. Marline was the girl that had helped Sue in the past when she was sick. Marline said she would love to live in Sue's house. So, all of her family moved up there to Sue's house. Sue's girlfriend, Marline, came to her rescue again. By now, Marline had a nice husband and two girls, just like

Sue. There was one difference, and that was the nice husband, which Sue didn't have. Sue's friend had a swell time in the North Country all the time they were there.

Marline's husband had a good job, which took him all over the country. He used to be the road manager for the group, Kiss. There were times when they would have the group up to the farmhouse; also, they would have parties, which Sue would come to and she didn't even know that she was partying with the group, Kiss. Sue was able to get backstage passes and meet the group in person with their make-up on, but when they were at the house, she didn't even know who they were because they did not have their makeup on then. Marline never told Sue it was the group Kiss at her house.

Sue and Marline were friends for a long time; they used to be dancers together and would party with each other. All through Sue's life, she had only about three good friends, and her dancing friend Marline was the best one at that time. Since Sue's girlfriend was all settled in the house, Sue and her family decided it was time to move on. So they did; they all went to Florida. Sue and her family were only in Florida for about a year, and she got a phone call from her neighbor, and the neighbor said, " your husband Jole, killed in a truck accident." Sue flew back to Cedar and found out that Marline and her family moved out of Sue's house. Sue didn't want the house vacant, so she told her dad and mom that it would be nice if they moved in. The reason Marlene moved out of Su's house was because of her husband getting killed. It was a shocking thing for Marlene when she found out how his death had was, all because when driving his Kenworth truck and somehow went off a cliff to his death. No one ever really knew for sure what happened. Sue's friend Marline was devastated. She moved out of the farmhouse, and at that time, Sue lost contact with her for a long time.

Sue's mom and dad decided to move into the farmhouse. It was time for Sue's parents to have a better life; to be able to live in a beautiful country, also. They sold the ranch they lived on in Detroit and brought what few horses they had left. The North was an excellent place for them to retire finally;, they were happy for a while. Sue's parents were up into their seventies now, and they were pleased up North. The number seven seems to be the end of things for many people, and it was the end for them. Sue got her parents all settled in, and Sue and her family moved back to Florida. Since Sue needed a companion, she took Guy with her, also. Things were ok for a while, and then Guy started becoming too possessive. Guy would try to be a father to the girls and was spanking Sue's son, Dana. Sue just could not stand this. Also, Guy didn't have a job, and Sue was tired of supporting him. So, Sue put Guy on a bus and sent him back home up North.

While Sue was in Florida, she felt that the good Lord gave her the talent to be a dancer, so why not? She went back to dancing. Her dancing talent always pulled her out of bad times, mentally and monetarily. Dancing made her feel like she was somebody. Sue's girls were old enough that they could watch Sue's son while she was at work. Usually, her son was sleeping when she was at work anyhow and Sue could be with all of them during the day and she worked at night when they were sleeping. When Sue first went down to Florida, she bought an old '65 Chevy and putt-putted her way down South. This car was so old that she never thought they would ever make it. When they finally reached their destination, the car croaked; at least they made it there. Later on, when Sue started dancing again, she was able to purchase a new car, so she decided to get another silver Lincoln similar to the one she used to have with Mike

Meanwhile, back to when they first got down to Florida. When they got there, luckily for Sue, she had a girlfriend living in the area, and they were able to stay with her. Sue's friend told Sue that they all could stay there. She said they were welcome to stay; Sue didn't want to impose, but she said they would remain there until she got a job. The girlfriend lived with an older man and worked for him. The older man had two daughters, and this was very good for Sue's two girls also. Sue and her family got spoiled; the house was a charming older Spanish style and was very large. Time went on, and Sue finally got a job. She also got her car, the silver Lincoln, and moved out of her friend's place. Before she left there, she helped her girlfriend with money to pay her for letting them stay there.

Sue found a new house for them to live in. Sue's new home was just a small apartment with only two bedrooms. It wasn't much, but it was suitable for a while. It was time for the girls to start school, and she put them in their new school. The girls didn't like it at the school because there were too many prejudiced kids, but they got used to it. It wasn't the first time they had to go to school with kids of other races; they did not mind living in Detroit, and they liked it there.

They were all doing fine, and then another jerk came into Sue's life. She was always picking the wrong ones. This one was a longhaired biker named Harvey. Sue had never picked one like this before, but she thought this would be exciting for her. They got close, and Harvey thought they should move in together and get a bigger apartment. Sue was not worried about Harvey getting fresh with Sue's girls because Harvey had two girls of his own; there were times when he brought them over. The girls all got along, and they had fun. Also, Harvey would take everyone to Disney World and many other places.

Things were going well for them, and also Sue was doing well at work. She decided she was making so much money that she would buy a new car. The car wasn't brand new, but Sue loved it. It was time for her to purchase another silver Lincoln Continental, just like the one she had before, that Mike had taken away from her. It wasn't quite the same, but close enough. The interior in this car was a color called lipstick; it was a rose color, which was her favorite color. Sue's boyfriend Harvey had a Chevy van; it was an ugly orange, but he had a mural of Sue painted on the rear quarter panel. Later, he had a painting of Sue painted on his motorcycle. Things were beautiful for a while until Harvey started to try to possess Sue. He was subtle at first, but after a while, he thought he had her under his control, and he changed. Harvey was turning out to be a mean person. This guy was teaching Sue's girls how to be thieves; he had them under his control also. When they would rebel, he would yell at them and threaten them. Sue's youngest girl Stacy would skip school, vandalize the school, start fights with the black girls, smoking and was even drinking. What was Sue to do now? Harvey was into karate and would teach Stacy all sorts of stuff. He thought it was cool that she was turning out like him.

Whenever Sue's youngest girl, Stacy, would rebel against this man, he would take out his heavy belt and whip her. What happened to this good guy? After a while, the men in Sue's life would always change. Then he started yelling at Sue's son. Sue knew she had to leave him somehow, but how? Sue decided to buy her own house. She thought that if it was her place that this guy wouldn't be so possessive. So, they all moved into this house. Things quieted down for a while until Sue and her family decided to go home to Cedar for a visit and pick up more of her stuff for the house in Florida. When Sue and the kids arrived back at the house in Florida, Harvey had stolen all of her furniture and sold it. Sue figured he knew that she would do something to get rid of him, so he beat her to the punch. Sue felt awful because some of the items were things that her mother had given her. A lot of them were priceless antiques of her grandmother in Nebraska.

Even though her things were gone, she was glad Harvey was out of her life, mostly for the kid's sake. At least she thought he was gone forever. Sue decided to let the house go back to the bank; Sue didn't want it now anyhow, basically because it was a wreck, and Sue was afraid of Harvey showing up again. Time was moving along too, and Sue met a real nice older man at the club she was dancing at; his named was Jack. This man took Sue and her family to a lot of lovely places, and he bought them a lot of things, also. This man felt sorry for Sue and told her they could move into a vacant house that Jack had. He was a lovely person and had a lot of property. Sue felt maybe an older man would be better for her. Even though this man was older, she liked him, but for some reason, she never could love him. At this point, Sue was having a hard time trusting any man. It was the first time anyone was decent to her and the kids in a long time. Jack had his own nursery business and also owned an asphalt company. Things were good for a while, and then Jack stopped coming around. Sue couldn't understand what was wrong. Come to find out, this man was married, and his wife found out about the arrangement with Sue. No wonder this man never said anything about marrying Sue. Sue knew something was wrong down deep inside, and that was why she really couldn't love him.

Oh, well, back to the drawing board. Sue and the kids moved out and got another apartment of their own. At least this situation with Jack didn't break Sue's heart like some of her other men did in the past. At the time, Sue was kind of getting used to the disappointments in her life. Their new apartment was charming. This new place had three bedrooms; they all could have their room. The girls were still in school, and Wendy was playing in the band. Stacy was getting into cheerleading again also. They were all doing reasonably well. Then, Wendy met up with the love of her life, and his name was Dave. Sue knew this wasn't a good thing for her, but she did anyhow. Wendy quit school and moved in with him at his parents' house. Come to find out, she was pregnant, and that's why she moved in with him. About ten people were living at Dave's family's house. Wendy's boyfriend had three sisters and two brothers living there. Dave and Wendy had to get married. Sue gave Wendy the dress she had from her last wedding. Sue had to alter it to fit Wendy, but it worked fine. Dave and Wendy had a real cute little wedding. About seven months later, Wendy had the cutest little girl named Mandy. This little girl made Sue a grandmother for the first time.

Time was going by, and Sue's youngest girl, Stacy, quit school. Here Sue thought they were both doing well and would never stop. At the time, Wendy was seventeen, and her youngest, Stacy, was about fifteen. When they were in school in Florida, they did well there; they were both in-band and both cheerleaders. Sue felt that since they were older, they were getting into the wrong crowd and changing their feelings about what they desired. Sue felt both of them were too interested in boys. But Sue guessed that lust for boys ran in the family and who was she to say anything? Since the girls didn't desire school, Sue felt they were too interested in partying and boys now. It looked like they were both on the same path that their mother and grandmother had. Hopefully, they would never go as far as Sue, and mostly their grandmother had gone. Sue hated to see them follow in her same footsteps, but that's life; lust is hard to control.

One day, Stacy brought over a hunk that she had met at the beach. This man named was Grant, and he was from California. H Grant was tall, dark, and handsome, had big dark, almost black eyes, and muscles that were just perfect. He had medium length hair and a mustache. He didn't have much hair on his body just like an Indian, which turned Sue on even more. They looked like they were perfect for each other. They were soul mates. Stacy wanted him for herself, but Sue fell in love instantly. Grant was fifteen years younger than Sue, just like her X-husband was, but Sue didn't care. Sue fell hard and fast for this guy because this was the first time Sue had felt anything for a man since Mike and Barry. Grant and Sue had a lot in common: they had the same zodiac sign, they were both water signs, both were interested in being vegetarians, scuba diving, sailboats, and much more. Grant liked Sue a lot also and decided to give up his apartment and move in with her. At the time, she had just gotten out of the hospital from having some reconstructive surgery; she had some stretch marks and scars removed. Grant was so polite to her that he didn't make love to her for over a month. He sure must have liked her a lot, to do that for her. Sue could not believe it; she was sleeping with a man that didn't bug her for sex. He told her that you have to become friends first before sex. Sue was so happy with Grant; it was like a match made in heaven. Another thing Sue's son looked like Grant and could have been his dad. The three of them looked like a cute little family.

Then later, they made love, and he was right; it was perfect. Sue was in heaven; she couldn't believe finally something good was happening to her. Later on, Sue made the mistake of spoiling him, like she did all of her other men. Hopefully, he wouldn't change on her like all the others. Sue bought him all sorts of stuff for his van, like a new paint job, new tires, and fancy rims. Sue couldn't help herself; that was just the way she was with someone she loved. Sue was generous with her friends also, but when she was in love, she gave everything. Of course, the color of the van was sky blue, which was their favorite color.

While Sue was in Florida, she went to get her cosmetology license. Sue wanted to get out of dancing for Grant. He never asked her to, but she wanted to for him. He never came to see her dance, either. She figured it would be nice to have a hairdresser's license. She had one in Michigan, so she wanted one in Florida. She thought she could get a job as a beautician and would be able to quit dancing. One day, she went over to a lady friend of hers, and this lady told Sue that she had just been to a fortuneteller psychic, and she told her a lot of real things, and she thought Sue should go to her. Sue thought, sure, why not? So, off the next day, she went to the fortuneteller. This woman turned out to be great. She told Sue all of the guys she was with and had been with were all negative people. And, she told her it would be a long time before she ever found the right one. At that time, Sue didn't want to believe that because of what she felt for Grant. Then she told Sue that she would be moving clear out of the state. As they were sitting there, she also said to Sue that she felt uneasy with Sue sitting there. Sue asked, "Why do you feel like that?" The psychic told her that she thought Sue was a witch. Sue told the teller that she always felt that she had powers, but Sue never wanted to explore them because she didn't want to hurt anyone. The psychic told her, "You must be a white witch." She said Sue could tell she was a witch because of her long black hair, and she wore white gold. The psychic told her she wasn't a wrong person, but she knew that Sue could manipulate people if she wanted.

Sue left the psychic that day and came back another day. The next day Sue found out even more. Then the physic told Sue that she could be doing what the physic was doing one day. Sue said I never really thought about being a teller. The physic said to her that the reason she couldn't do it now was that she needed to be more in the spiritual world and not the material world. Sue told her, "The reason I am like that is because of the way they raised me." The psychic told her she could see that. Then she said to Sue that her parents were so much older than her that they were old enough to be Sue's grandparents.

She also said that Sue's parents were not her biological parents and that soon both of them were going to die. The teller told her that after her parents died, she would be hunting for her birth parents, and she would meet her mother one day. Then she said to Sue that her mother would not tell her much, but she will have a letter for her at her death. Sue couldn't believe her ears. She was saying to her stuff that no one had ever known. Mostly, the part about that Sue had been with a woman. The teller could see what happened when she was working for the mob. Sue told the fortuneteller that she had never done anything to a woman, but the woman did things to her and that she hated, and it made her sick. The teller told Sue some women like that stuff. Maybe the teller wanted Sue that way. Perhaps it was a trait of her mother's, but it sure was not a trait of Sue. The fortuneteller then proceeded to tell Sue how she knew just what happened to her. The teller told Sue she was psychic and could tell what people were thinking.

She also proceeded to tell Sue more about the mob and how Sue made money off of men. The teller told her when she was involved with the Mafia how they made her do things with one woman, or else they would give her some cement shoes. The psychic told Sue that she was away from the Mafia and would never have to worry about them again. Sue guessed the teller was right about a lot of things. Sue said, "Yes, that was when I was in Detroit." Sue was so surprised that this woman knew what had happened in her past.

The next time Sue went to her, she told Sue that she would meet her sister, and she would find out that her sister was a lesbian. Sue was shocked by the things she was telling her; no one in the whole world could have known these things. Since this psychic knew all of these things in her past, Sue knew for sure that the other things she was telling her would come true one day. Then the teller said to Sue the exact day that Sue would hear about her cosmetology license and pass the test. That came true; Sue did pass the test and on the same day that she said. She also told her she would live a long time, and that in her past life, the physic told her, "she was reincarnated from Cleopatra." Sue did not know about all that. But she just listened to her.

Well, after Sue left the fortuneteller, she felt the psychic power was amassing. One afternoon, Sue and Grant, her boyfriend, worked on his van, and the phone rang. It was Sue's dad. He told Sue that her mother was deathly sick and not expected to live. He said that she was in the hospital now, and Sue needed to come home. Sue couldn't believe it because she had just talked to her a couple of days ago. When Sue heard the news, she remembered when her mother told her that she had cancer and hoped to die because Sue's father was so mean to her. Sue could understand why she was sick; Sue's mother smoked like a fiend and never ate right. Sue's mother would tell her she would never quit smoking. She said she was going to enjoy what life she had left. Sue felt real bad about the news. After she finished talking to her dad, she started making plans to move back to Michigan. She figured what the psychic had told her was beginning to come true. Sue sold her car and bought a train ticket for her and all of the kids. The train would be the quickest and cheapest way for them to travel.

A few weeks before all of the traveling, Sue had sent her youngest daughter Stacy, up to her x-mother-in-law, the reason was that she was getting too hard to handle. Sue figured because she was a good Christian lady that she could help her daughter. At the time, her daughter was doing so badly that she didn't want her to get into more trouble. Sue wasn't sure if having her at her grandmother's house would work, but it was worth a try. Her grandmother took her to Church and Bible studies.

It was time for Sue to go up North, so she got her daughter, Stacy, back from her grandmother's. Since Sue got her daughter back, she couldn't see any difference in her yet. Then she got the tickets for the train ride, and they all took off on their train adventure. They all had a good time on the train. Wendy didn't want to go because she didn't want to leave her husband. But she did because she needed to see her grandmother. Sue didn't want to leave her boyfriend, Grant, either, but she did. Sue also didn't want to leave behind all of her things in Florida, either. Grant felt bad for Sue and told her that he would wrap up the work he had there and come up and bring her things, including Sues Doberman dog. Sue thought this was wonderful of him to do this for her, mostly because of the dog. They had bought a Doberman Pincer together, and it was as a part of the family. Their dog was a black Doberman, and its name was Angel. The whole family loved this dog. Well, Sue and the kids were on the train and back to Michigan. They had the opportunity to ride on the train; it was indeed an experience, just like Sue had in the past when she was a kid and went to Nebraska with her mom. Sue's kids were never on a train before. They rode on the train for two days and nights. They all had a good time, considering the reason why they were going.

Finally, they all arrived in Michigan. Sue went directly to the hospital to see her mother. Her mother was in bad shape; she didn't even recognize her daughter. After a while, Sue went back to the farmhouse, hoping and praying that her mother would make it. Sue's dad was in bad shape, also. He was so bad that he would get nosebleeds, and they would hemorrhage. Sue felt so bad for her mother that she went out for a drink. Sue was depressed, and she ended up drinking too much. Sue wasn't a drinker, and it did her in. She didn't know what to do about the situation. When Sue came home, the room was just spinning, and she puked all over her hair, just like she did when she was on drugs, Sue got waisted. Since Sue had never drunk before, this was the reason she got so sick. After that, she knew why she never started drinking. It was a good thing, too, because of the alcoholic genes in her family.

Finally, her boyfriend, Grant, arrived with her dog and her stuff;

this indeed made Sue feel much better. The next day, Wendy's husband showed up, also. He had hitchhiked in the dead of winter with a thin Levi jacket. Sue and Wendy couldn't believe it when they saw him walking up the driveway with no winter clothing. Wendy's husband wanted her to come back home to Florida. He didn't care about the reason why she was there; he just wanted her back. Well, this went on for a day, and the next day, they both took off. Sue wanted all her family together, but there was nothing she could do about it. When Sue's boyfriend, Grant, and her dog arrived, they both were almost frozen. Grant did not have heat in his van, and it was cold up there. When Sue started to take her things out of the van, many dead cockroaches fell out into the snow. That was sure a funny sight to see them lying dead in the snow.

The next day, Grant and Sue went to the hospital to visit Sue's mom. Sue introduced her boyfriend to her mom, but she didn't even recognize Sue. Her mom looked awful. Sue felt even worse now, seeing her mom like that. They went home, and Sue was very sad for her mom. Sue's mom did not have a year to live in the farmhouse. Sue felt that year at the farm was one of the best in her life. The next evening, Sue and Grant were upstairs sleeping, and all at once, a dog started howling. They say that when a dog howls, someone has died. It was a pretty night; the moon was shining on the new snow. For some reason, Sue had an eerie feeling. When they heard the dog, she sat up in bed and just stared. Then she told her boyfriend, "My mother just died." Sue just knew her mom was gone. About ten minutes had passed after they said her mom was dead, all of a sudden, the phone rang. Sue was worried now and wanted to find out who it was. Then Sue's father told them that the doctor had called and that her mom had passed away. Sue felt awful. At the time, Sue was glad that her mom had met Grant. She thought this was the man she would be with forever, and she was thankful her mom had met him.

The next day, she started making arraignments for her mother's burial. Sue's dad couldn't handle it; he was devastated. Her dad probably was sad because he was always so mean to Sue's mom.

Sue thought her dad wouldn't care, but he did. They were together for fifty-some years. Sue's dad bought four burial sites for the two of them and two for Sue and whomever she would be with at the time of her death. Sue's mom's death made her dad lost without his wife. Sue's mom did everything for him, and he was spoiled. Sue didn't feel sympathy for him because he was so mean to Sue's mom for so long. She thought it was time for him to suffer now, just like the suffering he had put on her mom. It was out of Sue's hands now. Sue's dad and Grant didn't hit it off very well, and her dad ended up moved out and got his apartment. Later he bought a little blue house in Maple City. It wasn't suitable for two kings in a castle, Sue was thinking. So she felt it was a good thing for him to move out. Her dad had a paper route, which helped to keep his mind off of his wife. Sue and Grant got along fine for a long time. But, she did make the mistake of treating him like a king, and he was taking advantage of her. Sue's son, Dana, really liked Grant, and they became the best of friends. Dana would even call him "Pop" for a nickname. Sue, Dana, and Grant looked alike with their dark skin and dark black hair. They all looked like the perfect little family.

Sue was starting to run out of money from the little she had saved. Then, Grant decided he wanted a dirt bike. It was a good idea because everyone could enjoy it. But Sue told Grant that she didn't have the money for it, and he got mad at her. So, she sold some of her antiques and bought the bike for him. Yes, she was a dummy again. Sue had to sell some of her priceless antiques that her mother had given her to purchase the bike. But, Sue didn't mind selling her things; she loved him and would do anything for him. Sue should have seen the light at the time, but her heart was blindly in love again. Sue thought this was the true love she had always dreamt of; Sue thought they were so perfect for each other; they both wanted the same things in life. They both were vegetarians, they both loved blue and wanted to live in Florida again, and they both wanted to have a sailboat.

Another important thing was that they were very compatible in bed. What a dream world for Sue! Then it all started to happen again, but it was different from the others. Sue was never in love like this before. Their perfect life went on for a whole year until one evening. Sue's daughter's girlfriend came over and wanted a ride to the store. Then Grant said, "I will take you." Chuckle! Ha! Chuckle! Chuckle! Sue thought nothing of it, but later started to worry because they were gone for a long time; it seemed like hours. At the time, Sue could see nothing wrong because she was so blind. Sue didn't want to think the worst, anyhow.

Later on, Sue found out that he was fooling around with the girl that night, and other nights with other girls. But then, Sue still didn't know anything. There was another time when Stacy knew what was going on and didn't want to tell her mom. It could have saved Sue a lot of heartaches if Stacy had told her. Sue was blind and couldn't see the light for a long time. Grant didn't work, and Sue had sold all of her antiques and had to go on state money again. Sue didn't like to worry about someone else supporting her even though it was the state. Sue used to be so independent, and now she felt awful. Sue could remember Grant asking her if she knew what the word embezzlement was and that he would like to do it to someone. Well, Sue didn't have any idea of what he meant by fraud; she was so trusting. He used to call Sue illiterate and stupid because she hadn't gone to college and didn't even graduate from high school. Yes, Sue was gullible and believed everything this man would say to her. This guy was a very cagey person, and Sue didn't even see it. It was one reason why it was so crucial for Sue later on to get a diploma in high school and a college degree.

Then one day, Grant suggested that Sue should sell her house, and they could go back to Florida and start a business and buy that sailboat. He told her that all of their dreams would come true. Of course, she went for it. It was another one of Sue's big mistakes. So, she started selling the rest of her stuff, which wasn't much because she had sold most of it already. She put the house on the market, and in no time, it was gone. To this day, she could kick herself for selling her home.

When she was living there with Grant, they would have a big garden, have much fun in the snow, and even made their maple syrup. They would go out in the winter and cut down their tree for x-mass. They had a great time there. It was a fantasy world on Sue's "mini-farm," and she gave it all up for him. So, the house was gone, and she didn't have to worry about getting rid of her furniture because she sold it all so they could survive. Sue got thirty thousand dollars for the house; it wasn't much, but it was all she had.

Now they were on their way back to Florida. When they got there, they bought a tent, camping equipment and lived in a tent for months. They were at a campground that had showers so that they could take their showers. Sue loved it; it was an adventure for her. Grant didn't want her to spend the money on an apartment because he had other plans for her money. Dana liked the idea of camping. Sue was glad her son was happy about the move.

Then, Grant started brainwashing her again and wanted her to buy him a brand new Kawasaki motorcycle. Of course, Sue did it for him. Sue loved this guy more than anyone before. The bike she got him was all black, just like Grant's hair and heart. Buying the motorcycle set her back some bucks. There were only about four thousand dollars of Sue's money left. If that wasn't enough, he wanted a boat motor and trailer. Of course, Sue got it for him. They did have a good time on it; they would go fishing and skiing. Sue's son, Dana, was also having a good time. Dana and Grant looked like father and son. Sue's son was getting attached to Grant, just like Sue was.

The next thing Grant wanted was to take scuba diving lessons, and he wanted Sue to buy all of the gear. Sue was starting to get suspicious. She told him that it was fine, but she wanted to do it with him. He said, "OK," and they both got brand new scuba gear. Sue couldn't believe he let her spend some of her own money on herself. They had a good time at scuba diving. At that time, Sue had no idea that her boyfriend was embezzling her; she was still really having a good time and did not realize what he was doing to her. Sue started to worry now. Here, she was going through all of her money and didn't have much to show for it. Mostly was concerned because they didn't have a place to live. So, Sue put her foot down and told him she wanted to get an apartment at least. Sue really should have bought a house with the money, but the light of love blinded her.

Luckily for Sue at the time, the park they were staying at told them it was time for them to leave; they didn't let people stay there over three months. So, they had to move. So they got a small apartment. Sue was worried because she was running out of money, and neither of them had a job. Then, of course, Grant came up with another brainstorm for Sue to buy a business for him. At first, Sue was a little worried, but of course, he talked her into that, also.

Since he used to do carpet, he wanted a carpet business. Sue and Grant went to a lawyer and set up the company. They called it Van-Go Carpets. They had signs made up for the side of his van that looked very nice. However, they didn't get many jobs.

One day, Sue's boyfriend decided to call his mother in California and have her come out to help with the business. It was like he was trying to push Sue out of the picture. Then he told Sue he needed to go to California to make arrangements for her to get there. Of course, Sue went along with what he wanted. Then he told her he needed the money to fly there and some new clothing for the trip. Sue was blind again and took him to the mall and bought him a new suit and all sorts of stuff. It was time for Grant to go, and Sue bought him a plane ticket to California. She wanted to go with him, but he said no, and Sue couldn't understand why. Sue was starting to get worried again. As her love flew away, she felt like her whole world was passing away.

Finally, he came back and, "guess what." He brought his mother and so-called ex-wife with him and also his daughter. Come to find out he lied to her, he wasn't divorced. All of this time, he was still married. He had lied to Sue all along. Sue was devastated and could not believe this was happening to her. Sue fell apart. At this time, all of her dream comes, tumbling down again. But this time, it was her worst experience of heartbreaks. Her money and her man were gone now. Sue could hardly stand it. While Grant was telling Sue all of this, there was a hurricane.

Grant got stuck with her in their apartment because of the hurricane. Sue felt the world was feeling her devastation, also. Sue didn't want to see him again, but they were stuck there together for the whole night. After the storm blew over, he left the apartment and told her that he still loved her. It didn't help Sue. It made her feel even worse because she couldn't understand why he was doing this to them. It hurt Dana, also, because they were so close. But Grant had this planned in his mind the whole time; the word embezzlement was here, and she got it. She knew what the word meant now. He took all of the things Sue had bought for him and got an apartment for his family. Sue literally got sick. Sue didn't eat for weeks and went from one hundred pounds down to about eighty pounds. She tried to take some drugs to kill herself, but it didn't work; she just got sick and threw it up. One good thing happened. Grant's friend Rick came over and stopped her, and he made love to her that night, trying to help her forget about Grant. Sue was so out of it that night that she didn't even realize what was going on. While they were doing it, all of the pictures on the wall started falling off the wall. Then Rick got freaked out when that happened. Rick thought it was Grant putting a hex on them, but it must have been Sue's angels protecting her. God was still saving Sue for something. At first, she wanted to die because she felt so lonely, but later she started to hate Grant for what he had done to her and Dana. Sue always could harden her heart when she had to.

Dana felt awful, also. Grant was his "Pop," and he was losing him. He felt terrible for years after that because of this loss. Sue was a survivor and pulled herself out of it, but never really got over Grant. To this day, she still thinks about him often. Finally, Sue started to get her life back together; but she didn't have a car. Since she always had a little money left, she bought herself a cheap car. Sue needed some kind of a job and didn't want to go back to dancing, so Sue started to see if she could get a job at a beauty shop.

One day, she went into a shop to apply for a job, and they told her that they were selling the shop and asked her if she would like to buy the business.

Sue told them she didn't have much money and she didn't think she could do it. They told her she could put a small down payment on it and make payments to them. Well, Sue thought this was great. So, she put the last little bit of money she had down on the shop. This place was a small-sized salon with about eight shampoo stalls. It had the French provincial decor, which she liked, also. When Sue checked out the shop, she seen all the windows in the shop were beautifully trimmed in soft white sheer curtains. And here was a Crystal chandler hanging in the entry, and all of the furniture was in a light, pink, and white. Sue knew she needed to name the salon, so she decided to call it Crystal Cove. Since Crystal was her birth name, she thought it would be perfect. Sue had her daughter paint all new signs in front of the place; Sue's daughter Wendy was a great artist and could use the extra money. At the time she bought the salon, the lady that owned it first told Sue she would stay working there and have of her other girls work there also until she got on her feet. Buying this business was too good to be true for Sue.

As time went on, Sue was making a good living, and then the girls decided it was time for them to move on to another place. Well, Sue thought nothing about it at the time, until her business started to drop off. She was getting worried now because she needed to get more business in there. Her bills were coming in, and knew there was no way to pay them. Sue started to advertise, but it didn't help at all. Then one day, she ran into a man that she had worked for in Detroit; she was so surprised to see him. This man was Ron from the Dragon Lady Lounge, where she was Mrs. Flunger Dunger. He was great at getting businesses going and said he would help her with the publicity to get the shop back on its feet. Ron told Sue she should get a commercial on TV and that he had the connections to help her do this. So, that's what they did. He got the advertising going, and Sue starred in her own commercial. It was a good one, but she didn't see much change in her business. Sue's beauty shop business kept dropping off more and more.

One day, Sue saw a lady that used to be her customer, and this lady told Sue that the people she had bought the shop from took all of the business and opened up a new shop in a better area. Sue couldn't believe it; she got the beauty shop business all right. Here the two girls Sue had worked for her were now working in this new shop. It was no wonder that Sue didn't have any clientele anymore. Here she was still brokenhearted about Grant and broke financially, also. What was Sue going to do now? Well, there was only one thing she could do now go back to dancing. Dancing always pulled her out of depression and debt. Sue needed to get her body back in shape, so she started to exercise. Dancing to her rescue again; it always helped her feel like her own person and gave her confidence and hope.

Sue's youngest daughter, Stacy, lived with a boyfriend, so there was only Sue and her son, Dana, to support. With Sue dancing, she could spend more time with Dana during the day. It was an excellent chance for Sue. She went back to the place where she used to dance; it was called the English Pub. She thought it would be nice to get her old job back and look up all of her old friends. Sue would be a star again. Since she was in the limelight still, she got back into modeling. Sue got a lot of new pictures taken and was looking good also. The club that she was working at they even had her pictures in their TV advertising. All of her schooling at Patricia Stevens Modeling School was paying off. All kinds of good things were finally happening to her now. Sue even got involved with the Palm Beach Civic Opera. She had the great pleasure of singing with a famous opera singer, Beverly Sills.

Sue and unknown friend in opera

SECRETS ARE OUT NOW

The picture of Sue with her friend; she never knew his name. Sue performed in the opera The Daughter of the Regiment. It was an excellent experience for Sue. She made a little money, but she would have done it for nothing; it was great. This opera was beautiful. The costumes were long evening gowns for one scene and peasant dresses for the other. Sue was meeting all sorts of rich men. She even met a man that had an airplane, and she joined the mile-high club. Ha! Ha! Sue was on top of the world again. Sue was dating doctors, lawyers, Indian chiefs, rich men, poor men, beggar men, and thief. Ha! Ha! Sue was having the time of her life, and she deserved it.

One evening at work, a talent agent came into the club. This man had seen Sue in the club's TV advertising and asked her if she would like to audition for a movie, which they were going to film in Miami. Sue was skeptical at first. What kind of movie would this be? But she said, yes, why not? She didn't have anything to lose. The next day she went to the audition, and there were about one hundred girls there. Sue was anxious and nervous. As she lined up with all of these beautiful young girls, Sue's knees were knocking. They had each girl dance a little with their top off; Sue thought well, that didn't hurt. Sue figured next would be for her to take off her bottoms, but they didn't tell her that. Then they informed all of the girls that they could go home and they would get in touch with the girls that made it. Sue figured she would never hear from them again and just went home and forgot about the audition.

Even though Sue didn't want to think about the audition, she couldn't do it. Sue became glued to the phone every minute she could. Sue would take the phone even to the bathroom with her. Then one afternoon, the phones rang, and guess what? Yes, it was from the audition. They told her that she was one out of twenty girls chosen for the dancing part; Sue was so excited she could hardly breathe. All she could do was to jump up and down, screaming and yelling that she got the part. They told her to come down for fittings for the costumes tomorrow. The next day she went for the fitting and met all of the other people in the movie. She also found out what the name of the film was. It was called PORKY'S. The first day they were trying on their costumes, she felt like a star already. Sue tried on all sorts of outfits that were in all different colors. The one she picked was a pink top that had fringe on it and a black garter belt. She had pink feathers in her hair. Then they took them out to the stage, and they were practicing with a country band. Then the girls would come out on the stage and dance in a circle. Sue was the third from the last in the ring. She was having the time of her life.

The second day, they did the same thing, but this time they had artificial smoke to give it a bar atmosphere. The bad part about the smoke was that it gave Sue a headache. In the movie, one of the seans were a fake bar in the woods, but the real scene was filmed in a bar in Miami. The scene where Meat and Pewee were tearing down the bar was a phony front; they didn't tear up a bar. Also, they were having tryouts for the lead dancer, Sue tried out, but she didn't get it. Some other girl got the part because she went out with the director. Sue only had to work on the movie for three days and made seven hundred dollars. She definitely would have done this for nothing. Sue was on the stage dancing with six other girls and had some scenes sitting at the bar. The best part was that she didn't have to take off her top. She wouldn't be embarrassed to have her kids see the movie. Sue felt like a queen.

After they the rehearsing that day, they all went to the backroom and were taking snapshot pictures of each other. Some of the guys that were in the movie were hitting on Sue; one, in particular, was the one they called Meat. Sue didn't want to get involved with anyone there; all they wanted was a one night stand, and Sue didn't want anything like that. It turned out that this movie became very popular. Sue was really a star, now. She had a lot of fun, also. It was one of the best things that had ever happened to her in her life. After that, she got many other dancing jobs and many small parts in other movies, but nothing like PORKY'S. One of her other parts was in a B.L.Striker series on TV; it was called B.L.Striker, with Bert Reynolds. One of the other was a small part was in Miami Vice. She also had a small role in the movie Screw Ball Hotel. These were all filmed in Miami,

Florida. Sue was happy with the opportunity of being in films and also singing in the Palm Beach Civic Opera. Sue was on top of the world now.

Crystal in PORKY'S the movie

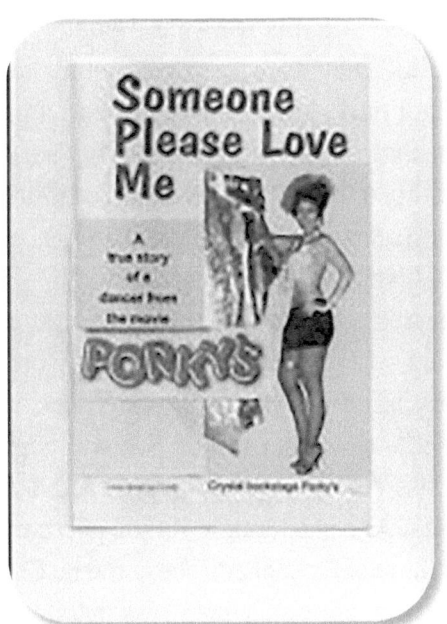

Crystal backstage PORKY'S

CHAPTER 9

NAME CHANGE TO CRYSTAL AND HUSBAND 4 MIKE THE DEVIL

Time was moving along again, and Sue met another cute young man at a bar that she was working. Usually, the cute ones were always her downfall. They were like a magnet for her. This one wasn't too tall, but he had dark, black curly hair and a nice body. He was Spanish, and his name was Mike, just like her second husband. Sue was lusting over this one. Sue was fascinated right away. He told her that he was in college to be a child physiologist and was presently working as an industrial painter.

Sue was surprised when he told her that he was in school. Sue was figuring this would be a good role model for her son Dana, and maybe she could quit work and spend more time with Dana. Another thing Mike told her was that he was a Vietnam Vet. Sue was hoping this one didn't turn out like her last Vet Steve. What was attractive to her also was his last name of Rivers. And she thought if they got married, she could go back to her birth name of Crystal and she could be Crystal Rivers. Sue's little philosophy about name's changes was that it was unlucky for the name of a ship to be changed, so it should be the same way for a person.

SECRETS ARE OUT NOW

So much for the philosophy and reasoning on ships and names! What a crazy reason to marry someone, but Sue was crazy anyway, at this time in her life. So, they got married, and Crystal Rivers it was. She figured this would make the right stage name, also. Since her adopted mother was gone now, she knew the name change wouldn't hurt her. Instead of this man, Mike, being a child psychologist, he needed a psychologist himself. At that time, Crystal should have known that Vietnam Vets were all crazy, just like her last X-husband. Well, after they were married, they moved into his mother's house for a while. The house was excellent, and it was on a canal; it was beautiful to live on the water. The wedding had been paid for by his mother, and it was excellent also. They got married by a justice of the peace in a little flower chapel. Crystal decided to get a triple silver Lincoln Continental, just like she had before, and she looked like a queen at her wedding. Crystal and Mike seemed so stunning in her car. They took many pictures, and they looked like they were made for each other because they were both so dark. Crystal liked redheads in her earlier days, but now she wanted mostly dark hair and skin men at that time.

After the wedding, it all started to happen. Crystal's husband got smashed. Since he had never gotten drunk before, Crystal was surprised. It always started after she married them. When this man got waisted, he looked different; he looked like a devil in his eyes. Crystal had never seen a look like this before. The next few weeks were weird also. Mike would get sick all of the time, and she couldn't figure out what was wrong with him. She even made him go to the doctor, but they couldn't find anything wrong with him. Crystal began not to trust him and figured something was going on. Since her husband was a Vietnam Vet, she just thought she should get a house out of him before he ripped her off or started some other sort of crap. Of course, she had to use her credit and money for the down payment, but she didn't mind. So, she got a house; it was a lovely house. It had three bedrooms, two baths, a fireplace, a pool, and a nicely landscaped yard. It also had a family room and a formal dining room. She loved this house, but what a price she had to pay for selling her soul to the devil!

One day, Crystal helped her son change his clothes; he was only about seven at the time. As she was helping him, she saw all sorts of bruises on his butt. Crystal instantly started questioning her son about the injuries. Dana was reluctant at first but finally owned up to it. Dana told her that his new stepfather was molesting him and spanking him. He said to her that one day, he even threw him into the canal, saying to him, "If you tell your mom, I will let you drowned the next time."

Dana told her that his stepfather would make him stay in the shower for hours while Mike was touching and pinching him in his privates. Crystal was sure there was more to this than what her son was telling her. Here all of this time, Crystal thought her husband would be good for her son. Come to find out; her husband was also lying about going to school to become a child psychologist. He was never in any school. Next, Crystal found out why her husband was so sick, and his eyes looked so evil. Crystal found out that he was a drug addict. He was one of the worst kinds; he would shoot up a drug called Dolata. While Crystal had done mild drugs in her past, she never had used anything like this. Crystal was so upset that she had gotten involved with the devil himself. She blamed herself for many years after what Mike did to her son. Crystal would cry herself to sleep over what had happened. Crystal carried this guilt around in her heart for years, and to this day, she still feels terrible about it. The day after she found out about what her husband did to Dana, she got an instant divorce and made Mike move out of the house. He also agreed to sign over the home to her. Crystal was only in this marriage for six evil months; thank God it was only a short time. Here is that evil number six again, just like the 666 sign of the devil that's in the Bible. Mike was the devil for sure.

After Crystal divorced Mike, he started harassing her. This animal was going crazy, and Crystal was distraught. He would go to her work and slit all four of her tires, not once, but twice. She would get them fixed, and he would do it again. Crystal was worried about leaving her job at such a late hour. As if the tires weren't enough, he took a sharp object and scratched the whole side of her Lincoln. One day, he called her at work and told her that he was seeing a witch, who would help him put a spell on her. The next night after work, Crystal walked out to her car and there was a monkey paw on her windshield. It freaked her out. She went and got someone else to take it off of her car. There was no way she was going to touch it.

If that wasn't enough, he started coming over to her house and harassing her. He would be outside her home, threatening her, yelling, and telling her he was going to kill her. If he didn't do enough horsing, then he ran over her mailbox with his truck, drove over all of the shrubs, and even put garbage and cement into her pool. At this point, all of this was getting her scared. She was too frightened to be alone with just her son. One day, when Crystal and her son were gone, he broke into the house, and Mike was going to shooting himself up with drugs, and Crystal came home. She saw his car there and told him she had called the cops on him, and he better leave. That scared him, and he left the house immediately. Later on, she found out that he stole a book of her checks and was cashing them. When he did that was when she did call the cops; then they put out a warrant for his arrest.

Crystal was getting upset about all of this, and she was afraid he was going to kill her or harm her children, Dana and Stacy. At that time, Stacy was living with Crystal. Stacy was also working as a dancer with Crystal at the club. They both felt they needed some protection, so Crystal got a hold of a charming guy she knew from the bar, and he moved in with them to protect them. He always liked Crystal and wanted to go out with her, but she never did. Crystal had him move in with her so they wouldn't be there alone. This guy was a big black guy with lots of muscles. He was a very handsome guy, and Crystal thought he was the right person at the time. Also, he had a daughter he brought over, and Crystal and Dana had a good time.

After he moved in, Crystal felt a little safer for a while. This guy was six feet, six inches, and had lots of muscles; he could scare anyone. One evening, Crystal's X came over and started to harass her from outside the house. So, Crystal sicked her bodyguard on him. You should have seen the look in Mike's eyes when this giant of a man came screaming out of the house, like the Tasmanian devil! Crystal's X started running back to his car as fast as his feet could carry him. Well, this kept Mike away from the house for a while. Later on, Mike would still call on the phone and harass Sue about getting her or one of her kids.

One of Crystal's lady friends hated Crystal's X-husband and also wanted to put a spell on him; it had been a long time since Crystal had done evil like this. She didn't want to tamper with black magic anymore, but she also didn't want her X harming her family either. So Crystal agreed to help her friend do a spell. One night with a full moon, they pulled out all of the utensils and started to do a magic spell. They found some of Mike's hair and some of his fingernail clippings that were in a wastebasket. Crystal was surprised it was still in the house. They lit some candles and made up a doll in her x-husband's image. Then, they got an old shirt of his and put it around the toy doll. Besides this, they got an old, ancient antique knife, which was very sharp. As they continued, they chanted some saying from an old witchcraft book of Crystal's. Then they proceeded to slice up the shirt and stab the doll. When they got finished with her spell, the friend left and went home. They had no idea if it would work or not. All Crystal figured was she hoped it would stop Mike from harming her and her family. It wasn't appropriate for them to tamper is the black arts, but Crystal was desperate. Crystal felt terrible doing this, but she didn't do it; her friend did it.

The next day, Crystal got a call that her X was in a car accident, and also, the cops told Crystal that he had scratches all over his body like someone was cutting Mike with a knife. Crystal found out that he was in a drug deal, and they arrested him for the drugs and cashing the checks he had stolen from her. Crystal was very relieved to find out Mike was in jail and would be there for a long time. He had been in prison before and was on probation at that time. Crystal never knew about this and learned they would be putting him back in prison. She could finally breathe more relaxed now. After a while, Crystal started to find out all sorts of things about her X. She found out he was screwing one of Crystal's best friends; she was at work; also, he was in prison two years before their marriage, and he had been heavy into drugs for years. Thank God Crystal got rid of this one! This one was the Devil himself.

The black guy that had moved in with Crystal was getting very possessive. Crystal told him he could leave now that her x was in prison, but he didn't want to go. He ended up being almost as bad as her x. Crystal was getting worried again. There was never a dull moment in her life. Crystal was always getting into a mess with men. This guy started to get verbally abusive with her. Crystal even found out that he was stealing from her, and she surely wasn't going to put up with that. This guy was aware of what she had done to her x, and he decided he better move out and leave her alone. He surely didn't want any spells put on him. Crystal could have had an excellent relationship with him if he did not turn out like another jerk. He was a very handsome man and very helpful at first.

Crystal's work was starting to get crazy, also. There were guys getting killed in the parking lot and girls getting raped in the parking lot too. One night, Crystal told a guy she didn't want to go out with him, so he went outside, got on his motorcycle, and drove it into the bar. No one had ever done this before; this guy was so mad he freaked out. As he was driving into the bar, he was yelling, "I am here to take Crystal away from it all. I am her knight in shining armor." Crystal surely didn't want this guy; he was crazy. Also, one evening, another guy was hassling Crystal. One of the bouncers took him outside with a hammer and caved his head. After many years, Crystal discovered that the guy with his skull smashed in was her daughter's brother-in-law. Crystal felt terrible for him when she found out who it was. That bar was a crazy place for a long time. After about a year, things started to settle down at work, and it was nice that Crystal didn't have a man living with her; that would hassle her or her kids for quite a while.

Crystal and Dana

CHAPTER 10

HUSBAND #5 DAVE, ALASKA, AND TRAGEDY WITH DANA

Crystal wasn't ready for any man at that time and didn't even go out with anyone for a long time. Crystal would pray for her knight in shining armor to come in and carry her away from it all. Then, one day, it happened, Crystal's prayers were answered. One evening when she was at work, he came in. She didn't know at the time, but she fell harder for this one, more so than any of her other husbands. It was true love, not lust like she had for Grant. This one was tall, with sandy brown hair, big blue eyes, and big broad shoulders, and his name was Dave. He was quiet and a real sweetheart. He was an electrician and worked very hard. While he was in the club, he tried his hardest to get Crystal's attention, but she didn't want anything to do with him at first. After a few months, she gave in and started dating him. She fell hard when she got to know him. He drank a little beer, but he was a swell person. Time went on, and she started going out with him even more. She knew right away; he was the one for her, so she had him move in with her.

At that time, she still had her lovely house with the swimming pool. Dave helped Crystal with a lot of work she needed on the house. She had finally found a nice person that wasn't ripping her off. Dave was from Texas. Dave had his mother, a brother, and a sister still back in Texas. One day, Dave requested that Crystal goes to Texas with him to get his motorcycle. Crystal loved the idea. She thought it would be fun. Since Stacy was still living at the house, Crystal could leave Dana with her. It would only be for a short while, anyhow. She was only gone for a week,

So, off they went to Texas. They had a wonderful trip. When they arrived in Texas, Crystal loved it there. She met all of his friends and relatives. They were all charming people. Crystal loved Texas, and she felt it was beautiful. It was time for them to go back home, so they rented a trailer, then he put his bike on it and towed it back to Florida. They arrived back in Florida, safe and sound. The reason Dave left Texas in the first place was that he had some trouble there. He got in trouble way back when he was a kid, and he never really wanted to talk about it. So, she respected his wishes and never asked questions or talked about it.

While they were back in Florida, they rode his bike all of the time. Crystal had a lot of fun on Dave's bike. Dave became a perfect friend with all of Crystal's children, mostly Dana. Crystal's daughter Wendy wasn't around much because she had a life of her own then, but she did come over on occasion. One evening, Dave came up with a brainstorm. He wanted to have a get rich quick scheme. There were people at the club that could get Crystal some cocaine to sell, so she bought it. Crystal and Dave got a scale to weigh it out and bagged it up to sell. The plan was that they would go to a Z Z Top concert in Miami and try to sell it. Crystal didn't need the money; she must have been bored at the time. Crystal and Dave never used that kind of drug, but they thought they could make some money. Dave had some acid and told her they would have a good time selling the cocaine at the concert. Acid and marijuana were the only things she liked to do. Crystal thought it was the lesser of the evils. She never did do the cocaine.

The evening of the concert came, they dropped the acid, and off they went to the concert. When Dave and Crystal arrived at the concert, Dave told Crystal to put the stuff in her purse because security never checked ladies' handbags. So, Crystal had all of these little baggies of cocaine in her bag. As they were entering the gate, Dave went in first, and Crystal followed. When they got up to Crystal, they told her I was time to checking purses, and they demanded her to empty it. So, she did, and they found it all. They called the guard immediately, and off she went to jail. She did not pass go and did not collect two hundred dollars. Ha! Ha! Here, she was in jail, tripping on acid and freaking out. Crystal had to stay overnight, and she thought this time was going to be like the last time when she got put in jail in Detroit; when her boyfriend in Detroit never came to get her out. But this time, it was different; Dave came to her rescue. Dave got Crystal out, and they went home. This man loved Crystal and felt terrible that this had happened to her.

As time went on, it was getting closer to Crystal's day in court, and she was freaking. She was afraid they would find out about the Detroit charges she had and lock the jail door and throw the key away. Crystal got another brainstorm. She thought they should go to Alaska, where she had gone before. She knew she could get a job in the same bar she had worked at in Alaska. The Great Alaskan Bush Company was the name of the bar there. Crystal's Dave figured it was a good idea also.

Back when Crystal visited her dad, and Dana was visiting his dad, she got a brainstorm and flew to Alaska. Some people told her about a bar in Alaska where she could make a lot of money, so she thought she would try it out. While Crystal was there, she met a lot of friends, and they helped her out. She worked at the Great Alaskan Bush Company for only a week. It was a beautiful place, but she needed to get back home. However, this trip to Alaska would be different for Dave and Crystal since she ran from drug charges. They knew they would need a few rugged gears for the journey. Crystal put the house up for sale and told the real-estate person she would get in touch with them. She never did sell it for any money; she just signed it off to get out from under it. They bought a brand new Chevy truck. It was a four-wheel drive, and it was cool. It was brown, and they purchased a camper top for it. They bought all sorts of camping gear for the trip, also.

Of course, they took Dana along. He was about eight years old and was excited about the trip. They made a bed in the back for him to be able to sleep. There was a sliding window that he could crawl through to be up in front with his mom and Dave when he wanted to. Of course, he was small enough to be able to fit through the window. On the way up there, they stopped at Crystal's Dads so that he could meet her new man Dave. They hit it off right away. They didn't stay very long because they needed to get on their way.

They finally arrived in the Yukon of the North. On this trip, they saw a lot of wildlife. Going to Alaska was very educational for Dana. On the journey, they saw wild mustangs, rabbits, eagles, elk, and moose. The mountains were magnificent and massive. It was a crazy time for them to be traveling. It was in the dead of winter, and the roads were treacherous. As they were driving, they were on roads that went straight down on both sides of the way; it was high up in the mountains. It was so scary for them all because the gravel roads were gravel with ice underneath. They were on the Alcan Highway, and they have a saying. "I drove the Alcan Highway and survived." The roads were so slippery that they were swerving all over them. At one time, Dave was taking a nap in the back, and Crystal was driving. Dave woke up and here, Crystal was going sideways down the road. Dave instantly came to the front and told her he would take over driving; Crystal was relieved.

When they finally arrived in Alaska, they stayed at Crystal's friends' house that she had met when she was there before. Anchorage was the name of the town. Crystal got her old job back at The Great Alaskan Bush Company, and Dave got a job as an electrician. They were making all sorts of money. Crystal made over three thousand dollars a week, and Dave would make a thousand a week. Crystal put her son into school, which he did very well. Dana liked Alaska except for the snow. There was not much snow, and he couldn't make snowballs or a snowman. It was so cold that the snow was dry and fluffy, and it wouldn't pack together. The part Crystal didn't like about Alaska in the winter was that it was dark all of the time. The sun came up at eleven A.M. and went down at one P.M. It was too cold there for Crystal, but she still loved it. Alaska had what was called silver frost. It was a beautiful sight. In the morning, there was a frost on everything. It was so cold that you had to plug in your car at night so the battery wouldn't freeze up.

When winter was over, and summer came, then the weather was beautiful. It was light all the time in the summer. The only bad part was you needed shades on your windows to be able to sleep at night. It was beautiful there in the summer, although it was only warm for about one month. Because of the long days, they could grow giant vegetables because there was so much sunlight. Another bad part about being in Alaska was she missed her daughters and her granddaughter. But they would be back to visit as they could afford it.

Crystal and her family were doing so well they decided to buy a house up there. Crystal's friends moved into the house with them. At least they could help with the bills. The house they found cost seventeen hundred dollars a month. They found one right on a bay that led into the ocean. The house was huge. It had four bedrooms, a living room, a dining room, a family room, two-and-one-half baths, and a fireplace; it was massive. They started buying all sorts of new furniture. They all were very happy for quite a while.

Since Dave had brought his motorcycle up there, he decided to set it up in the living room, and he and Dana re-built it. After they finished it, Dave decided to ride it in the snow. He was a crazy person. As time went on, everyone was pleased there for a while. Crystal even got into the Anchorage Civic Opera. Crystal was happy for the first time in a very long time. Crystal was really in love with Dave; he treated her better than anyone ever did. There was only one problem, and it was she missed her family back in Florida. Will she ever be totally content? Crystal's Dave had a few faults, but nothing like the other men in her life. He treated her like a queen, and Crystal loved him with all her heart. Of course, there was still bad luck in her life to come. One evening while she was at work, some drunken people smashed into a whole row of parked cars, and, of course, her new truck was one of them. He struck the fender and back bumper. This drunk even hit an older man who was crossing the street. Crystal got her truck fixed and went on with her life.

Then one evening, someone smashed in her windshield, and she couldn't figure out why that happened to her. She figured it was some guy she said "no" to at work. Some guys did not know how to take the word, "NO!" Well, she got the truck fixed again, and the next night, someone slit her tires. Dave was ready to go into the club and kick some, but's; Crystal told him that might jeopardize her job and not to go in there. The problem with Alaska was that everyone in the winter would get what was called cabin fever and go crazy. People could not get out much because of the cold and would get bored. It was so cold there you could get frostbite and never realized it. Despite all of this, Crystal could handle the little problems because she was a survivor.

One day, Crystal and her man were going to a place to get a costume for the opera she was to sing in; then, her man backed into a woman in the parking lot. Dave didn't do hardly any damage to the woman's car, but she freaked out and started yelling, "Police!" Police" This woman could not speak English very well and thought something had happened that was bad. Dave wanted to give the lady money; he would have given her three times the money for the damage, more than it was worth, but all she keeps on saying was, "Police!" Well, the cops came and inspected the scene, gave Dave a ticket, and everyone went on their way. Crystal and Dave thought everything was all right, until that night. The police came to their door with a warrant for his arrest. They immediately put handcuffs on him and took him away; Crystal and Dave freaked out. Dave hitting this car was the ruination of their lives. Next, the police took Dave off to jail. Crystal was devastated. Her heart drooped to the ground. At that time, she lost the best man ever.

The next day, Crystal went to the jail to find out what it was all about. Dave poured his heart out and told her what the whole problem

SECRETS ARE OUT NOW

was. He said to her that when he was in Texas, he was riding with one of his girlfriends in his uncle's car. At the time, his girlfriend was drunk, and she got into an accident and killed a woman and her baby. Of course, they were thrown all over the car, and when the police came, they accused Dave of driving the vehicle, and he went to jail for it. Well, it was court time, and he didn't want to go to prison for something he didn't do, so he ran from Texas. It all took place when Dave was only about twenty-five.

Dave told Crystal all about everything. While Dave was in jail, they did an ID searched on his license, and found out he was wanted in Texas for a crime. Dave had his court hearing, and they were going to extradite him to Texas. Crystal went crazy. She was so heartsick that she got physically ill. Crystal got him out on bond, and they told him if he would get himself back to Texas that they would go easy on him, and he would only have to do maybe a year or less. Crystal and Dave were trying to get a new life together, they felt Dave should get his problems cleared up, so they went for it. Dave decided to drive himself back to Texas and turn himself in. Crystal figured since Dave was clearing up his life, she should clear up her mess back in Florida. It would be a while before Dave had to go back to Texas, and Dana was still in school, so Crystal left Dana there with Dave for a time till Crystal got her mess cleared up in Florida. She couldn't take Dana with her because she didn't know if she might put her in prison for her cocaine offense. Dana didn't mind because he liked Dave; he was so good with Dana. Dave and Crystal's girlfriend helped take good care of Dana for her until it was time for Dave to go to Texas.

When Crystal flew back to Florida, it was a good thing she didn't have Dana with her; she was sick on the plane. The stress and heartbreak of the situation got her sick. When she got there, she stayed with Stacy and Tony, her boyfriends. Because of her getting deathly ill and was in bed for two weeks. Crystal was so upset because of the whole mess that she got sick and also lost a lot of weight; she dropped almost twenty pounds. Crystal stayed with Stacy and her boyfriend while she was getting better. After she recovered, she hired a lawyer, and he told her that she was acquitted of the cocaine offense, and he could get her on probation. Crystal wanted her probation to be move to Texas so she could be with Dave. And they did allow her to move her probation to Texas. It was time for Dave to drive the truck to Texas to turn himself in. Dave put Dana on a plane after he was out of school to come back to Florida, and then Dave left for Texas. Before he left, he took Dana to all sorts of festivals that they had in Alaska. They had a good time together before Dana went back to Florida. Dave had to leave their house and all of the things they had acquired. All this was the most devastating time in their lives together. Crystal's dream came tumbling down again.

Crystal didn't want to go back to dancing for a living, but she had to get back on her feet. So, she decided it would be a good thing for her to go to a truck driving school. Crystal and Dave could get a rig when he got out of prison, and they could go on the road. There were a lot of jobs that were in the Texas area, and they could drive at night and go on short runs. So, Crystal went to truck driving school and received a CDL. There wasn't anything she wouldn't try to do; Crystal could do it all and did do it all.

Crystal finally got back on her feet; then she flew to Texas. Before they flew to Texas, she found out that her man made it to Texas with her truck. When they arrived in Texas, before Dave's appearance in court, they could see each other. Dave took Crystal all over Texas, and she met a lot of Dave's friends and relatives. When he turned himself in, they put him right into jail. They kept him locked in prison until his trial. At least Crystal was with Dave before he gave himself up. Crystal loved meeting more of Dave's family and friends. She became very close to everyone and loved them all. Crystal felt these people were the most beautiful she had ever met, he had a heart of gold, and she thought she wanted to live there forever.

Crystal and Dana were living at Dave's mothers' house while Dave was going through his trial. Crystal and Dave's mother became the best of friends. Dana was attending school there, and Dave's mother would help him with his homework. Dave's mother was a wonderful person and very intelligent. Dana was doing very well in school in Texas and made many new friends. Crystal needed to get a job because she needed to pay the truck payments. Crystal went to a place looking for a dancing job; Crystal worked one night and couldn't do it anymore. She loved and missed Dave so much that she felt guilty taking off her clothing for other men, so she quit. The next day, Crystal went out looking for another type of job. She found one detailing cars; it was challenging work. She had to wash, wax, and clean the interior and exterior of the vehicles. It was a different kind of job for her; eventually, it became too hard on her. She worked detailing cars for two months and had to quit because she couldn't handle it physically.

In the meantime, it was her boyfriend's court date. Crystal and his mother came to the trial. It was a big thing in that little town of Center, Texas. Dave's trial and the situation we're in the newspapers and even on the radio. It was Dave's turn to go up and testify; they were all so worried about him. Everyone was so sure they were going to be easy on him because he turned himself in. He got on the stand, and they went through their procedures. They verbally dragged him through all of his so-called old crimes. Then, there was a recess while the judge made his decision; they were all going crazy during the wait.

Finally, it was time; the judge told him to stand for his sentencing. They told Dave he would get seven years for one crime and seven years for the other. Crystal and Dave's mother almost fainted. They could not believe it. He brought himself in for nothing; they tricked him. Dave should have kept running, but he tried to do what was right, so much for the honest court system. Crystal and Dave's mother were in tears. Crystal was allowed to talk to him for a short period and promised Dave she would wait for him and never go out with anyone else. Crystal meant it with all of her heart; she had never loved anyone like this ever before. It must have been her loyal Indian background that made her want to wait for him.

Then it was time for them to put Dave in prison; Crystal wouldn't be able to see him for six months, and then she could visit him. When she finally was able to see him, all she could do was see him through a glass window; she couldn't even touch him. It went on for several months until later it was a screen that she could see him through. Then they sent him to a prison in Huntsville, where real killers and mafia people were. In this prison was the man that committed the chain saw massacre. Crystal would pray that Dave would still be the same person he used to be before he went to prison. It seemed cruel that Crystal finally found the best man in her life, and she lost him that quick. Thank God for giving her more courage to fight her battles. God was still saving her for something, and she did not go crazy through all of this.

Crystal was broke and needed to get a job or something. She decided it was time for her to get close to God again, and her son needed it, also; so they started going to Church. Dana liked going to Church. Everything was better with them going to Church until another crisis happened to her. Dana needed to know his father, and Crystal didn't want to keep him from having a relationship with his dad; so, she got in touch with Dana's dad. It was the beginning of summer, and Crystal felt she should let her son go to Detroit and see his father; so, she got some money together and flew him up there. Dana was about nine years old at the time and was very capable of being alone on an airplane. The airlines also kept an eye on him. Dana was a big, brave boy at nine years old; while he was on the plane. Crystal missed him very much, but she couldn't be greedy. He needed to see his father, also.

The Church they started going to was a real nice Methodist Church, and the people there were great. Crystal was making plans to take her son back to the Church just as soon as he returned from Detroit. The preacher and his wife just loved Dana, and they missed him too while he was gone. Crystal was very lonely now and then, guess what? Here comes Crystal's daughter Stacy and her boyfriend, Tony. They knew Crystal was alone and needed her loved ones by her. When they arrived there, they all required jobs, and so they started hunting. Tony found some small carpeting jobs to hold them over for a while. Since they were all staying in Dave's mothers' house, they were all getting on each other's nerves, so they decided to move into a trailer together. It was helpful for them, but the only bad part was Stacy and Tony would be having sex, and the whole trailer would start shaking. That would make Crystal miss her man even more.

Crystal needed to get a job also. But, not too much luck until one day, Crystal saw an ad in the paper for a manager, waitress, and cook for a little restaurant called the Pit Grill. They all went to apply for jobs, and they all got their jobs. Things were going well for a while. One evening, a funny thing happened. Stacy rang up five thousand dollars for a man's five-dollar burger. It wasn't funny at the time, but later they laughed about it.

Things were going good for Crystal now, and the kids were getting their heads above water, also. Then the shit hit the fan again. The district manager checked up on them and asked Crystal to come over to the adjoining motels. He told her he kept his office in one of the rooms. When she arrived there, he told her he would give her a raise. Then he told her he wanted to have sex with her. Crystal's reply was, "I suppose if I don't have sex with you, I will lose my job." His response was, "No, I wouldn't do that to you." Crystal's answer was, "No way." She would never do that to her boyfriend. Crystal left the motel and knew something would probably be happening the next day.

A couple of days went by, and Crystal got a letter, which said they were all fired. Crystal was upset. What were they to do now? Tony got some more jobs doing carpeting to hold them financially for a while. Crystal decided not to work for a bit and met one of Dave's uncles, which he was a famous oil painter. He gave Crystal a discount on her oil painting lesions. Crystal had a good time and painted many beautiful pictures. Crystal tried to sell her paintings, but with no luck at all. Crystal still needed a job, and Dave's mother's job was selling produce at the Houston market; so, she asked Crystal if she could get a trailer, and Crystal could pick up produce and deliver it to the market in Houston, and she could sell it for her. Well, Crystal was excited about this. Here, with her trucking experience, she was able to put it to use. To get her license in Texas, Crystal had to take her road test in a dump truck. She took the written test and the driving test and passed them all. So, a trucker she became with her CDL and her little rig. She got a 19-ft Flatbed trailer, and off she went.

Crystal would get up at 2 a.m. and go to Tyler, Texas; there, she would pick up peaches that weighted about six thousand pounds and drive them over one hundred miles away to the Houston market. Crystal only had one unfortunate incident. A tire blew out, and her trailer and was weaving all over the road. But, she was an excellent driver and pulled it out of the weave. At first, she thought she was a goner, but she kept her little rig under control.

They were all doing well and decided to rent a little house; they were even able to get a horse. They thought this would be great for Dana when he came home. Crystal was visiting her boyfriend almost every other week. She would have to drive very far to be able to see him. It had been nearly a year since Dave was put in prison. Crystal was hanging in there and was loyal to him all this time. When she visited Dave, he told her that he could get out for a week to see her if they were married. Also, he told her if she got a lawyer, he might get out sooner if they were married, and if he had a place to come home too. Crystal was so excited. She went right out and to got some money for a lawyer. Buy selling some of her antiques to get the money. Crystal was refinishing antiques and selling them, so now she had an even better reason to sell them.

When she was at the lawyer's office, he told her the same thing Dave had told her. So, Crystal decided to have a wedding by proxy. She got the preacher he was from the Church she was going to, and he agreed to perform the ceremony. Crystal got one of Dave's best friends to stand up for her. She went out and bought a dress at a thrift shop and some cheap rings, also. It was a real different wedding. Everything went well, and they were married. All along, she wrote to her man every day and told him day by day in detail of what she was doing. Now she had some excellent stuff to say to him. She told him at what time they would be married and everything. She had some pictures taken and sent those to him, also. The next time she went to see Dave, she gave him his wedding band.

It was about a month later, and the lawyer told her that her husband could get his leave to be with her. She was so excited; she had more plans to make now. She got the little house all fixed up. She went to a thrift shop and got a new nightgown for him to see her in. Well, it was time for her to go and get him; she could hardly wait. Everything was perfect. Crystal's husband was a lot quieter than he had ever been before. Everything went along nicely until it was time for them to make love. He couldn't do anything because in prison, they gave him saltpeter and he couldn't get hard. Crystal still didn't mind because she loved him so much. They didn't do much; they just hung around the house and enjoyed one another. It was time for Crystal to take Dave back to prison; they couldn't believe how fast the time went. While she was driving him back to prison, all she was doing was crying the whole way.

Time was moving on, and Crystal, Stacy, and Tony were all having a good time until it was time for Crystal's son to come back home. At that time, Crystal did not know there was a plot going on, and she didn't even know it. Crystal called Dana and asked him about his visit with his dad and told him it was time for him to get back because school was about to start up again. Dana said, "My dad told me I would be living here with him now." Crystal was in shock, so she got her X-husband on the phone. He told her, "I told you I would get even with you one day." He said that he got a lawyer, and Dana was his and in his custody legally now. Crystal didn't know what to do. She felt like killing herself; she was so heartbroken about her husband and now her son. Dana was his now, and she could not do anything about it.

In the meantime, she was still going to the lawyer trying to get her husband out early. She had an appointment with a lawyer where he was going to tell her what could do. Since they were married now, Dave was supposed to be able to get out early. She arrived at the lawyers' office; she was so excited. She didn't even have time to sit down before the lawyer yelled out that there was nothing he could do. Dave had to serve the full time of seven years still. They had lied to her; here she spent all of her money, one thousand dollars, married her man, and they still couldn't do anything. She was devastated again. Even though she didn't feel that marriage Dave was a mistake because she loved him more than any of her hubbies and would still wait for him, no matter how long it took, it wasn't right that they had lied to her. But she could do it; she was a healthy person.

Crystal didn't know what to do about her son; she tried to get a lawyer in Texas, and they told her they couldn't do anything for her there. So, she decided to fly to Detroit and get a lawyer there. When she got there, she had to borrow her dad's car to get to court, which was four hours away from where she was staying with her dad. She couldn't afford a lawyer, so she got a court-appointed one, a woman. It turned out to be a bad idea. The judge she got did not like court-appointed lawyers, especially female lawyers, so she had lost before she began.

When she got to court, she found out that her X-husband Mike told them, "Crystal left Dana and Mike had to go to Texas and pick him up." All of this was a lie. Then he told them she was an alcoholic, a prostitute, a drug-addict, and a dancer; when she wasn't any of those things. Crystal wasn't dancing anymore. It had been written in stone, and there was nothing she could do. Crystal went back and forth to court all most every day, sometimes twice a day, trying at least to talk to her son. The court told her she was sent letters and was nowhere to be found, which was a pack of lies! Crystal wasn't allowed to see her son for almost a year. Because they wouldn't let Crystal see her son, she felt she should just go back to Texas and be with her husband. She told Dave about the situation, and he didn't seem to care about any of it. He was a different person now that he has been in prison.

Crystal got a hold of a different lawyer in Detroit because she came up with more money from selling more of her antiques. This lawyer told her that the judge said that if she got permanent residency in Detroit, she could get visitation rights. And after a year, he could come to visit her. So, back to Detroit, Crystal went. Going to court again meant that at least this time, she could talk to her son on the phone. Then finally, Crystal started getting visitation privileges. She could go over to Mike's house, but she had to sit on the porch with him; she wasn't allowed to go inside or take him anywhere. She could only see him for half an hour at a time. It was awful for her because she lived so far away. Later, she started having more extended visits. Finally, after a year, she could have him come to her place. She would go and pick him up and have to take him back to Detroit. It was a 5hour drive from her dad's to Detroit. Crystal was getting real tired of all of this. But, there was nothing she could do. Crystal's husband Dave didn't care anymore about her or her problems. Since he would never be able to move to Detroit, she decided she had better start divorce proceedings. She needed to be able to see her son. Crystal's kids always were the most important things in her life, and she needed to see her son. She was brokenhearted about both situations. To this day, she still cries about all of this.

Later on, her father died. She lost the three men she had loved the most in her lonely life; this all occurred in one-year. At least she spent a lot of time with her dad before he died. No matter where Crystal lived, she always came home to be with her dad in the summer. Here Crystal was, all alone again, living at her dad's house. How was she going to pay all of the bills without a job? Luckily for Crystal, her dad had a little nest egg. The problem with all of her dad's accounts and all of the vultures came trying to collect. Some of them were even her dad's best friends. It seemed like Crystal was in the courthouse all of the time for one thing or another.

Crystal's dad's house was a little blue one in Maple City, Mich. The house had a roof shaped like a pyramid, and she figured she might have better luck in her life because of this. Since the house wasn't paid off, it was something for her to work own. Crystal finally got all the bills paid so she could continue with all of her problems. Also, she received visitation rights with her son, and it was extended later; she was able to have him visit her in the little blue house. Crystal would get him on the weekends, holidays, and even for a month in the summertime. Not seeing him for a whole year was hell for her, but things were getting better now. It meant that Crystal would have to pick up her son and take him back to Detroit, but she didn't mind. The bad part was when she had to take him back; this would break her heart, but she was a lot stronger because of her new faith in God.

When Dana would come to visit, Crystal took him to Church with her, like she was doing before he got taken away from her. Crystal's power and strength pulled her through a lot of rough times. Later on, her daughter, Stacy, and Tony came back to Michigan from Texas. It seemed like throughout Crystal's life; her Stacy would stick by her and follow her wherever she went. Stacy was Crystal's okay buddy. Now, Crystal had almost all of her family up in Michigan. She took all of them to Church, and she was trying to live a healthy, clean life. She quit all that witchcraft thinking and got close to God.

Being in her dad's house hurt her; she missed her dad. Crystal would look at all the things in the cupboard that she had canned up for him the summer before he had passed away, something that he did not have a chance even to eat. Crystal didn't like being in that house, but there was nothing she could do about it at the time. Before she lost her dad, Dave and Dana, there were twenty acres that Crystal had purchased the year before; she was planning someday to move there with Dave and build a house. So much for a home on the twenty acres! Crystal had to sell the land because she couldn't afford to pay the house payments. The lady that bought the property from Crystal became Crystal's real good friend for years. Her friend's name was Barbara. Barbara was a teacher and would help Crystal with her schoolwork since Crystal decided to go back to school.

Cedar Michigan

CHAPTER 11

HUSBAND #6 BUTCH AND FAMILY, GRANDSON DAVEY

Crystal, her daughter Stacy, and Tony lived in the little blue house for about a year. Crystal was running out of money again and decided to rent out rooms to a couple of girls; this was a mistake. Since these girls moved in, Stacy seemed to side with them. Stacy would get into arguments with Crystal and call her a bitch. Crystal couldn't believe her ears, from her own flesh and blood, to turn on her. If that wasn't enough, the girls started having all sorts of boys over. After a while, the house got the reputation of being "the little blue whorehouse" of Maple City. Then on top of that, people in the town started shunning Crystal. They never liked her because she was not a born and conceived Pollock-like the rest of the town people. If that wasn't bad enough, the girls started having parties. The people in town didn't like her living there now.

Crystal was still very lonely even though she had a lot of people around. While Crystal figured she needed to get a divorce and move on with her new life, she felt she needed someone. To find someone new in her life was the answer. Crystal was getting a divorce from Dave; it was a hard thing for her to do because Dave was the nicest man, other than Louis, that she had ever been with. Because Crystal would never be able to go to Texas and Dave would be on probation for years after he got out, she felt divorcing Dave was the only thing she could do then.

Another thing her staying in Michigan was the only way she could see her son. Later on, Dave got out of prison; then, about ten years later, Crystal found out that Dave had died of colon cancer. Maybe Crystal's situation with her son, making her have to stay in Michigan, was God's way of protecting her from a worse heartbreak at that time, Dave was only thirty-five years old. What a shame. Crystal loved Dave more than any other man in her life. He will always be in her heart.

One night, the girls had another party, and sure enough, Crystal spotted a real cutie. It looked like husband number six had been found! The thing that got her interested in this man was pure loneliness and lust, but Crystal felt he was a hunk in her eyes. This guy's name was Butch, and he looked like a Butch. Butch was dark because he was a Mexican. He was not too tall and was thin, with short black hair, a mustache, and small features. This guy looked like he was made for her; they looked good together. This man looked like he could be Dana's dad, also. It seemed like Crystal was always looking for a father figure for Dana. Since the girls were older now, they didn't need a father figure anymore. They could take care of themselves. Another reason she was attracted to Butch was that he was Mexican, and the Mexicans were descendants of the Aztec Indians. It is also where the Apache Indians originated. So this made a good match for Crystal. The bad part was, he was fifteen years younger than her again, just like some of the others. At the time, Crystal was feeling very old and needed a younger man to help her boost up her ego.

Here he was, another military man; at one time, he was stationed in Germany and presently was still in the reserves in Michigan. Crystal was a fool for a uniform. At least he was not in any wars so that he wouldn't be beating her up like her third husband. As far as Crystal could see, there was nothing terrible about Butch; but he was a drinker, also. Crystal didn't mind at the time; she needed the attention and overlooked his drinking. He made her feel young again and gave her hope for the future.

At the time, Crystal was still going to Church, and there were times when she was able to take Butch with her. When Dana came to visit, all of them would go to Church. It was terrific for Crystal, Dana, and Butch to all go to Church together. They all looked great, too. They all had such a dark complexion, and they looked like a family made in heaven. Butch was friendly to Dana, also. Thank God for that. During this time, Crystal's oldest daughter, Wendy, had moved back to Kentucky from Florida. Wendy's husband's family lived in Kentucky, and that's why they moved there. Wendy had a son while she was in Florida; his name was Davey. Now Crystal had a new grandson; he was blonde with big blue eyes. Davey loved his grandma. As time went on, Davey and his grandma became very close. Later, Davey kind of took the place of Crystal's son, Dana.

Crystal and Butch went to Kentucky to see the new addition to the family. They all had a good time, but of course, Wendy's husband had to get Butch drunk. Crystal didn't know how long Wendy would be with her husband, either. He used to get drunk and sniff transmission fluid; then, he would get mean with Wendy. One time, Wendy called her mom and told her she wanted to come home and asked Crystal to drive to Kentucky and pick her up. Crystal immediately got in her truck and went to Kentucky. As soon as she got there, Wendy told her mom she changed her mind and didn't want to leave her husband. Crystal was so mad after driving eighteen hours that she turned right around and went back home. Crystal had always done a lot for her children, sometimes with no appreciation. It was bad enough for the men in Crystal's life to mistreat her, but her children did the same thing to her from time to time.

A while before, when they were all in Florida, Crystal signed for a car for Stacy, her youngest daughter. Then, Stacy decided she didn't want to pay for the car anymore, and the bank repossessed the vehicle. A while later, Crystal wanted to sell her little blue house, and there was a three thousand-dollar loan on it. Crystal only received two hundred dollars for her home, and the bank took all the rest of the money to pay for Stacy's car. What a rotten trick for her daughter to do to her. Crystal's daughter never tried to pay it back either. After Stacy had her car repossessed, she decided to borrow her mother's new black and white mustang; Stacy was driving it one night, and yep, she smashed and totaled Crystal's new car. Crystal didn't get mad at Stacy because she was just glad she wasn't hurt. Is there any more bad luck out there for Crystal? Crystal's youngest girl, Stacy, was still living with her in the blue house with her boyfriend, Tony. Things weren't working out very well with Tony. He was from Florida and didn't like the winters. There wasn't much work up there, and he started dealing drugs. Crystal told him that he couldn't be selling drugs and living there at her place.

    Tony finally looked for a job and found one, but he didn't have a way to get to work. Crystal offered to drive him back and forth to work, so she did. Well, driving him ended up being a long trip, and she was getting tired of it. So, it was good old Crystal to the rescue. She decided to let Tony drive one of her dad's cars. That was a dumb thing to let Tony drove her dad's car, but he pushed the hell out of it. Tony would lie and tell the girls that he was working, but he wasn't. Tony lost the job that he had and even started stealing from Crystal and trying to sell her things. Tony took some antique guns from Crystal that was her dad's, and he was trying to sell them. Thank God she got the arms back. Crystal couldn't stand the situation, so she told Tony he had to move out. Tony got ahold of his father in Florida to wire him some money for the thief to get a bus ticket and got out of there. Crystal was very relieved that was over.

    Crystal loved finally being back in Michigan; she got to visit all of her old friends, and she got into canning and going to yard sales again. She picked up many antiques that she had to get rid of through the years; she was happy, too, for a while. Crystal even started restoring furniture again and selling some of the pieces at the flea market. That did not do that good, so she decided to open up a hair salon. Since she opened up a hair salon in her house, she called it the Hair Hut.

There was a little business for her, and it was enough for her to pay her bills; at that time, she was thrilled not having a husband. Her antique business was profitable in the summer, but nothing to brag about in the winter. But, she loved it, anyhow.

Crystal and her new boyfriend, Butch, would do a lot of things together. For a while, they were inseparable. When her son was there, the three of them would do a lot of things together. They would go fishing, canoeing, hiking, and all sorts of outdoor situations. Butch would have been perfect had it not been for the beer. There was only one problem with Budweiser; "Bud does not make you wiser." Ha! Ha! It made her boyfriend dumber. Butch's mother hated Crystal because they were the same age, and she was jealous that Crystal looked so much younger than she did. His mother would do everything possible to try to break them up. At first, she was kind to Crystal until she found out that Crystal didn't have any money. Money was essential to his mother, and she wanted her son to have a woman with money, which could give him kids.

Time was moving right along, and Crystal was pleased. Crystal was always wondering about her biological birth parents. One day, Crystal got a wild idea; she would start looking for her parents. Crystal was thinking about when the fortune-teller told her she would meet her biological parents; she felt it was time to find them. In an attempt to locate them, Crystal decided to put an advertisement in the Detroit newspaper. The ad read, "Looking for anyone related to Peter Gellata." She was going by her last name, and she called information to find out if there were any Gellata's in the phone book. There was only one, and the first name was Peter. Gellata was the name that was on her adoption papers. So, she tried that name to see what would happen.

She waited a long time, and then one day, the phone rang. A lady called her and said, "I have some information about your ad." She told Crystal that she read her ads, and she knew a woman with the last name of Gellata. This lady thought it could be Crystal's mother and that if so, she had a half-sister, also. Crystal was so surprised she had to sit down because her knees began to get weak. After the shock was over, all Crystal could do was jump around and yell, "Finally, Finally!" She was so excited. She thought. Finally, she would get all of her questions answered. The lady proceeded to tell her that she would set up a meeting for her and her mother, but only after she called her to find out if it was all right. Crystal was going through the most ironic thing that had ever happened to her in her life so far. The lady that called told Crystal that she and another friend would be coming to see her before she would call Crystal's mother and sister. Crystal said, "That would be fine with me."

About a week later, the lady and her friend came all the way up from Detroit. This lady felt she needed more proof before she would let Crystal get involved with her mother. All along, the whole thing was very suspicious. Crystal was so excited; she knew better things were starting to happen to her, finally. She felt all of the good she had done for others was coming back to her. Hopefully! Finally, the lady arrived with her friend. It was hilarious for these people to come up there. One of the ladies looked like Crystal; she had a split between her teeth like Crystal, but she didn't tell her that she was any relation to her. But, Crystal was still suspicious and skeptical of everything. Crystal looked at everyone, always wondering if it was her relatives.

At their meeting, the ladies were both very nice. They had some lunch with Crystal and took a lot of pictures of her and the kids. The two ladies didn't tell Crystal much about her mother or sister, only that her sister lived in Florida, and her mother lived in Detroit. The lady said to her that when she got back to Detroit, she would contact her mother to see what she had to say about their meeting. The lady also said to her that she would give Crystal's phone number to her half-sister. The ladies left, and Crystal was even more excited than ever now. She was anxious to find out what her mother and sister had to say.

A few weeks went by, and one evening, she got a call from her so-called sister. Crystal was ecstatic; she couldn't believe it. Crystal's half-sister started pouring out her heart to Crystal on the phone. One extraordinary thing was that she told her was that her name was Crystal, also. And here, her first, middle, and last names were the same, too. She told her all sorts of things that were ironic. Their lives seemed to be so much alike. Crystal's sister told her she didn't like that they both had the same name, and would she mind if she called her Crisy. Well, Crystal was a sweet person and agreed to let her call her Crisy. She didn't mind, but it hurt her. As they were talking, Crisy found out how much they both had in common. Crisy was amazed.

Crystal's sister decided she would give her a phone number. It was her mother's number and this excited Crisy. Right after Crystal and Crisy's conversation, Crisy immediately called her mother. She got a hold of her mother and told her who she was; the woman was quiet at first, and then all she could say was, "This is a nightmare, This is a nightmare. I can't believe this is happening." Crystal (Crisy) felt very bad about her mother's response. Crystal (Crisy) didn't give up, and she kept calling her mother until finally, after a year, she started to come around. One of their conversations was about Crystal trying to get her to come around for a visit. Crystal told her she wanted at least to be friends. After one of Crystal's conversations with her, Crystal told her mom she loved her. Her mother's reply was, "Friends do not love each other." Crystal couldn't believe her response. What kind of person was this woman?

Then, Crystal finally got her to open up a little. Crystal told her that she was planning a trip to Florida to meet her sister and asked if it would be all right if she met her in Detroit on her way down. Her mother was still leery but told her it would be all right. Crystal's mother said that she was still not admitting that she was her daughter, but she would see her. They made plans for Crystal to meet with the two women that got in touch with her first. The one-woman that called Crystal initially phoned again and told her where she lived so they could meet.

A few weeks later, Crystal set out for her trip. It was hard for her to afford it, but she would make it somehow. First, Crystal went to Detroit; she was used to the trip because she had to visit her son so often. She then went to the lady's house where she spent the night. The next day was to be when she would meet her mother. Crystal was worried now. Would the woman reject her totally or admit anything?

The next day arrived, and Crystal and the two ladies took her to the bar to meet her mother. Crystal was so excited she had diarrhea. As Crystal got out of her truck and approached the bar, she didn't know what to expect. As she walked through the door, she got a lump in her throat. Then the ladies walked her to a booth in the back of the bar. After that, the two ladies introduced Crystal to her mother. Crystal took a deep breath and saw her mother's face for the first time. Crystal knew right away that it was her mother. She could see the resemblance, and she felt it, also. Crystal wanted to cry, but her mother was so stunned that she didn't dare. Crystal's mother looked a lot like her. She was short with tiny feet and hands and small features. The most significant difference between them was her dyed, red hair; she looked like a tramp. Crystal's mother spoke and said, "Well, this is the girl that claims to be my daughter. Sit down and have a drink and let me talk to you." Right then, Crystal was very disappointed with her mother; it was not a very warm welcome. Then her mother started asking Crystal all sorts of questions. She asked, "What makes you think that I am your mother?" Then she asked her questions like what kind of food she liked, her favorite colors, her hobbies, and all sorts of stuff.

As the evening went on, Crystal's mother and the other ladies got pretty well lit. Crystal could see that her mother was a drinker. At this time, Crystal's daughter, Stacy, was having a drinking problem, and Crystal could see now where it came from. Her mother still didn't want to admit that Crystal was her daughter. Crystal dragged out all sorts of proof like her baby bracelet that had her mother's name on it and her adoption papers with her name on it. It was just like the same name as her sister's in Florida. But, nothing worked; her mother was still skeptical, or was she just playing a game?

It was time for the big reunion to end, so they all left the bar. As they were going, Crystal could hear her mother telling the other

SECRETS ARE OUT NOW

lady, "Oh, no! Now there are three of them running around." Crystal didn't know just what that meant. Then her mother told Crystal to follow her to a restaurant, and they would talk some more and get something to eat. As they were at the restaurant, her mother was asking her more questions. A little later, she told Crystal that she had something to say to her, and she would say to her after they had a bite to eat. Crystal was anxiously waiting for her to tell her something. After they had a bite to eat, Crystal was almost falling off the edge of her chair, waiting for her to tell her something constructive. Then, her mother began telling her a little about herself; that she had Indian blood and Dutch blood. Crystal asked the woman, "What nationality do you think I am?" The woman replied, "I think you are Italian and Indian." She told the truth about her being Italian,

Then finally, her mother said, "I have to tell you something." Crystal said, "Yes, what is it?" Then she stated, "I'm not your mother, I only have one daughter, and she is in Florida. But I would like to give you an Indian name." So the woman told Crystal her Indian name would be Tinawa, which meant tiny one. Crystal couldn't understand why she would give her an Indian name, but deny that she was her daughter. This woman wasn't rite. She probably was bummed because she thought Crystal was dead. Now her sin was haunting her.

Crystal was so hurt to hear her say that she was not her daughter. Crystal's heart about to drooped out of her chest. She knew the wicked woman was lying but didn't know why. Crystal knew this woman was her mother, and there was nothing that would change her mind. After that, Crystal and her mother left the restaurant, and Crystal put her tail between her legs and went on to Florida to meet her sister. She was hoping that the next meeting would be better than the one with her mother. As Crystal was driving, she felt her meeting with her mother was an awful experience and that the woman had a deep, dark, secret buried down inside that she was hiding. Crystal knew she was lying and knew she could make the woman come around one day. Crystal could see where she got her powers from; her mother was a real mean witch, and Crystal would break her evil spell someday. While she was driving and thinking about all of the crap her mother put her through, Crystal cried all the way down the road and couldn't believe her mother had a chance to make her sins right, but wouldn't do it.

Crystal finally arrived at her sister's safely after two days, and one night, she was tired. It seemed like the drive was the longest one she had ever experienced, even though she had driven it many times before. As she arrived there, she saw that her sister lived in a little trailer in the suburbs of Fort Lauderdale. It was a beautiful place with lots of plants. As soon as Crystal's sister opened up the door, she knew this was her sister. This girl looked precisely like Crystal's oldest daughter, Wendy. This reunion was a lot different than the one with her mother. The two Crystal's seemed to unite instantly, although the whole thing seemed very mysterious. Her sister poured out all of the good and bad experiences to Crystal. Even though they got along, Crystal's sister was very jealous of her, mostly because they had the same name. Crystal's sister still wanted her to be called Crisy the entire time she was there. She was insistent on this that Crystal being called Crisy. The so-called Crisy was telling Crystal, her sister, about the meeting with their mother and how she couldn't understand why she didn't want to admit anything. Crystal said to Crisy that she had just met her mother five years ago also, but she didn't deny her. Crystal said to Crisy that her mother gave her an Indian name; also, it was Tionka, which meant little one. Their mother was nuts to provide them with almost the Same Indian name, too.

Crystal and Crisy decided to call it a night and continue their conversation the next day. In the morning, Crystal went on to tell her how her stepfather, Peter raised her throughout her childhood. Crystal's mother was going to Arizona, and she was hitchhiking. A trucker picked her up, and that was how Crystal was conceived. Crystal's father must have been a blonde because her hair was a brownish color, not like Crisy's black hair. Crystal looked a lot like Crisy's oldest daughter, Wendy, because of having the lighter colored hair. Crisy and Crystal had the same body frame: short, small feet, and tiny features. Despite this, there were several differences between them. Crisy was prettier, had more going for her, and this made her sister jealous.

Then, Crystal told Crisy how a repulsive black man had raped her and how she was into prostitution, and she was a dancer, also. It was so ironic how they both had experienced the same lifestyle. Crystal used to be a stripper in Detroit. Then Crystal told her she was currently working as a cardiac technician. Strangely enough, Crisy became a CNA and later, a phlebotomist. They were both in the medical field; that was really ironic. Then Crystal told Crisy how she was madly in love with a guy when she was very young and how they were living together; Crystal was pregnant, and she was pleased because they were going to get married. However, one day, Crystal came home from work, and here she found her man in bed with another man. It wasn't bad enough for him to be in bed with someone else, but here it was another man. Crystal found out her man was gay the whole time they were together. Crystal was devastated. She immediately left him and went to try to get an abortion, and did it. Crystal went to her stepfather for the money, and he gave it to her. She had a stepfather that only gave her a material love, just like Crisy. Similarly, both of the girls were raised by fathers that only gave them material love and not genuine parental love. As a result, Crisy and Crystal both looked for love in all the wrong places.

Since Crystal's father gave her money for the abortion, she needed to find someone to perform the abortion. Back in those days, abortions were illegal, and it was hard to find someone to do them. The only one she could see was a quack in an old building in Detroit. Crystal proceeded to tell Crisy how she found a black lady to do the abortion. The abortion was done in a dirty, gloomy basement where a black woman put her on a sheet on the cold cement floor in the middle of a room. Crystal was telling Crisy how there was a light bulb hanging from the ceiling, and Crisy instantly could see the time she was raped where there was a light bulb hanging from the ceiling, also. This made Crisy feel eerie. The black lady was not clean and didn't have sterile instruments, of course. Crystal didn't have any anesthetic and was screaming with pain when the woman did the procedure. When her abortion was over, and she was almost dead, she ended up getting an infection. Luckily, the black lady gave her some antibiotics to take home; she ended up okay. After her abortion, Crystal couldn't have any children because of the way it was performed.

Then Crystal told Crisy more; after all of that, Crystal got raped by a horrid black guy and got a nasty disease and had to have a hysterectomy. Crystal was never the same in her mind after all of that. Crystal's life went downhill from that point on. Her downfall was when she got into dancing; prostitution, drugs, and alcohol, just like her biological mother. Crystal decided to hate men forever. Instead, she stopped being a prostitute, became a lesbian, and never married any man. Crisy had a lot of the same experiences but was a stronger person. Crisy took drugs and was involved in prostitution only because she was in with the mafia and had no choice. Even though Crisy had a bad life, she never let it get the best of her. Crisy had too much power to make anything spoil her life, no matter what happened to her. Crisy never became an alcoholic or hooked on anything. Crystal was an alcoholic and got hooked on shooting up drugs real bad; Crisy could see the track marks on Crystal's arm.

After all of this was when Crystal became a medical technician. She never had anyone in her life and lived a very lonely life because of the wrong choices she made in the past with men. While they were telling each other all about their history, they both broke out in tears for one other. It was a magical night for both of them. They both were, ripped off in life by not having the parental love that they both needed desperately. Crisy was always searching for that true love in life. Crystal has given up and ended up choosing to be alone forever. There was a big difference between them; Crystal had a chip on her shoulder, and Crisy was a very loving, forgiving person. Crystal never forgave her mother for giving her away. And, she didn't like the idea that her mother denied Crisy. Crystal, deep down inside, knew that Crisy was her true sister, but she was still jealous and told Crisy she wanted more proof. Crisy didn't have any more proof for Crystal; she just needed to accept the evidence she had.

That third day after they poured out their hearts to one another, Crystal seemed to turn on Crisy. Crystal also told Crisy that she had to buy her own food while she was there and had to pay rent. Crisy could not believe it, especially after all they had been through the night before. Crisy told Crystal not to call her Crisy anymore, and she was leaving to go back to Detroit. Well, that was par for the course for Crisy's life. Crisy had a pure heart and deserved to have the name of Crystal and Crystal it was from then on. Her heartbreaking experiences, made Crystal harden her heart towards her sister and mothr. Time for crystal to get on with her life. On Crystal's way back home, she picked up her son and forgot all of what had happened to her. Crystal's X-husband was supposed to share expenses with her but never did. So, she killed two birds with one stone by picking Dana up. Mike owed her five thousand dollars in back child support and never paid it. She figured that was why he took her son away from her, so he wouldn't have to pay child support.

Crystal and Dana finally got back to Maple City. Crystal was glad to be able to get back to her boyfriend, Butch, also. He was younger than she was, but she loved him anyhow. But more crap was coming up for Crystal; the alcohol problems were escalating. She didn't know Butch had an alcohol problem at first, but as time went on, she was finding out. Crystal figured she could heal him so he wouldn't be a drinker. Crystal always thought she was Florence Nightingale, trying to help everyone, but some people can't be helped. One time, Butch was so drunk he put Crystal's truck into a ditch. The same old crap was starting again. Crystal was stupid to continue to stay with him, but she was too in love and let him get away with it.

Crystal loved Florida and found out that Butch was born there; he also had many of his relatives there. They decided that they would rent a travel trailer and go to Florida on a trip. It was in the dead of winter when they started out. They rented the travail trailer and towed it with Crystal's truck. On the trip, the roads were all icy, and they almost got killed. The travel trailer was sliding all over the road. But, they survived and made it to Florida. They had a good time there when Butch wasn't drinking. Crystal figured the reason he drank was that he had been in the army stationed in Germany, or it could have been his alcoholic mother. In Germany, they would drink warm beer and liked it because it would get them drunker. Crystal thought for sure she could help him. At least he never cussed at her or hit her all of the time they were together. Also, he was acceptable to Dana.

While they were in Florida, they would go fishing on a pier with Butch's grandfather. Crystal got to visit her girls also; they were still living there. They had many memorable times as a family in the warm tropical weather, with all of them living close to one another. One evening, Butch's grandfather had a birthday party for Butch, and he proceeded to get drunk. Well, his mother ganged up on Crystal and told her she needed to leave because she wasn't welcome there. While Butch was lying on the floor drunk, and Crystal couldn't get him up. So, she moved out of their trailer and went to stay with another man. This man, for the longest time, wanted Crystal to marry him. But she couldn't because she was in love with Butch. This man even bought her an engagement ring, but she couldn't marry him. Crystal had met him in Florida several years before.

Moving in with another man was a dumb thing for her to do; she must have been crazy herself at that point. Crystal went back to the trailer to get some of her belongings and found out that Butch was sick and lonely for her. He told her that he loved her and would quit drinking; he even wanted to marry her. He said he didn't care what his mother thought of her. Well, she stayed with the other man for one night and then came back to Butch. Butch convinced her to go back to him. Crystal told him that they should get married, and he needed to quit drinking if he loved her. He promised he would.

They started making plans to get married. They had an adorable wedding. They went to a little chapel and had a notary public marry them. After their marriage, they decided it was time to go back to Michigan. When Butch got back there, he told his mother that they were married. She called him a dumb son of a bitch, that wasn't saying much for her. At that time, they wanted to start a new life, so they sold the little blue house of her dad's and bought an old farmhouse. The house they bought needed a lot of work, but they had a good time doing it together. Crystal had a garden and got into canning again. She even sold some of her veggies at the co-op in town. Crystal's son, Dana, also had a great time there when he came to visit. Dana and Butch went fishing a lot and became excellent friends.

Now that they were married and Crystal couldn't have any more children, they decided it would be nice to have foster children there at the farm. They both started going to classes to become foster parents. Butch hadn't touched a drink in almost a year; he was doing so well. After the classes were finished, they still had to be accepted. They thought for sure they would take them. Here right at the last minute before they were to get approved, they told Crystal they couldn't have the children because she used to be a dancer. Crystal was devastated again. What a low blow for her. She was one of the most beautiful people in the world, and they didn't want her. It had been years since she was dancing. Their rejection hurt Crystal very much.

After this disappointment, Crystal decided to change her goal; she decided to go back to school and become a nurse. Since she never finished high school, she needed to go back to adult education to get a high school diploma. Crystal was tired of working as a beautician and wanted something different. She picked out the most challenging career ever, being a nurse. She made it through her high school and graduated with a cap and gown; now, she had a high school diploma. Eventually, she went to college received an associate's degree in art and science. Later on, she worked as a phlebotomist, a certified nurse's aide, and an emergency medical technician. For three years, she rode with the voluntary fire department and the ambulance in Cedar, where their new house was.

Butch and Crystal were reasonably happy for the longest time; the winters were hard up there. But, having a husband made it easier for her. Crystal, Butch, and Dana had a lot of fun together; they looked like the perfect little family. Butch and her son looked so much alike that people thought Dana was his son. Everything was perfect for a long time until a friend of Butch came from Germany to visit. This man's name was Mentsie, and Butch loved him a little too much. Butch fell off the wagon and started drinking with his friend. Butch even quit work so that he could be with his friend. The whole two months that his friend was there, Butch never made love to Crystal. Crystal felt awful about this. There were nights when Butch and his friend would go out into the cherry orchard and just sit there for hours. Crystal felt there was something wrong. She didn't want to think about sick things, but they would even go out there when it was raining. What could they be doing outside in the rain?

There was one time when both men were drunk and slipped up when they were talking. Butch would tell his friend that he loved him; Crystal would say, "What?" and Butch would say to her, "Not you. I mean him." Was Crystal's husband gay? What were they doing? Crystal and Butch got into arguments all the time over his drinking and not paying any attention to her. Then Butch would get mad, go over to Crystal's girlfriend's house, and sleep with them. Butch did this to two of Crystal's lady friends. It was terrible for him to do this, but at least he was with Crystal's friends.

There was one night when Butch and his friend, Mentsie, were invited over to Butch's mothers' house for a party. It hurt Crystal because they told her she couldn't come. Butch was always siding with his mother, and she was still trying to break them up. After Crystal got her high school diploma, she just couldn't stand anymore, and she decided to divorce Butch. Crystal quit going to Church again and was very depressed. This situation hurt Dana, also, because he was getting close to Butch. If Crystal wasn't upset enough, she called her biological mother again and got more disappointments. Then Crystal decided to call her mother and talked to her; her mother told her, "Don't call me anymore. You are not my daughter." If you do call again, I will have the police after you." Crystal's mother was a witch; Crystal was hurt again. However, she didn't give up. Months went by, and she called again, and again, and finally, her mother talked to her a little, but not much.

Crystal decided to call her sister and see what she had to say. Her sister told her that her nationality was a Chiricahua Apache Indian, and if they were sisters, she was one, also. Then Crystal's sister said that they had two half-brothers somewhere, but her mother wouldn't tell her where they were. Crystal could remember the fortuneteller telling her all about her having two half-brothers somewhere. It was all coming true, what the fortuneteller had told her. Crystal was even lonelier now, and she called her kids; they all moved up North to be with her in the farmhouse. It was summertime, and Crystal was fortunate to have her son there all summer. Crystal was in heaven for a while. Also, the girls had their boyfriends and husbands there. It was like one big happy family. They had chickens, turkeys, and started growing a garden; everything was great, but not long. All of this was after Tony came back to Stacy. He was there at the farm, also. Having too many kings in the castle was not good. Everyone was fighting, and Crystal's Stacy and Tony decided to go out and party. Crystal left Wendy, her husband, and the grandchildren and went with Stacy and Tony, just to get away for a while.

Things were okay at the party initially; they were all drinking, doing drugs, and having a good old time. Then Tony smarted off to Crystal. Crystal stuck her tongue out at Tony, and Tony told her where she could put her tongue. Crystal was highly insulted by her own daughter's boyfriend. Crystal was so embarrassed and hurt that she decided to walk home. When everyone realized Crystal was gone, they all began to look for her. Crystal had to walk five miles in the black of night; it was so dark she couldn't see her hand in front of her face. This walk kind of reminded her of when she walked home in the snow, but the moon was shining then, and she could see. At least this time, it was summer, and she enjoyed the warm summer air.

As Crystal was walking, if she heard a vehicle coming, she would jump back into the weeds so no one would see her. Crystal felt like a deer in the night as she hid down close to the ground in the tall grass; she loved every minute of it. Her Indian background reappeared in her life once again. When no one was coming, she would start running a little. Then, Crystal decided she wanted to get home sooner, so she went cross-country and got away from the road. As she was walking, she stepped into the swamp. She had on white jeans, and they were just covered with mud clear up to her waist. It was funny to her, even then.

Finally, she got to the top of the hill in her back yard. At the top of the hill was the cherry orchard, and she could see the lights on in the house. She didn't have far to walk now. When she got to the house, her son-in-law was standing there and asked where she had been. He stated, "We are sure glad to see you." Here Stacy and Tony were out searching for her with a gun. There was a creepy guy at the party, and her family thought this guy had kidnapped Crystal or something. It was a good trick she pulled, but everyone felt better when she came home.

A few months later, a beautiful thing happened. Crystal found her old Indian girlfriend, the one that nursed her back to health after her husband left her home alone. Crystal hadn't seen her in over ten years, and she was so glad she found her. The Indian girl's name was Marline, and back when Crystal's name used to be Sue, she would never have found her with her new name. Crystal told her about her new name, and Marline said she would try to get used to it. It was a hugging and kissing reunion for them. Crystal and Marline were closer than she was to her blood sister in Florida. Crystal was so glad they were close again; here all of the time, Marline was still living in the area. Crystal was delighted to have her friend yet; people were jealous of her, and she didn't have many friends. Marline was a beautiful woman, and people were jealous of her, also. All of Crystal's children decided there wasn't enough room for all of them at the farm, and they all moved out. Wendy and her husband went back to Florida, and Stacy went to Arizona with Tony. Since Crystal was getting lonely without her children, she started going out with the local girls. Crystal was having a good time for a while. But she needed more than just to hang out with the girls.

One evening, she met another creep. It didn't last long; she found out he was going out with one of her friends at the same time he was with her. So, she ended that romance fast. At this time, it was in the dead of winter. Christmas and New Year were gone, and it was cold, gloomy, and lonely in her old house. Crystal was so alone in her big old house that she started to get physically ill. She got so bad that she was right down in bed; she couldn't even put wood in her antique wood burner. Crystal called her old friend, Bud, and asked him if he would come over and help her put some wood in the stove, and he did. Crystal and Bud were friends for years. He was twenty years older than Crystal and had a lot of money, but Crystal couldn't like him the way he wanted. So Bud and Crystal were just friends for a long time. They used to go out for lunch and dinner all of the time. Then one year, Bud died while she was in Florida. She was coming home, but he died before she got back; Crystal felt awful because of losing her friend. It seemed like she was losing a lot of her friends to death.

Crystal's mind started playing tricks on her, and because of this, she was getting physically ill; she figured she better do something about this. Here she was in the depressing winter, no money, getting sick; it wasn't worth it to her. So, Crystal got smart and decided to go to Arizona, where Stacy was. Crystal put her dogs in the truck and was off to the sun. Crystal was off to a place where she had always wanted to go. When Crystal had the name of Sue, she had been to Arizona and had gotten a speeding ticket for going one hundred miles an hour. She had to pay one hundred dollars to get out of jail. This time, she was going to stay awhile and also check into her Indian ancestry.

Crystal remembered her sister telling her how her grandfather was an Apache Indian chief from Arizona, and she wanted to check it out. Chino Valley, Arizona, was where her mother was from, also. While she was on her way, she stopped off in Texas to see all of her old friends. Crystal went to visit the preacher and his wife that married her and Dave. Crystal thought Dave was still in jail, and she wouldn't get to see him. She didn't want to hurt him by seeing him, anyhow. Come to find out; Dave was dead. Crystal felt awful for him. Crystal always had a soft spot in her heart for Dave. God had saved her the hurt of being with Dave when he passed away.

While she was there, Crystal was able to stay with the preacher and his wife in their house; it was a beautiful place. Crystal was treated like a queen; she even had her own room. These people were the most beautiful in the world; they also told her she could stay as long as she liked. They were too kind to her dogs. Crystal had her Doberman, Angel, and Angel's pup; the pup was a red Doberman. At least on the road, she wasn't alone. Crystal only stayed for two days, and she was on the road again. She didn't have any trouble on the road. It took her four days and three nights to get to Arizona. When she finally arrived there, she found Stacy and Tony staying in a recycling shop where they were working. It was disgusting because there were no facilities, and they were peeing in a can and sleeping in their car. At least they got their showers down the road at a truck stop. Crystal was glad she had come there to rescue them because, in the past, Stacy always came to Crystal's rescue; now, it was her turn.

While Crystal was there, they all went to Indian ruins, and she got to see Chino Valley. She never found any of her relatives, but she figured it was worth a try, anyhow. They went to a place where there was a beautiful river in-between some mountains. Also, they went into the mountains and walked through a giant cave that was in the mountain. While they were in the cave, they found some turquoise and brought it back with them. Crystal felt right at home in the old Indian ruins. It even gave her a mystical feeling, like she had been there before.

Crystal was getting tired of staying in her car and figured she should make some money to get a place for them. Crystal decided to try to get a job dancing in one of the local clubs. It had been a long time since she danced, but she knew she still had it. So, they all got into Stacy's car and set out to find Crystal a job. They went to several places. Crystal was such a fussy person; it had to be just right, or else she wouldn't have even tried there. Well, she finally found one; the lights were just right for her, and she liked the atmosphere. Crystal and the kids went in, and she asked them if they needed a dancer. Their reply was, "We are always looking for dancers." Crystal said, "Great. I will be in tomorrow night." The next evening came, and they went back to the place. Crystal was a little worried now, but she grinned and bared it. HA! HA! She was a sensation, just like she used to be.

After she had danced, the owner of the club came up to her and said her costume was too skimpy and she had to get new ones. Well, Crystal had designed and put together all of her costumes; she was not about to change her image now. So, Crystal told them she was not going to work there; she only made one dollar in Arizona. Crystal told Stacy and Tony it was time for them to go back to Florida, where she could make some real money. At the time, Stacy had a horse, and they needed to get a trailer to bring it back to Florida with them. They found a horse trailer, put the horse in it, and off they went to Florida. They were having trouble with Crystal's truck; the fuel filter was sticking, and her vehicle would just conk out. Come to find out; it was the fuel pump. The pump was always going out on that truck. So, they put a new pump in and off they went

If that wasn't enough, the axle broke on the trailer, and the horse trailer was all over the road; sure was a good thing that Crystal was an experienced driver, or else everyone would have been dead. Stacy and Tony were driving behind Crystal in their car, and they freaked. At least they were almost to their final destination. They went to a truck stop, and no one could fix it. So, Tony called his dad, and he came to pick up the horse in his big truck. Even though they had some troubles, they had a good time traveling. They both had CB radios and were ratchet jawing on them. When they arrived in Florida, they all stayed with a friend who also had horses, and they were able to keep their horses there. All four of them were staying in a little travel trailer. The trailer was fun at first, but later it started to become cramped. Crystal was glad to be back in Florida, no matter what she had to do. People used to think Crystal had Gypsy blood in her because she traveled around so much; her CB handle was Gypsy Star.

Crystal was back in Florida; she looked up the old fortuneteller that she had seen before; it was hard, but she found her. She hadn't seen her in ten years. The fortuneteller told her all kinds of new things. She said to her that her daughter would meet a new man with the initials of J, and she did. Then she told her she still felt Crystal was a witch, and if she would ever get out of the material world, she could develop her spiritual powers. It was true; Crystal was on an earthly plane, and this was because of the way she was raised. Every time Crystal got hurt, she would turn to the material world because it would make her feel better. Dancing was another thing that made her feel better. The teller told Crystal that she would be dancing again, but only for about two years. Then she would meet a man that would take her off the stage for good. The teller told Crystal that this man would be from her past, and they would be together for the rest of their lives.

At this time, Crystal thought this man would be the last one, but was it? Another thing the teller told Crystal was that the club she would be working at was the one that she had been at years before. And she said to her that the club would be going through a lot of changes. The teller said she could see all sorts of flashing lights. All that the teller told her did come true. The teller also said that Wendy would be getting a divorce from her husband, which eventually came true. Well, Crystal took it all with a grain of salt and went on to her new life. She did go back to the club she had worked fifteen years before. The people at the club had a lot of respect for her because she was a clean dancer, didn't get drunk, and didn't hang around with the guys that came into the club.

Crystal was working hard to get herself on her feet once more; she was making more money than she had ever made before at this place. Since she was making so much money, she bought another '75 Lincoln Continental, somewhat like the other one she used to have, but this one was white with the lipstick-colored interior. Crystal was on top of the world again, her material world that is. Crystal also bought herself some diamonds; her motto became, "Diamonds are a girl's best friend." Crystal was a classy lady once again. However, Crystal wasn't doing well in that little trailer, so she moved in with Wendy and Dave; this was before they split up. It was fun for a while; she could spoil her grandchildren now because of her money. Crystal's granddaughter thought grandma was rich, but not quite. At the time, Crystal would take them all sorts of places.

One night at the club, Crystal met a blind man. He was different. The blind man's name was Joe; he would come in and grab the girls, telling them he was seeing them using Braille. Crystal and Joe became the best of friends. Joe would take Crystal and her family to lots of different places. Crystal liked Joe, but she couldn't get close to him because he had too many problems. He would do sleeping pills to sleep because Joe said he could dream in color, and this was the only time he could see.

Things were going fine at Wendy's house until Dave came home drunk; he was harassing Wendy, and Crystal told him to stop. This man was always drunk and beating up Wendy. Then he started in on Crystal. He called her a whore; bitch, dancer, and that he didn't want her whore money again. Then he told her to get out of his house. All of the time, Crystal's grandkids were crying as they were hiding in the closet. It brought back many memories of how Crystal's dad used to treat her mother, and Crystal would be sobbing behind the couch as he beat up her mother. Crystal's grandkids were going through the same thing.

He told Crystal to get out of his house. It wasn't his anyhow because his father paid the rent for them the whole time they were married and lived there. Wendy was following in her mother's footsteps, where husbands were concerned. Crystal felt so hurt that she moved out immediately. She didn't have anywhere to go, so she moved in with one of Wendy's friends. It didn't last long. Crystal hated to impose on people, even though she helped them with rent. Then Crystal decided to stay at one of Wendy's sister-in-law, but she didn't even stay there one night because they all started to get drunk, and she didn't need that. So, Crystal spent the night in her car. Then a cop came by and told her she better move or she might get into trouble. Crystal needed to get a place of her own.

The next day, Crystal was driving around her old neighborhood, and what do you think? Her old house was for sale. Crystal loved this house and how she used to lay out by the pool. Could it be real; she might get her home back? It seemed like Crystal was getting all of the things back that she had before. Crystal went immediately to the house to set up an appointment to see it. She found out it was for sale by owner. When Crystal talked to the guy, he said he wanted seventeen thousand dollars down. Wow! How would she ever get that? Then the guy said he would take five hundred dollars a week. It would still be hard for Crystal. But she could do it.

Luckily, all of her kids were pulling for her because they wanted her to get the house. Stacy moved out of her boyfriend's and started dancing again. Crystal brought two other dancers from work and rented out rooms to them. It went on for a year, and she finally got the down payment money. Stacy and Wendy helped also. Crystal finally talked Wendy into moving in with her, to get away from her creep husband. Crystal loved her house, and she fixed it up like a palace. She went to the thrift stores and brought all old French provincial style furniture. In the dining room, she put a Crystal chandelier over the table. Crystal had it real nice. She planted a lot of rose bushes in the yard, also. Crystal loved the pool, and she had a lot of parties there. In the winter, Crystal used to have her natural fireplace burning in the evenings. She even bought a white baby grand piano for the family room and started taking lessons.

Crystal was on a roll now. Crystal was even fortunate enough to get her son to come to Florida for a visit; he was older now, and his Dad didn't mind. It was great for her to have her old house back, and she had all of her kids in one place again. At the time, she could afford to spend a lot of money on them. Crystal was trying to get her sister to acknowledge her, but she still didn't believe her. There were times when Crystal would set up meetings with her to give her gifts, and she wouldn't even be home for Crystal. So Crystal ended up giving the gifts to someone else. You see, when Crystal was in Arizona, she bought a turquoises cross; that was the gift for her sister. Her sister would stand her up, so she gave the necklace to another friend of hers.

Time was flying by in her life now. Crystal was still trying to get her mother to acknowledge her, also. She tried for four years, and then finally, one day, she started coming around. One day Crystal called her and told her that she just wanted to be friends with her. Even though Crystal told her this before, her reply was different this time. Her mother's response was, "As long as that is all you want from me." When the conversation ended, Crystal told her mother that she loved her, and her mother's reply to that was, "What do you mean, you love me? Friends don't love one another." Crystal couldn't believe how cold her mother was to her. Crystal knew she had to bribe her by telling her that she would fly her to Florida to get her to accept her. Well, the bribe worked. Her mom said she would come and that she had something to tell her, and she wanted to do this in person. After all of this, she came to Florida, and she admitted that she was Crystal's mother. Although Crystal's mother never told her anything about her father, she would lie and tell her all kinds of different last names for her father. Crystal still felt it was the Italian man she was married to at the time.

It was Turkey day while her mother was there, and she enjoyed meeting her grandkids and great-grandkids. Crystal spent a lot of money on all of them. This was some reunion for them. Crystal and her mother had many talks while she was there, and she told Crystal a lot of her dark, hidden secrets. Crystal wasn't at all like her mother personality-wise. Looks-wise, her mother was short, with small feet and hands like Crystal's, which was the only similarity. Crystal never figured out anything about her father. Crystal asked her why she named her and her sister the same name, and the only thing she said was she liked the name. Crystal could tell her mother was a liar, but she just ignored it and went on having a good time. Also, Crystal's mother said to her that when she was young, she had slit her wrists because she wanted to die. She told Crystal that she used to be a hooker. Eventually, she told Crystal that when she got pregnant with her first Crystal, she did everything to get rid of her. Crystal's mother never admitted how she tried to get rid of Crystal. Later on, her mom would say she never told her those things. After their reunion, Crystal got an unexpected phone call; she just about fell off the couch. Her sister was coming over to visit her. It was a pleasant visit, but all she wanted was money.

Crystal on her sailboat

Crystal on her sailboat

CHAPTER 12

TERRY #7, SAILBOAT, JAMAICA

Meanwhile, back at the old dance club, Crystal was still dancing her butt off. One day, Crystal had a brainstorm; she was tired of dancing and wanted to do something different. So, she thought it might help to start up an antique shop, and she did, although she still had to dance to get the shop going. It was hard on her at first, but things were moving along reasonably well. The shop was a small one, right on Lake Worth Road in Lake Worth, Florida. Crystal used to buy stuff for her shop from garage sales to sell. Crystal had her shop named Crystal's Antiques. The shop was doing reasonably well at first.

Crystal was getting pretty bored and was tired because she had to work at the club and in the shop. As she was sitting at her desk day dreaming out the window and was half asleep, a guy was riding his bike in front of the shop. Come to find out; he was one of the guys that came into the club years ago. This guy used to tip her a lot of money. This particular time he rode by and stopped in. He told her he had wanted to talk to her but didn't know what to say. Crystal told him to come to the shop, and they could speak. So, he came in, they talked a while, and then he left. This guy told Crystal he would go back into the club she worked at and see her more often now that he had met her personally. Crystal didn't think anything of this man at that time; she didn't know how involved they would get. Crystal used to see him in the club and figured he was just another guy. Well, he did come into the club again. One night, in particular, he came in, and he started tipping her twenty's and fifty's. The money got Crystal to notice him now. Crystal went over to his table and started talking to him, and she found out his name was Terry. This guy was so cute; he had black hair, but not much of it; even though he was young, he was balding on top. Crystal never thought she would ever go out with a bald man. Terry was an aviation mechanic, and this fact about him turned her on. He didn't stay too long at the club that night before he left.

The next night, he returned again, and Crystal found out that he had a big truck with oversized tires. It was all jacked up; it was a Chevy like the one she had, but he was black with red pinstripes, and Crystal's truck was an ugly brown truck. Terry's vehicle was the coolest truck she had ever seen. This made him even more appealing to her. Crystal liked Terry and wanted him to come over to her house and visit her. The night he was to come over to her home, Crystal waited and waited, but he never showed up. One night, while Crystal was at work, she saw Terry and got on his case for not showing up. He said, "I'm sorry. I will come over tonight." Crystal said, "That would be great. You can see my baby grand piano." Terry said he could play the guitar and would love to see the piano. Terry finally came over, and they made mad passionate love. They fell for each other right off the bat.

Crystal's antique shop never did have much business. Crystal was getting tired of working two jobs, so she decided to close up her shop and started making more money in the club. Having two jobs was just too much for her. Crystal ended up taking another loss on her shop, but she was used to things like that happening to her. Back when Crystal lived at her dad and mom's in Michigan, she had a beauty shop there, and it went under, also. So Crystal always had losses.

One night at the club, a significant change took place, just like the fortuneteller told her. The club put in a D.J. booth and all sorts of lights; they even changed the name to the Landing Strip. The reason they decided to call this club the Landing Strip was because it was directly at the end of a runway, where the airport was. They hired a lot of new girls, and they were all young girls. Crystal was previously told that this would happen and that these things would happen, and they didn't believe her at first until they started to happen. All of the people believed Crystal now. The fortuneteller also told Crystal that her next husband would be a person she had known for a long time. Could this man Terry, be the one? Could it be Terry, the guy she saw now? Well, time would tell the answer to this new man. Of course, Crystal always wanted good things to come out of her relationships, but not too much ever did. At that time, all of her children were grown up and on their owne now, and she didn't have to worry about them. She could work on a good relationship with whoever she would be with now.

One evening, it was a full moon, and Terry picked up Crystal from work, and they went for a ride by the ocean. The moon was shining on the sea; it was a blue moon, you know, "Once in a blue moon." That night Terry proposed to Crystal. He had bought an Indian ring from the flea market and gave it to her under the moonlight. From then on, they were engaged. Terry moved in with Crystal, and they had a good life for a long time.

Another night, Terry came into the club and told Crystal that he got a job change. He said to her that he had the opportunity to work in Jamaica and make about one hundred thousand dollars a year. Crystal was glad for him, but she would miss him. Terry told Crystal that after about a month, she could quit dancing and come there with him. Crystal was ecstatic; she told him she would go there to be with him, with bells on. Is this Crystal's knight in shining armor to take her away from it all?

Terry was gone, and it had been about a week since she had heard from him. One day, he finally called her. He asked if she was ready to come to Jamaica. Crystal replied, "I sure am!" Terry paid for her plane ticket, and off she went. Terry's job was working for the D.E.A. fixing their helicopters. He would work on the helicopters looking for the marijuana fields, and then they sent people to burn them up. Crystal was very proud of her man. Crystal's son was with his dad, and the girls had their men, so Crystal would not have to worry about them. Now she would be able to do something for herself.

It was time for Crystal to hang up her dancing shoes. Crystal literally hung them up; she took a long nail and nailed the suckers right to the wall. The next day she flew off to Jamaica. As she flew over the big mountains, it took her breath away. Here she was, in the lap of luxury, and would never have to dance again. Crystal's man was going to take care of her. This was the first time anyone had ever done this for her. Terry was even paying all of Crystal's bills, also; the payments on both houses.

Crystal loved Jamaica; all of the people were so nice. There were a lot of Christians there, too. Crystal and Terry even started going to Church. All of this was a dream come true. She felt as if she was in a fantasy world. While she was living there, she got treated like royalty. They were going out to eat all of the time. They also went for a taxi ride to the other side of the island. On their trip, they went through what was called fern gully. There were places where you could stop, and the natives would describe the plants that grew there. They had lemongrass and many others. Once they were there, they went to Duns Falls. It was beautiful, and Terry even walked up the falls, but not Crystal; she was a wimp. It was beautiful, behind the motel where they stayed on the ocean, and they could go on a glass-bottom boat ride. Crystal could see all of the fish and shells in the water. The water was so clear and was such a beautiful color of aqua.

After they left there, they went to a park where they had more waterfalls and a bird sanctuary with a large museum with fish in it. On their ride back, they went through fern gully again. It was beautiful and was like a jungle ride through there. They saw the villages where people lived in tin houses; Crystal felt sad for them, but they seemed happy. The people there wore beautiful clothing, and it was very colorful. They wore bright gold, reds, purples, blues, and much more. Goats were running free all over the place, and people would invite them to eat with them. One sad thing was that there weren't many tropical birds because they had to eat them; these people were impoverished.

Crystal was only allowed to stay there for six months, and then she had to go home and renew her passport. Crystal needed to see her family, anyhow, so she went back to the States. She stayed at home for a month, and then she was allowed to return to Jamaica. After the next six months passed, she was allowed to return. Then for some reason, Terry called her and told her that he was coming back home, also. Crystal couldn't understand what was going on. One day back in the states, Crystal got a call from Terry; guess he was coming home, Terry's job was finished there, and they did not need him anymore. Crystal was very upset because she had to go back to dancing again. At least Terry got his old job back at the airport.

Crystal was dancing her butt off still, and they were surviving the change in circumstances. Then, Crystal got a brainstorm and decided to purchase a forty-two-foot sailboat. It was a beautiful boat; it had two masts, two bathrooms, and two bedrooms. The ship was all rigged out and was blue and white. The name of the vessel was Le Hair Blue, which meant the hour is blue in French. Crystal went and put a down payment on the ship, now that they had their boat. Crystal had always dreamed of having a sailboat, and this dream came through. When she was with Grant, he always wanted a sailboat, and now she would have one. Ha! Ha! To Grant, Crystal has her sailboat.

They decided it would be nice to live on the boat, so that is what they did. At that time, Terry and Crystal were paying for two houses and the boat. They were working their butts off. They had gotten a good deal on the boat because it needed a lot of work. They were happy on the ship for about six months, and then Terry started drinking heavily and with Crystal's daughter, Stacy. They were drinking when Crystal was working at night. Crystal later on always wondered if Terry and Stacy had something going on. Crystal never trusted too many people because of what she had been through in her life. So Crystal was still happy with the way her life was at that time anyhow. She loved Terry very much and overlooked his flaws. No one is perfect in life, mostly her.

Crystal has decided to reveal the most heartbreaking experience that has ever happened to her in her life. She is not putting it in sequence form, or she is not adding names or places. Crystal is doing it this way, so she doesn't hurt anyone involved with this incident. So that is why she doesn't want to implicate anyone. At one time, one of Crystal's daughters' boyfriends did a terrible thing to both Crystal and her daughter. Crystal was living away from home at the time and was very lonely for her children. Crystal's daughter's friend would call her all of the time, telling her to come home and that he loved her and missed her. Well, Crystal thought nothing of this at the time.

When she finally went home, she lived with her daughter because she didn't have any other place to go. At first, things were beautiful. Then, this boyfriend started making jokes about how beautiful Crystal was and how she had a nice body for her age. At first, Crystal was flattered, mostly because she had just broken up with one of her husbands and was very vulnerable. At that time, Crystal tried just to take it as a compliment and leave it at that. To keep peace in the family, she would give the guy complements back, never thinking he had more in his head than just a compliment.

Time went on, and this guy started giving Crystal hugs. Crystal still thought nothing of his actions. But next, he was giving her kisses on the lips. Crystal was getting worried now. She just didn't want to believe he had anything else in his mind other than a friendly gesture. Later on, this guy started grabbing at Crystal's butt and boobs. Crystal was really worried, confused, and shocked now. At this time, she just didn't know what to do. This situation with Crystal's daughter started to eat at her. She wanted to tell her daughter, but she didn't want to hurt her. So, Crystal put it out of her head for a while, hoping it would stop.

As time went on, this guy started grabbing Crystal and telling her he wanted her to show him her privates, also. Crystal figured he thought since Crystal was a dancer, she had done this in the past. She would flash him. Crystal had him do some work for her around the house because she needed the help. He had done the job, so he would tell her that she owed him now. Crystal didn't want him thinking she owed him, so she went out and bought him some tools. She was not going to be obligated to him in any way.

Now things were getting worse. This guy would come into Crystal's room when she was asleep and put his hand under the covers. He would try to grab her crotch. Crystal couldn't believe this was happening. She felt so bad for her daughter. Crystal's heart broke for her daughter, and she didn't know what to do about the situation. It just had to stop. Crystal should have stopped it way before it got this bad, but she didn't know how to handle the situation so no one would get hurt. When this guy couldn't obtain what he wanted from Crystal, he would argue with her. He would accuse her of running up the phone bill and not paying it, which was not valid. Crystal gave them money and bought groceries all of the time. Since Crystal was so sensitive, this arguing would put her into tears. At the time, she just had to keep her mouth shut because she didn't have any place to live.

Then one day, she had a big fight with her boyfriend. She just couldn't take it anymore. She went crying out of the house in tears. Instantly she decided it wasn't worth it, and she started moving her things out. Since she had no place to go, she was living out of her car for a while. At this time, she had her birds and dog with her. It was hard enough for her to find a place to stay, but people especially didn't want animals. When Crystal moved out of her daughter's, she felt so awful. Crystal thought she better be honest and tells her daughter just what kind of a man she was married to and why she was leaving. Some people told her she should say to her, and some told them she shouldn't tell her. Well, out of a fit of anger right after she left her daughter's house, she did tell her. In a way, it was good, and in another way, it was terrible. The good was that at least her daughter knew what kind of a man she was married to. The bad thing was that her daughter didn't believe her. The next response from Crystal's daughter was that she didn't want to see or speak to Crystal. It went on for a whole year. The fact that her daughter didn't talk to her about devastated her. Crystal loved her girl with all of her heart, and it was killing her.

Crystal just couldn't get it off of her mind, and she couldn't sleep or eat. She was heartsick. Because of all of this, Crystal lost about ten pounds. Later on, Crystal became physically ill. The separation between her and her daughter was intolerable. Crystal was always trying to make amends with her daughter. Then one day, she had an idea. Her daughter loved animals, so Crystal got her some little animals. Well, this finally broke the ice for them. Since then, Crystal and her daughter have never discussed the incident again. The sad part is this guy is still trying to seduce her to this day. Crystal just humors him not to make problems.

Now, returning to her life with Terry and his drinking. The drinking that Crystal's loved ones were doing wasn't too bad, but Terry started getting violent with Crystal. He would push her around and cuss at her. Terry was acting nuts. One evening when he was going crazy, he got out the 22 shotgun Crystal had bought for him. Terry told Crystal that the gun was the only thing he had ever trusted. Terry was lying down in the back bunk of the boat when he said to her how he felt about the gun. Then he came out from the back bunk, pointed the gun at her, and told her to get out. He ordered her to "crawl up the porthole-like the rat that you are." As he was doing this, he called her all sorts of nasty names. Crystal was shocked and heart-broken again in her life. Then, he came after Crystal and tried to shove her out of the porthole. He finally gave up, went into the back bunk with his gun, and passed out.

The next day while Terry was at work, Crystal packed her things, rented out the house in Florida, and went back to her home in Cedar. Crystal thought Terry was crazy, and she didn't want anything to do with him. He lived on the boat for about four months and wasn't making the payments; the boat company came and confiscated the vessel, and Terry had to find somewhere else to live. Crystal loved Terry and did miss him. She needed to move on again. Later she found out why he was crazy. He was doing some crazy drugs, no wonder he wasn't rite.

Since Crystal was back at her farm, she was having a good time in her old house. Crystal had a friend move in to help her with the bills; she rented one of the rooms upstairs to; a guy named Bob. Crystal tried to forget all about Terry by growing a garden and canning again. Terry was out of her mind for a while, but not entirely out of her heart. Crystal had to go back to dancing to keep up with the bills; she was dancing at a club in Fife Lake that she danced in the summer when she came up there. Also, she worked at a beauty salon during the day. Then Crystal decided she wanted to do something with her mind instead of her body. She could still remember when Grant told her how she was illiterate. Since Crystal did get her high school diploma when she was with Butch, she decided it was time to go to college. First, Crystal decided to take an emergency medical technician course to get some medical experience. Crystal became an E.M.T. and did volunteer work with the Cedar Volunteer Fire Department in her hometown. Crystal worked with the ambulance for three years; she loved to be able to help others. Crystal was experiencing a lot of gruesome sights, but it didn't bother her. The bad part about working for the fire department was that she was the only woman there. When the men came in for a meeting, they wouldn't even sit at a table near her. Crystal guessed they were afraid of their wives coming in and seeing them sitting next to her. Crystal thought nothing of it and went on with her work there.

One day, Jehovah's Witnesses came over and talked her into starting a Bible study with them. For about three years, they came to her door when she was home in the summer and bugged her to study the Bible. This time she told them yes, that she would start a study. Crystal became very involved with them and stopped dancing altogether. Since she was not making very much money, she lost the house in Florida. The people weren't paying the rent, and she couldn't make the payments.

Crystal got very close to Jehovah and wanted to clean up her life. She started going to all of the meetings and was very close to getting baptized. Crystal loved the religion and felt this was the right one, finally. She had been searching for years for the right one, and she was so happy with Jehovah's Witnesses. The thing that made her feel good was that they didn't get paid for their work. And, they didn't beg for money. Their goal is to teach the word of God, just like Jesus did. Then, Crystal decided it was time for more college; she started attending Northwestern Michigan College. Crystal was doing very well and received an associate degree in science and art. After that, Crystal went for her A.D.N. Crystal had all of the prerequisites to become a registered nurse. Time was moving along, and Crystal was thrilled in her religion and college. It had been about three years since she had heard from Terry, and guess what? Yes, he called her in the dead of winter. Terry proceeded to tell her that he had changed and that he went to drug rehab and A.A. Of course, Crystal was glad to hear all of this. Terry was always in her heart, and now he was popping back into her life again.

A few months went by, and Terry was all she could think about; he would continuously call her, and she was falling into his trap again. So, in February, she decided it was time to go back to Florida. Crystal told Terry she was into a beautiful religion, and she wanted him to do the same. Of course, he told her all of the things she wanted to hear. Crystal closed up her house in Cedar, quit school, and took off to Florida. When she arrived in Florida, it was a very loving reunion. The beautiful thing about Florida was that all of her kids were still there. Since Crystal had quit dancing and couldn't afford the payments, she no longer had a house in Florida like she previously had. Terry was living far away from where her home had been anyhow, so she just moved in with him. At the time, Terry was living with his boss, and it wasn't too bad at first, but after a while, Crystal felt like a burden on his boss, so they moved out.

SECRETS ARE OUT NOW

Crystal was sleeping with Terry for a month and wouldn't let him have sex with her. She told him they needed to be married before she would do anything like that. Crystal loved her new religion and figured her life would be better by doing things the right way. Terry agreed and started a Bible study with her. Things were fair at the time, but Crystal didn't like living at Terry's bosses' and decided it would be best for them to move back to her farmhouse in Michigan. Before they moved back to Cedar, a preacher married them; the ceremony was in his back yard. This preacher was an extraordinary person, but they were glad to be married, anyhow. They had a honeymoon in a cheap motel close to the ocean. It wasn't much of a honeymoon, but their sex was better than ever. Crystal felt closer to him than ever before. The love she had for Terry would always be there no matter what. Then a few weeks after their honeymoon, they moved back to Cedar.

They arrived in Cedar and quickly settled in. Terry got a job working with an elder from the Kingdom Hall; Terry never really liked the work he was doing up North. He was like a fish out of water. They were regularly having their Bible study and having a great time even though Crystal thought Terry loved the religion just like she did; she thought he was getting into it and straightening up his life, like her. Then one evening, all hell broke loose. It had been almost a year since he got drunk, and then everything blew up. He started hanging in the bars and didn't want to go to the Kingdom Hall anymore. One evening, in particular, when he was coming home, he fell off the wagon. Terry was returning from work with his paycheck, he got drunk in the bar, and someone took all of his money. As if losing his check wasn't enough, he went over to Stacy's house, and they had a party going on there. Everyone was drunk, and Stacy and Terry got into an argument. He went into a rage and punched Stacy in the nose, broke her nose. Stacy was going to press charges, but she didn't because of Crystal.

When Terry came home, he was a mess; Crystal was angry with him for doing this. She was distraught that he punched her daughter.

Terry started in on Crystal; he was arguing and cursing at her. Then, he literally was taking furniture and beating Crystal with it. Then he tore up their whole living room. He knocked the pictures of Crystal's kids off the wall and said terrible things about them. Crystal couldn't believe it. Terry seemed to be jealous of Crystal's children. He was like an insane person, and Crystal felt she didn't even know him anymore. He might have been on drugs again.

The next day, Terry got up and saw the broken furniture and dirt from the plants. All he would say was, "Who in the hell did this to the house?" Besides the house being a disaster, Crystal's body was bruised from head to toe. She had been beaten before, but never as bad as this. When Terry saw all of the mess in the house, he said again, "Who in the hell did this to the house?" Crystal didn't know whether to believe him or not. At the time, Crystal knew she had to do something, and quick. About several weeks after the fight, Crystal came up with a brainstorm. She knew Terry didn't like working at the job he had there, so she told him, "Why don't we find a new job for you somewhere else that you might like?" Terry said Crystal, "That sounds like a great idea." Little did Terry know, but Crystal was just trying to get him out of her house. Crystal felt that if this didn't work, she needed to find another way to get him out. So, they got an aviation paper and started looking in it for jobs. They found some jobs, and Terry began getting his resume in order. A few months went by, and one of the places in South Carolina called him. The people in South Carolina told Terry they wanted him, and he accepted. Crystal rented out her house, and they were off to South Carolina.

When Terry and Crystal arrived there, they loved it. They rented an apartment and started buying new furniture. Crystal even went back to college. She was studying phlebotomy and became a nationally registered Phlebotomist. Terry loved his new job. For a while, Crystal thought Terry was happy and would quit drinking. But no luck, he was getting drunk again. Crystal helped Terry by letting him trade in her truck for a new vehicle of his own. It wasn't one month, and he started drinking even more and smashed up the new truck. Crystal's heart was broken again. Terry was so drunk one night that he urinated in the closet, thinking he was in the bathroom. That same night, he was freaked out, he yelled, saying that the devil was after him. It looked like he was the devil's son now. Crystal was about ready to leave him over all of his drinkings, but she loved him and tried to make it work. Love is blind. "Ha-ha."

The next year, Terry got transferred to North Carolina. The company moved all of their furniture, and off they went. They were in North Carolina, and they didn't like it there; they liked South Carolina better. Time was moving along, and Crystal was accepted into the nursing program at Lenoir Community College. Crystal was doing very well there and would have made it through the program, but the crap started to happen again. Terry and Crystal were doing well monetarily; they had all new cherry wood furniture and a large 32-inch T.V. They also had a poster bed, which Crystal always wanted. Crystal even had a job in the hospital as a phlebotomist. They had it all again, but Terry was still drinking. He used to take money out of the handy teller and not tell Crystal, then their checking account would over-draw, and all of their checks would bounce. There were times when Terry would take Crystal out to dinner and start arguing right in the restaurant about money. Crystal would catch him lying about money, and he would say, "You witch. Are you calling me a liar?" Crystal would be so embarrassed and hurt that she didn't know what to do.

One evening, Crystal tried to join him in drinking, but that didn't work either; she got so sick and knew that this was not for her. But Terry wanted her to drink anyhow. Crystal tried everything imaginable to make it work, but nothing ever helped. Crystal wasn't going to any Church at that time; she was just drinking and going crazy. Terry was pulling her down into his gutter, making her just like him. Terry's drinking and being so mean to Crystal was making her physically ill. There were times where he would get her so worried that she would frantically be crying, shaking, and sobbing like she did when she was a kid. Crystal would have diarrhea, lose weight, and even lose her hair. Crystal was becoming very afraid of Terry.

After all of that crap, that was the straw that broke the camel's back. One night, Terry and Crystal were over to a friend's house, and the other wives were asking Crystal how she liked the bonus check the guy's received. Crystal was shocked; she had no idea there was a bonus check. Here he was hiding this from her so he would have his drinking money. When they got home that evening, Crystal confronted Terry about his bonus check. Terry got very angry and told Crystal, "You greedy witch, I'm going to kill you." He was embarrassed that Crystal caught him trying to deceive her. Terry always told Crystal he would never hit her with his fist, but this time he had the pillow in his hand and connected into Crystal's nose with his fist. Crystal got her Indian temper fired up and kicked him out of bed. All of the things on the nightstand came down with him. Crystal was finally standing up for herself, but this was a bad idea.

A little later Terry got even angrier and came after her as she ran out of the bedroom; he got a hold of her hair and dragged her out of the apartment. He was having a hard time getting her to move, so he grabbed her arm and pulled her out the front door by her arm. Crystal was in her nightgown, lying in the doorway outside, with her hair still in the door. Then he shut the door on her and locked it. After a few minutes, he decided to harass her more; he opened the door and pulled her back into the house by her arm. Crystal's hair was falling out, now. Then, Terry went into the bedroom, filled up her suitcase, threw it at her, and told her to get out. The last time he kicked her out, she did leave. Finally, after that, he went to bed, passed out, and left her alone.

The next day, Terry was supposed to go on a run for his work; he would go out of town to work on airplanes. Crystal waited until he left; she decided this was her chance to escape this beast forever. Stacy was living in the same town at the time, and she came over and helped Crystal pack everything she could get into her car. The following day after Terry hurt her, Crystal had to go to the hospital because he had dislocated her shoulder. Before she left the hospital, she filed a police report. She wanted a police report just in case he tried anything else. Then, she quit school. Crystal was very sad to leave school; she had to give up her dream again of becoming a nurse. Next, she went over to Stacy's for a while and stayed with her. She was safe there because Terry didn't know where Stacy lived. Crystal was there at Stacy's for a month; then, she decided to go up North to stay with her oldest daughter. So, she flew up to Wendy's to stay with her for a while. Crystal stayed there almost all summer; until Wendy's husband began harassing her. Then the fighting started. Crystal decided she needed to move again. Well, she ever gets peace in her life?

When Crystal was living with Terry in North Carolina, her granddaughter, Mandy, came to live with her. Mandy didn't live with them too long before she found the love of her life, Mike, and moved in with him. Mandy was living with Mike for a long time and ended up giving Crystal a great-granddaughter. Mandy decided to name her Abigail, Pretty good Crystal, only being 60 and a great grandmother. The sweet baby was so cute. It was starting to get cold, and Crystal needed to go someplace where it was warm and try to create a new life. So, Crystal went to Florida again.

At the time, Dana, her son, was about twenty-five years old and had his own house and business in Detroit. If it weren't for Dana, she wouldn't have been able to afford to live in Florida. Dana set her up in a condo, and she was there for the winter. While she was down there, she got back into the religion of Jehovah's Witnesses again. She also got a job in a hospital drawing blood. Crystal was a humanitarian and loved to take care of people. Being able to help them pleased her very much. She was a gentle person, and the Patients loved her also. Crystal was only in Florida for a short time before she was lonely for her children; Stacy came to Crystal's rescue once again and stayed with her until she was ready to leave. Then, they all drove their own vehicles back up to Michigan. On their trip, Stacy's car broke down, and of course, Crystal had to pay to have it fixed.

Crystal always helped her children out when they needed it. It was a long drive back, but they all arrived safely.

Crystal came home and stayed with her daughter Wendy, all summer; she couldn't go to her house because she had rented out. Staying with Wendy allowed Crystal to be with her grandson Davey. She had a great time with Davey; they would go for ice cream, go to the movies, and do lots of things together. It was helpful for Crystal to be in Cedar again, but Crystal missed her granddaughter Mandy because she was still in North Carolina living with a boyfriend there. Will Crystal ever have her dream come true of having all of her children together in one place? While Crystal was with her daughter Wendy, the situation became tense, and she didn't stay with them very long. Wendy's husband didn't like Crystal living with them and started fighting with her.

Crystal decided she needed to make other arraingments. After a while, she decided to move back downstate to Detroit and live with her son, Dana. At her son's, Crystal was getting a little bored, so she decided to try to get a job. She met up with a lot of her old friends like Phyllis and the girls from her old neighborhood. Then one day, Phyllis told Crystal she had Louis's phone number. Louis was the boyfriend that she had after she had divorced Barry, her first husband. Louis always called Crystal Sue Ann, so it seemed like Crystal was Sue Ann again. Since she came back to Detroit and was around all of her old friends, theycalled her Sue as Sue. So, back to Sue, it was. Louis used to call Sue his "pachino," which meant "little one" in Italian. It was thirty years since Louis had seen Sue, and they went out for a while. Nothing ever transpired because Louis lived with a woman for twelve years and didn't want to leave her. So, Louis and Sue quit seeing one another.

Crystal was getting tired of being alone and looking for love in all the wrong places again. It seemed like Crystal was always looking for men and love in bars. This time, Crystal got a brainstorm and decided to put an advertisement in one of the lonely heart's columns. She put an ad in the paper that stated, "Looking for a man that is a non-drinker, non-smoker. And guess what happened? Crystal found her perfect match, or so she thought. This man was Indian and Mexican, just like Crystal. His name was Paul; Crystal had never gone out with a man named Paul before. This man was five foot four, with black eyes, dark smooth skin with almost no hair on it; she liked that. It was just what she had always wanted in a man. He wasn't rich, but he treated Crystal like a queen at first. Crystal thought she had finally found her perfect man, but he became too possessive, and Crystal had to end it. Paul would yell at Crystal and tell her that he didn't want her to spend time with her children; he felt her time was only to be with him. Crystal couldn't tolerate that because her children meant more to her than any man. In the past, when Crystal was with Dave, the love of her life, she gave Dave up for her son, Dana. Crystal's children meant more to her than anything in the world, and no man could change that.

One summer, much later, Crystal's friend Marline needed to move into Crystal's house for a while. Crystal thought this would be fine for a short time. After Marline was there for about a week, she decided she would sell her house and stay at Crystal's permanently. Crystal couldn't believe it; Marline was trying to possess Crystal's home, now. Marline seemed to be jealous of Crystal and her home. She took over the house and started cleaning it; this was fine, but she started rearranging everything and changing paint colors, and Crystal did not like that.

Marline told Crystal that she needed to sell her furniture so she could bring her things there. Then Marline said that she would get renters in the house to help both of them earn money for expenses. Since Crystal didn't want to hurt Marline, she went along with it all. A month had passed since Crystal and Marline discussed having renters, so one day, Crystal asked Marline if she had gotten any renters yet. The crap hit the fan then; Marline told Crystal that she was pushing her. Marline got all defensive, and the next day, she moved out. Crystal couldn't believe her friend got so mad. Marline wrote nasty letters to Crystal, calling her every name in the book. Here Crystal's best friend forever had turned on her, as everyone else had done to her. Marline lost the best friend she had ever had, also. Crystal and Marline had secrets that no one ever knew, and now it was all gone over jealousies. Here it was again, heartbreak for Crystal. Her best friend now had ended their friendship; it was no more. Is there no end to Crystal's disappointments in life?

Crystal was about fifty-nine years old now, and not much is going on in her life. She was living up North in her farmhouse and doing fine. Crystal got a job with an agency for home assistance. One of Crystal's patients was an American Indian lady. The Indian lady took Crystal under her wing and brought out all of Crystal's Indian qualities. The lady taught Crystal how to make Indian fry bread and dream catchers and lots of crafts. Crystal was feeling her Indian spirit powers, now. The Indian lady told Crystal she should go to the pow-wows and make Indian fry bread and sell it. Crystal thought this was a great idea and did just that. She made dream catchers, Indian clothing, and jewelry, also. Crystal's first time selling her Native American goods was at a rodeo; it was great. She didn't make much money, but she got a lot of experience. Back in North Carolina, Mandy, Crystal's granddaughter, was still doing great with a little one of her own. Little Abby still had blonde hair and big brown eyes; she looked like her Dad, Mike. Now there were five generations in the family. Crystal, being in Detroit, didn't get to see her great-granddaughter and missed her very much.

Crystals leather fringe jacket she made

CHAPTER 13

DON THE 8TH HUSBAND AND INDIAN WEDDING AND INDIAN DANCING

On the first night of the rodeo, there was a full moon in the sky. Crystal was selling her Indian things, and a crazy thing happened. Wendy and her husband and a lot of friends were all at the rodeo camping out. Wendy gave Crystal a lucky shirt she had and told her to go out and find a cowboy. So, off she went to find a cowboy. And guess what? She found one. Her new cowboy happened to be a lot like her adopted father. Crystal didn't think much of it at first, but they became very close later on. Crystal and her new man met on a full moon; it was so romantic for them.

The next day, Crystal didn't think he would be back, but sure enough, he was at her fry bread stand again. Crystal's cowboy was named Don, and he was her age for a change. Don was the oldest man she had ever been with, which was good. Don was German and Dutch; he had a farm, horses, cattle, sheep, goats, chickens, pigs, dogs, cats, and ducks. Don had everything just like Crystal did at her dad's farm and even more.

After the rodeo, Don called Crystal two to three times a day;

Crystal was Don's dream woman. He had always wanted an Indian woman. Don always figured that it was time for the Indians and cowboys to get together. After a month, Don wanted Crystal to move to Grand Rapids, where he lived on his ranch. Crystal didn't have to think too hard to decide to move to Don's place. Before Crystal met him, she planned to go on the road and sell her Indian things, but Don changed all of that. Crystal was living at Don's for a year, and one romantic evening, Don proposed to Crystal; he gave her two-and-one-half carat marquise diamond ring set in white and yellow gold; just the one she had always wanted. After their engagement, they proceeded to make plans for their wedding. Don and Crystal wanted a non- traditional Indian and cowboy wedding; Crystal worked hard to pull this one-off. She had never heard of a wedding like this before. Since Don was Crystal's eighth husband, Crystal wanted the wedding to be on the full moon, just like their meeting and engagement. They started seeing each other on a July full moon, got engaged on the July full moon, and were married in June on the full moon, also because there was no full moon on a Saturday in July that year. Crystal was such a compulsive romantic! So Crystal was a June bride, just liked she had dreamed when she was a child. She had never been a June bride before.

Crystal wasn't into any religion at that time. She was into her Indian spiritual tradition of nature. Crystal would pray to her spirit God and thank him for her health and her family's health. Also, she thanked God for her new life with Don. Crystal was kind of afraid to get into any religion because she felt something would happen again. After a while, Crystal wanted to get a job, so she got a job as a phlebotomist in Grand Rapids. She worked there for a year and got bored with that and decided she wanted to go to school again. Crystal received an Indian tuition waiver Grant, went to a university, and would become a nurse. But because her feet were hurting, she couldn't stay in the nursing field any longer; she was 60 now, and her age was partly the reason her feet were painful. Time went on, and Crystal became bored with that and quit school.

At least she could say she had gone to a university, which she had never attempted before.

One day, Crystal decided to get on the internet and found this website called Classmates; she joined it, and she found her old high school friends. Then she saw all of her old school friends, like Terry, the one that both of them had gone out with the Italian redhead. Also, Crystal located Diane from across the street. She used to come over a lot. Then she found Margie, the one who beat her up after school. The best one of them all was Bonnie, her best friend forever. They lived far apart at that time, but they got close again and talked on the phone almost every day. Crystal and Don even went to Florida, where Bonnie and her husband live in the winter. Also, Crystal went to her high school reunion with Don. They had a great time. It was strange for Crystal because everyone knew her as Sue. Also, everyone looked weird. It seemed like to her; she was looking at strangers that had her old friends inside of those bodies. It felt eerie to her.

It was approaching the date for Crystal's wedding. Crystal worked all year to make her Indian wedding dress. Crystal's dress was white buckskin with all sorts of feathers and beads on it. Crystal sowed by hand the dress and did all the beadwork. The colors of her accessories were purple and a small amount of turquoise. Crystal had a wedding party, too. She had a girlfriend who is Indian, also was at the wedding. She also dressed in traditional Indian regalia at Crystal and Don wedding ceremony at the ranch. They had the wedding in Dons the arena. When Crystal and Don came out, they were both on horses. Crystal's horse had a turquoise blanket she had put on it, and her friends also painted it in Indian designs and a feather. Her horse was a brown and white paint Indian pony named Apache. Don was on his Appaloosa gelding named L.O. Besides; the preacher was riding a longhorn cow named Miss Kitty. The whole wedding was unique. Crystal made the gifts for the people that came to the wedding. It was an Indian tradition to do it that way. She made small dream catchers and gave them to her best friends. For their reception, there was a country band that played in the barn at their ranch.

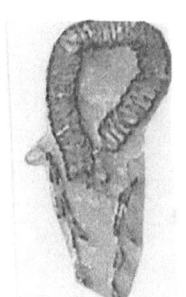
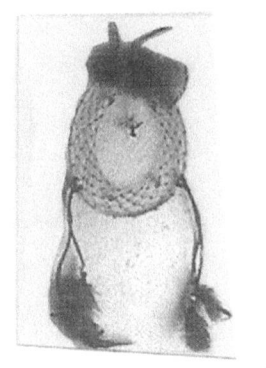

Crystals Indian Regalia that she made.

Before the wedding, more guests arrived, and there were about a thousand people there with their horses, trailers, and campers. Channel 3 was there to get a clip for the news. It was a big thing for them. They had a lot of pictures taken and even had an aerial view taken. Crystal and Don have been together for three years, and she is the happiest ever. Crystal is sixty years young, married to her eighth husband, and is finally satisfied, so far. Crystal also became involved in Native American dance. She turned her Indian wedding dress into a dance dress. She made a shawl and a fan for her dance regalia. Crystal has been dancing in all of the pow-wows in her area. The dances in the pow-wows are very spiritual, and she loves her new style of dance. Since Crystal has gotten closer to God and her Native American heritage, she has felt much better about her life. Crystal Sue has a different style of dance now. She started as a stripper and now is a spiritual dancer. Later on, Crystal got back into the religion of Jehovah's Witnesses and is working hard to become baptized someday. God has been saving her for something, and now she thinks she knows what it is.

CHAPTER 14

THE ENLIGHTENING OF DONS INFIDELITY AND 9TH MARRIAGE WITH TERRY AND HER NEW LIFE AS A JEHOVAHS WITNESS

Crystal should have known from the start that her 8th marriage wasn't going to be a good one. She gave "Don Won" the benefit of the drought and started over again. Well, here, Don goes again. At Crystal's son's wedding shower, a strange thing happened. After the wedding shower, a few people came back to Dana and Sarah's house, and then they all decided to have some drinks. In a little while, Dana, Sarah, and Davey, Crystal's grandson, decided they wanted to go out, so they did. They wanted Don and Crystal and one of Sarah's friends to go, but they were tired. Crystal was tired also, and she went into the bedroom to lie down. After a while, Don and Sara's girlfriend decided they needed more beer, so they went to the store. Don and the girl weren't gone very long, so Crystal thought everything was O.K. Crystal could not sleep, so she was just lying there; there was a crack in the door to see and hear what was going on in the living room. All at once, she listened to the girl say, "I don't want to be your friend. "Here, Crystal saw Don chasing the girl from couch to couch, telling her, "all I want to do is hug and kiss you. You are so beautiful." The girl could not stand it and keep saying, "Leave me alone, I don't want to be friends;" as she jumped from couch to couch, she was trying to get away from him. Crystal could hear and see it all. Then Crystal had enough, and she got up to go to the bathroom. Crystal did not want to embarrass the girl; she probably was embarrassed enough.

In the morning, Crystal confronted Don, and all he could say was, "It was all alcohol-related." Well, Crystal did not say any more. At that time was after Don and Crystal were only married for a month. Crystal couldn't believe he would be doing such things already, mostly since Don and Crystal were still newlyweds. Don and Crystal were living to gather for a year before they got engaged. Before they got engaged, a lady comes to Don's to sell him an engagement ring for Crystal. Crystal was so excited to be getting a new engagement ring. They picked out a 2K-Marquise diamond ring, like the one she had received from Terry a long time ago. Although the ring Terry got her meant much more to her because she still had a soft spot for him, it was prettier and more significant. Even though the ring Don got Crystal was beautiful also. After Don paid for the ring, the lady went home. A couple of days later, the lady called Crystal. The lady warned Crystal about Don. The lady said, "I have known Don for a long time, and he is not to be trusted," She told Crystal that, "All the time he was picking out the ring, he was flirting with me and grabbing my behind; when you were not looking." This lady knows Don's neighbor across the street, and the neighbor would tell the lady all sorts of things about Don. Something like what he did with his other women and how he treated his X.

Also, the neighbor told the lady, "When Crystal was up North with her kids, he would have his X girlfriends up in the barn screwing her." Crystal did not want to believe what the lady had told her. Crystal felt that the lady was jealous. Why would he do this if he was going to marry Crystal? So Crystal just put it out of her mind and went on with her slapping her, he said, "You don't mess with a cowboy." Well, Crystal showed him, you don't mess with an Indian; she gave him a run for his money. Crystal drugs it out for a long time, just to give him a hard time; she had the divorce go on for 12 months. During the ten months, she also had him pay for all of her insurances. Don and Denice's little escapade did Crystal a favor. The dirty old was a deceiving jerk and was out of her life for good.

One other lousy time when Crystal was with Don, Crystal was in the hospital with an emergency gallbladder attack. Don comes in to visit her late in the evening. When he came in, he would bring a different young girl in with him. One time, in particular, the dirty old man brought in Nicole, a girl that lived with them before. Then one time, he brought in Nicole; she wanted to go to the Right Tavern, it was a Friday night, and Nicole wanted to drink.

Nicole knew Don would pay for her beer. Crystal told Don, "I don't want you to go out was Nicole's and her sister; Her nickname was brat, and she surely was. What if I get sicker and need you?" Nicole begged him and begged him, "We won't be gone long, "Don replied. Crystal did not think it was a decent thing to do; while she was lying in the hospital needing an operation. Well, Don promised that he would go home. By the time he left, it was already 11:30; it was time for them to kick him out of the hospital. It was late. After they left, Crystal tried calling home with no answer. Crystal tried and tried, with no response. Crystal did not need to get upset, finally, at 3:30 in the morning. All at once, Nicole answered the phone. Crystal found out Don went to the bar and was dancing with all of the women in the bar. What a heck of a thing for Crystal. When she is sick in the hospital and Don is out dancing with all sorts of women. The craziest thing was what was Nicole doing at Don's house at 3:30 in the morning? All of that make Crystal wonder, did she make another mistake? It looks like another heartbreak for Crystal. As time went on, things got worst.

Later on, Crystal found out things that Don did at his bachelor party. At the bachelor party, he had a lady that was supposed to be at Crystal's bachelorette party. This girl went to Don's and then to Crystal's party. At Don's party, this girl was dancing for the men. Crystal found out that she was dancing naked on the back of his truck. Then after the dance, she went into the house for a while, with Don. Crystal was so hurt when she found out this crap, she should have ended it right then, but she went on with everything despite the crap. Another thing, at Crystal and Don's wedding; he was flirting and being sexy with other women by dancing very hot with all of them. He even had some sitting on his lap; there must have been more going on that Crystal did not know. Later on, some of Crystal's friends told her that they thought it was awful how he was acting, mostly at his own wedding. After all of that, she felt what people were telling her must have been confirmed. But it was too late now. Time went on, and things weren't getting any better. One day after they had been married for about a year, the phone rang. Crystal answered, and there was no one there, so she listened for a moment. Then Crystal heard the most shocking thing in her life. Sometimes with cell phones, if you bump the last number you called, it will accidentally ring back. So, that is why Crystal received this call, and she could not hear anyone.

 Crystal keeps saying hello, hello, and no one answered. Then Crystal listened and could hear Don's voice, and it sounded like he was in his truck. Suddenly she heard Don says, "Honey, how much do you want?" As Crystal listened, she listened to a woman's voice; she sounded like a black woman. The woman replied, "You can give me fifty dollars." Don's reply was, "oh, honey, that is not enough. I will give you more than that." Then the girl said, "Can I have your phone number?" Then Crystal could not here if they exchanged numbers or not.

 Next, Crystal heard Don drops the girl off somewhere. After all, that crap, Crystal, was devastated again in her life. Crystal was so shocked; she never had anything like that happen before. Things in their life went downhill from then on. Crystal called Don on his cell phone and confronted him about the incident. Crystal lied and told him someone called her and told her that they saw him with a black woman in his truck. Of course, Don lied through his teeth and said he has never had any women in his truck, mostly a black woman. The black woman was a shock for Crystal because he was so predigested. Don used to cut down black people and Mexicans; all of the time. Don was a two-faced person. Crystal always loved everyone and was never predigest.

When Don got home, Crystal told him how she knows about everything. Finally, Don admitted everything. Crystal asked him, "Where did you do this black girl?" He said, "In the truck stop, in between two 18 wheelers." Crystal always had an inkling of what went on in Don's truck. 'She was very wise about things. She has smelt perfume, found makeup, and other stuff in his truck. When they first got together, Crystal made Don a dream catcher, and he had her picture on his visor; eventually, all of these things come down. He must have felt guilty with them there. Crystal was seeing different signs all along but just did not want to believe it. After all of that, Crystal just did not wish to have Don touch her anymore. She was a nervous wreck. She had to go to a doctor for sleeping pills, tranquilizers, and antidepressants. Crystal had never had to take any drugs like these before. Before all of this, they had a fair sex life. Even though Don was a minute man and he was self-centered. He did not have time to satisfy Crystal, but she was a good wife and did not complain. If Crystal could not have sex, she would always sexually satisfy Don somehow. Now that he did these disgusting things, she did not want to do anything with him anymore. Crystal was so broken-hearted after all of this, she started E-mailing her X, Terry. It was soothing to know that he still loved her and supported her. Crystal was with Don for four years before he did this; it was six years together. There is that evil six again. Crystal was always loyal to the men she was with all through her life. Crystal never deceived Don, but she needed someone she could talk too. Terry was her best husband; he was a drinker, and Crystal was controlling when they were together the first time. That was why things did not work out for them back then. Way deep down inside, Crystal probably loved Terry and did not even realize it.

As time went on, things got worse and worse for Crystal and the dirty older man. This situation has made Crystal very bitter; she has never felt like this with her other husbands. Don deserves to be called the dirty old man. For a while, Crystal had a young girl move in upstairs to help with bills. The dirty old man never gave Crystal any money for herself; all she had was her money from her rent up North and her S.S, which was not much. With most of her money, she bought all new furniture and new dishes that were badly needed for the old man's house.

For a long time, Crystal has been studying with the Jehovah's Witnesses. All the time that she was with Don, she was a good Christian woman and went to the Kingdom Hall regularly. Someone needed a little bit of God in the family. At that time, Crystal was very close to being baptized. Crystal had a friend named Denice, which was her Bible study teacher. Crystal would confide in Denice all of the time; she trusted her with her life. Also, Denice helped Crystal edit her book. And Crystal dedicated her book to Denice. They become perfect friends; they would go out to the mall and go to movies and lunch all of the time.

Crystal was so close to being baptized; she was even going out in service, which meant she was going door to door as Jesus did. Crystal had studied with the witnesses for a long time, but she never got baptized before. Meanwhile, Crystal was telling Denice everything about her past and thing that was going on with Don. Then one day, Denice turned on Crystal; she was telling Crystal that she needed to read scriptures about lyres. Crystal could not understand why Denice wanted her to read scriptures about lyres. Crystal asked her, "Why do you want me to read scriptures about lyres?" Denice told Crystal, "Because you have been lying to me." Crystal was devastated again. If that was not enough about the dirty old man, now her best friend was turning on her. Denice told Crystal, "You lied to me about riding on a wagon in the 4th of July parade, and it is not time for you to bet baptized now. Crystal told Denice she was sitting in a truck taking pictures of her kids riding a horse in the parade; Crystal was not riding in the parade. Also, she told Denice she was riding in a wagon on an all to gather different occasions. You see, the witnesses do not believe in any Government events. Crystal always went by all of the beliefs of the witnesses. At the time of the accusations, Crystal was very sensitive because of the old man and how her life has been going up till then; it was more than she could stand. Crystal broke down and went into total depression. Well, Denice saw how upset Crystal was, so she began to cry also. All of these confrontations happened at one of her Bible studies. Crystal just could not stop crying, so Denice left Crystal's house.

Crystal still went to the Kingdom Hall, and what happened there was not pleasant. All of the Witnesses shunned Crystal. Mostly Denice and her family avoided her. After that, she just did not want to go anymore. At the time, she did not realize what was happening, but later she felt it was the Devil's doing. All of these things that happened to her and Denice were the Devil's trick. Satin did not want Crystal to be baptized as a Witness, so he threw a wrench in her works again.

A while back, when her first book comes out, she met a lady friend named Denice, who sees her sign in the window for her beauty shop. Her name was Denice also, like her witness friend. This lady was the first one to buy Crystal's book. As time went on, they became good friends. Denice was a divorced and lonely person, Crystal thought, so Crystal would ask Denice to come along with her and the old man out to dinner. After a while, she was with them all of the time. Crystal started to get clues about this but never could pinpoint her feelings.

Later, Crystal told Denice she needs to get a horse and come camping and the rodeos. Crystal felt close to Denice and trusted her. Crystal started confiding in her, which turned out to be a mistake. Crystal made the mistake of telling Denice all about the old man going out with the hooker. At the time, Denice had two daughters; later on, one of her daughters did marry the old man's son. Denice's girl was a sweetheart, and the old man's son Greg was kind-hearted also. Greg was the only kid that was nice to Crystal. Crystal loved all of the old man's kids, but they never returned the kindness. Denice's daughter was named Sally, and she had a for year old daughter that was a sweetie also.

Well, anyway, Sally's daughter would be with the old man and shun Crystal all of the time. Later on, the old man would ignore Crystal to be close to Denice and their kids. One day the dirty old man took the four-year-old grand-daughter upstairs with him when he took a shower. Crystal was dying to see what was going on, but she did not want to start an argument. Crystal felt that the situation was uncalled for, but she did not say anything. Crystal wanted to sneak upstairs but, she was afraid of what she might see. So Crystal never said anything; at that time, they would not have believed her anyhow.

A little while later, Nicole moved in upstairs. Things were fair for a time, and then Crystal would notice something. Crystal would come into a room, and the old man would quietly pull his hand out from the backside of Nicole's, but. Incidents like these were going on all of the time. Also, Crystal would find out things about Denice and the old man. Times like when Crystal would go up North to see her kids, people would tell her they saw the old man and Denice out in the bars, going out to eat together, and they were always riding horses alone. When they all were at a rodeo, the old man would shun Crystal and hang around Denice and her kids and neglected Crystal.

One evening at a rodeo, the old man had been shunning his wife all day. Nicole saw how he was treating Crystal, and because she was drinking, she decided to empty her heart. Nicole told Crystal, Wendy, Stacy, and Robin was one of Crystal's friends. Robin's daughter Heather was there, all about an incident that the old man did to her. You see, Nicole was in college and studied upstairs at night. Nicole told everyone that, "When I was studying in my room upstairs, Don would come up to take his shower, after his shower he comes into my room, with a towel wrapped around him. Then he jumped into bed with me and started trying to touch my private parts. Then he started to kiss me, I told him to stop, and he finally did and went downstairs."

After Crystal found out all of the trash that Nicole had to say, Crystal was mad as a wet hen. Crystal went directly to Denice's trailer and poured out her heart to Denice. Crystal, in the first place, should have never confided in Denice, and in the second place, Crystal was so upset; she said things she should not have said. Crystal told Denice, "If the old man could try nasty things on young girls, he might even try on little girls." That was the wrong thing for Crystal to say to her. Denice went directly to the old man and exaggerated by telling him Crystal accused him of trying something with her four-year-old granddaughter. Here come to find out Denice had been using everything Crystal would say against her all along. Denice exaggerated everything.

Well, all of this was the old man's way out. The old man lied to Denice, and she believed him. She was a fool. As far as Crystal was concerned, Denice was a lying, conceiving, cheating, two face, whore. Crystal feels she will never confide in another woman or trust them anymore. People are out for their selves, mostly these days. Later on, Crystal feels they both deserve each other, and they did her a favor. The old man and the witch made a good pair. The old man can't keep a good woman. Crystal was the best he ever had; she cooked, cleaned, went to God's house regularly, and even prayed for the old man. Since all of this has happened to Crystal, she was a bitter person now. It has changed her for the worst. She has an attitude now, cussing, and is ready to get wild again.

One day Crystal was trying to move her things out of the old man's house because he told her he was going to divorce her. He said, to Crystal, " we will be divorced in six weeks." Crystal went up North with some of her things; when she got back, she talked to Stacy on the phone. The old man told crystal he wanted the title to the truck, which was in her name also, and he wanted the keys too. As she was on the phone with Stacy, he told her, "Hang up the phone witch and get me the keys." Because she did not do what he wanted right away, he slapped her face and knocked the phone to the floor. Crystal was shocked and started to cry; the more she cried, the more he yelled at her. The crazy man has been cussing at her a lot lately, but she never thought he would hit her. Stacy was still on the phone and heard everything. The old man had no reason to be like that. Crystal's other husbands all did drugs or were drunks when they would get violent with her. This dirty old man had no excuse to get violent with her. Crystal's daughter Stacy was still listening on the phone at all the yelling, and she got scared and quickly called the cops. Crystal got ahold of Robin, and she came straight over, she came to Crystal's rescue. One night Nicole told Crystal and the others about the old man with trying things with Robinhe tried on her in the barn one day. All of the skeletons were coming out of the closet now since the crap hit the fan.

    Later Crystal found out about at least ten other girls that he had tried sex on. This husband turned out to be the worst one of them all, lying deceitful jerk. Crystal had never been hurt like this before. This marriage made Crystal hate and not trust anyone, mostly all men. Meanwhile, back at the old farm dump, which Crystal never really liked anyhow. The farm was like a dingy dungeon, it was dark in there, and everything was in brown, which she hated the color and her last name. Crystal tried to brighten it up, buy all the painting, getting new windows, drywall upstairs, and much more, but it did not help. The only good thing about living there was the animals. This man was so gross he used to spit on his own basement floor and pea in his sump pump which pumped water out of the basement. He was too lazy to go upstairs to pee. He probably thought it was sexy.

    Back to the time when he was hitting Crystal. The cops came, and then he told them that Crystal was drinking and on drugs, which was a lie. But they believed the old man because he has lived there all of his life. The cops were out in his yard drinking with him and laughing at Crystal. Since they believed him, the cops told Crystal she had to leave. Crystal said, "But what about my things?" They said that "Don will let you get them later." Well, Crystal had all of her antique furniture, her mother's china, and much more in that house. So she got kicked out of her supposedly home.

Finally, Robin got there and was mad at the whole situation; eventually, Robin took Crystal to her home. Crystal stayed with Robin for a long time, while she was going through the divorce. Crystal was so devastated she went into a deep depression. Crystal was at the wrong age to be still going through things like this. She did not know what would become of her life now. Robin told Crystal she should go and get counseling; it would be a good thing for her. Well, Crystal never had to do anything like that before, but she went. Crystal's doctor put her on valium, antidepressants, and sleeping pills. Crystal lost a lot of weight, which was right in a way and wrong in a way. Bad because her skin stretched and did not want to go back.

Crystal decided to go up North for a while to Wendy's, Crystal needed to be with family. While she was up there, she saw her X husband Butch; he was always a good friend. He built up her spirits by telling her she was still beautiful and one of a kind. He took her out a couple of times, and that was good for her. Butch never hit Crystal thought he was too involved with his family for Crystal. Crystal needed a lot of attention, and Butch had a daughter that needed his attention more.

Time went on, and Crystal needed to get her furniture and things out of the old man's house. Crystal went over to Dons, and there, he had the locks changed. Robin and her family decided to help Crystal get her things out. Crystal had to break into his house to get in. Well, she got most of her things, but not everything. Crystal hoped that he would have haunting dreams because of what he has done to her. Time was moving along, and Crystal was feeling a little better. She went from 135 down to 105lbs; she looked good, even with what she had been through. One day she was feeling low and decided to E-mail Terry her X. Crystal told him about her situation, and she asked him if he might want a live-in. Terry said, "Sure, come on down. I have lots of room." So off she went, back to NC. So She packed up everything she could get into her suitcase and flew there. Crystal wanted to make sure that he really wanted her and still loved her. Crystal did not wish to impose on Terry. All the time she was away from him, she knew that he was still the one for her. She always knew deep, down inside that she truly loved him. He was always a part of her life, and her family's also. Everything went well at Terry's, and she flew back to Cedar to tie up some of her business.

Crystal's family always loved Terry; they considered him their dad and grandfather. Crystal's great-granddaughter Abby even loves Terry also. When Crystal was with the old man, Crystal and her family all went to the beach; as little Abby was playing in the sand, the old man came up and sat next to Abby. Instantly Abby told him, "You need to leave, you scare me, and I don't like you, you need to leave right now." "Out of the mouth of babes" Abby knew that he was a nasty person, and where Crystal was concerned, she had no clue for the longest time, Crystal had to put her stuff in storage; she sold most of it, and she gave a lot of her stuff away. It was hard for her to give up her stuff at her age. Then Crystal put everything else into her car, even her dog and her bird, and drove herself to NC. It was a hard drive, but she did it. Terry was glad to have her there, and they got along better than ever. It was a new start for Terry and Crystal, which was a new beginning for them. They had an understanding that they never had together before.

It took about eight months, and Crystal was a free woman again; here, This divorce was her eight on, "quite a record." The old man said it would only be six weeks; she sure fooled him. Crystal drugs it out for over a year. Enough about the dirty old man; he's not worth talking about. Now her Terry, who would ever think her knight in shining armor, would be her X hubby, lucky number seven. Seven would always be her lucky number. Later they joined a bike club called the Ghost Riders. They were still going to bike rallies and having a great time. Terry and Crystal have never been so close before. Terry was the best man in her life. After about three years of being together, they got married again. They had a biker wedding at the clubhouse.

Their date was 7/7/7 and at 7oclock in the evening. They could not get any more special dates than that. Terry and Crystal have a bright future ahead for them now.

The wedding was so cool, Terry in his biker attire and Crystal had made a red leather fringe top. Also, she had a headgear with red and black flowers and an Indian eagle feather in it. They ride in on their Harley, and the preacher was a biker also. So that was a very cool wedding for them. Later they bought a charming house out in the country on 1.acre ½ lots. Crystal got her antique furniture from the farm and put it in their new home. Later on, Wendy moved into the farmhouse to take care of it. Terry and Crystal plan to move to the farmhouse when they retire.

Another thing Crystal found out later in life was, she had another sister. She guesses her mother was popping out kids all over the place. Crystal found out her name was Linda, and she lived in Texas here all the time Crystal was in Texas, she had a sister there and didn't even know it. Well, Linda was born in Florida and was probably there when Crystal was down there also. Linda's is three years younger than Crystal. She has blue eyes and blond hair; their mother had blue eyes too. In the future, they're hoping to meet finally, it will be so wonderful for them.

Eventually, Crystal started a new enterprise; it was a beekeeping business. She is getting honey from the bees and beeswax. And with the beeswax, she makes candles. She is making good money from her new enterprise. As for the Jehovah's Witnesses, Crystal has been Baptized in the religion and is the happiest she has ever been. She is going to all the meetings and going out in service, doing what Jesus did, going door to door, and teaching God's word. She guessed the reason she had a hard time before with the witnesses was because of Satins doing his thing, and blinding her, just like he is doing to the whole world. Crystal feels very bad for her witness friend Denice; she just got tricked into Satin's trap and hoped the situation does not harm her heart. Crystal understood the situation and still loves Denice. Another thing she has forgiven every one that has damaged her in her past. Crystal has a new life with Terry now, and being a Witness has made her the happiest she has ever been. Now in her life, she has a better future with her sisters and brothers at the Kingdom Hall. Her life is better than ever now, with the spirit of Jehovah God with her and guiding her. Also, she looks forward to her new, renewed life on paradise earth one day.

CHAPTER 15

MORE TRAGEDY FOR CRYSTAL AND TERRY

Things were going good for Terry and Crystal; she was doing her beekeeping for a while and getting money to sell. Beekeeping was not an easy profession. Terry was working hard; they were doing fine. Crystal was able to go to Michigan to visit her kids; she had a wonderful time up there. Crystal and Stacy flew up, that was good since Crystal was getting older, she did not like flying alone. While they were up there, her son Dana took them all over the place, they went kayaking, to casinos, to the zoo, of cores out to eat a lot. Crystal and Stacy both had a great time. Crystal loved to see her babies up there. Then it was time the girls got back to North Carolina. They were happy and sad about that.

When she got back, Terry picked her up from the airport as usual; he was glad to see her. Terry didn't look very well, but he never said anything about feeling bad. A few weeks went by, and Terry did start to tell her he didn't feel well. He said he had blood in his urine and his stool. Crystal felt that it was not a good thing. About five years ago, he had the same thing, and that turned out to be prostate cancer. He had it taken out, and of course, there went their sex life. No Sex happening to him sadly brought his morale down. He was never the same cheerful, happy guy, he used to be. Their life was never the same. He never wanted to go anyplace, never took Crystal any place before, and after that, all he wanted to do was hang in his shed, with his Harley drinking his beer and chain-smoking. Crystal told him he would get sick if he didn't slow down, but her nagging never helped. A few weeks later, Terry wasn't feeling well at all. He was peeing blood again and blood in his stool. This time it was worse. Terry didn't want to eat and was throwing up. Then in a couple of days, he could hardly stand up. Crystal told him, "that's, that, I'm taking you to the hospital." It took some coaxing, but she finally got him in the car. When they got to the hospital, they had to help him out of the car; he was so fragile. Crystal has never seen him like this before. Terry never really was a complainer. As soon as he got in the hospital, they admitted him. They started doing all kinds of tests on him. The next day the doctor told us he had ten cancer spots on his liver. That was the worst news. I told him and told him he should have quit that smoking and drinking when Terry had prostate cancer the first time. Terry would never listen. Terry was not getting better; he was getting weaker every day. On the third day, Crystal went in to see Terry, and he was totally out of it; he was like sleeping and could not wake up. At that time, the Dr. told Crystal that it did not look good for him.

The next day came, and Mandy took Crystal in to see Terry, and he was the same way; the nurse told him they were going to move him to the hospice care. While Terry was in there, the Drs were giving him morphine. They said he might not make it, and they were just trying to keep him comfortable. Well, Crystal could not talk to him, and she decided to have Mandy take her home. She was so tired because she hadn't sleep in 3 days. At home, Crystal was trying to think positively and was praying for Terry. It was about seven in the evening and she heard the phone ring; she was so afraid to answer it. So she did, and it was the hospital. They gave her the bad news. Terry had passed. She just could not believe it; it only was about four days since she took him in there, and here he was gone.

Crystal was devastated. Even later on still could not believe it. It didn't seem real. It all happened so quickly. It was like a nightmare, and Crystal thought for sure it wasn't real, she wanted to wake up from it, but it was real.

Here Terry was only 62 years old; Crystal was 78. Here she thought that Terry being younger than her he would be taking care of her when she got old. This fairy tale romance was not what she thought would ever happen. Now Crystal was a widow for the first time in her life. To this day she still can't believe it happened. Now Crystal is all alone and so sad. She was never a widow before. Crystal needs to pull herself out of her depression, Crystal never had this kind of lonely ness. Time to get closer to Jehovah; she knows he will help her. Crystal will look for a new mate one day. The next one will be in the truth. Maybe then she can have her storybook love one day. Be looking for another book to finally have her storybook ending.

CHAPTER 17

THE MEETING OF HER HALF-SISTER LINDA AND THE PASSING OF HER DOG

One day Crystal decided to go on ancestry.com to find out her DNA; all her life, her adopted parents told her she was Dutch, German, and Irish. She never believed that because she never looked like that Nationality. When Crystal got the test back, it told her Crystal was 80% Italian and 20% African. She figured that was the reason she was fantastic in the arts of music and dance. Also, the papers said that there was a close relative that is a girl. Again, her sister was doing the same thing and found out she had a half-sister. So that was amazing for the two girls. They were talking on the phone for one year, and Linda decided to come and visit Crystal. Lind stayed for five days and had a wonderful time.

Way back when Crystal first started liking for her first sister, and when she met her mother, she could remember her mother saying, "oh no, now there are three of them." At that time, Crystal had known idea there was a third sister. Now she knew why her mother said that. Linda was seven years younger than Crystal, but it did not seem like they were. Linda spoiled Crystal; she took her out to eat every night she was there. The two girls bonded instantly. They had a lot in common. They could feel lots of love between them.

Then Linda had to get back to Texas where she lived. They will be friends forever now. While Linda was there, Crystal's little dog Scooter was sick; he died of liver cancer. Here her hubby died of liver cancer, and then her dog dying of liver cancer. When Crystal cane back from taking Linda to the airport, she found her little dog had passed. Now Crystal was extremely devastated. First, her hubby dies, and now her very best friend Scooter died. Crystal was never so lonely at that time. It was a good thing Linda came to visit her at her sad time; her presents helped. There were two other times, she had felt this much sadness when David got put in prison, and when Grant left her. They were sad times, but she felt losing scooter was the worst heartbreak she has ever had. This devastation made Crystal age a lot, with all her crying, her eyes were all puffy with bags under her eyes.

One good thing that helped her was she knew that God was with her, helping her not to flip out and get sick over it. All of her Witnesses' friends sent many cards called a lot. With Jehovah God with her, she knew she would survive. Crystal will get another dog one day, and she is praying for a new mate, but the next one would be a Witness. No happy ending for this story, but she always prays and knows there will be one for her in the future. But if not in this life, but for sure in her next life on parodies earth. She knew for sure because God promised it.

A MESSAGE FROM THE AUTHOR

The best thing in my life has been my children. I have always been a family-oriented person. I have always strived for love in my family, with my children, grandchildren, and great-grandchildren. Besides, I have always sought for their happiness. In return, my children have been the most prominent love and joy for me. I also have three children, five grandchildren, and one great-grandchild. All through my life, the lessons that I have learned is that (life is a learning experience), and what you put out, you will get back. It's called karma. Put out good, and you will receive good things. Put out bad, and you will receive bad things. The main thing is to be kind to others, to have a relationship with God and study his word and follow Jesus

I wish I had learned these lessons earlier in life. I guess everyone feels that at certain times in his or her life. No one is perfect like Jesus, and we have to learn the right way to live. I have searched all of my life for love and the right relationship and never found it until now. I have looked for love in all the wrong places, and here it was their right in front of me; it is God. God is a forgiving God. He forgives us through Jesus for all of their wrongdoing. Some people think God today rules the world, but this is wrong. The devil is the one who is running the show on earth. That is why there is so much trouble in the world.

Another thing I have been searching for was the right religion. Through all of my searching for the true faith, and it was here right in front of me all along, it was in the Gods word, the Bible. I have tried every religion imaginable. I felt there was God in all religions, so many of them would be good. The problem with the other religions was that they did not go by what the Bible teaches.

The one religion that came closest to being the right religion was the Seventh Day Adventists. Being a vegetarian myself, I felt it was good that they believe the spirit of God lives in them, and we need to put only pure and natural things into our bodies; that is a good outlook, but there's more to a religion than that. Good faith needs to be one hundred percent from God's word, which means it must come from the Bible. If it isn't in the Bible, it's not true.

Being a vegetarian is a good thing. I have not eaten meat for 55 years, and I am seventy-eight years young, I am very healthy. Also, I try to eat organically and grow my veggies organically. I try to grow all my herbs and dry them in containers for my spices. We are fortunate to have a loving God that gives us all of the varieties of food, animals to be our friends, and all of the beautiful sites of the world. We need to thank God every minute of the day for all of the good things he gives us.

When I found the Jehovah's Witnesses, I feel they are the true united religion. I know they are the only true religion. Everything they do is in unison with each other. The Witnesses do not teach for money; they just want you to hear and teach the good news that we all can and will live forever on parodies, renewed earth. His word is what Jehovah has taught us in the scriptures. The Witnesses go out and teach the truth to everyone, the same as Jesus did. I would have to write another book to tell you all about Jehovah's Witnesses.

I know having the spirit of God in your heart is the most important thing. You cannot find happiness in people or material things. You need to search for God first, and then everything else will follow. The problem with the world today is that people want to control others, and they are too greedy. If all people had the spirit of God in their hearts, there would be no assault, crime, drugs, stealing, or murder.

God created us to be perfect, and greed started us off on the wrong foot. God gave us a beautiful earth for us to have everything that we need forever. We are not supposed to die. We are all created to live forever, and I plan to live forever on God's beautiful earth. God wants us to go out and teach his word, just like Jesus did. Now that I am a Baptized witness, I am a happier person and look forward to the future when I see my passed away family and animals with God's Holy Spirit; I can handle anything, and I will be able to fight of Satin's sneers.

Here are some quotes from the Bible.

(1Corinthins 6:11) "And yet, that is what some of you were, but you have been washed clean, but you have been sanctified, but you have been declared righteous in the name of our Lord Jesus Christ and with the spirit of our God."

(Revelation 21:4) "And he will wipe out every tear from their eyes, and death will be no more, neither will mourning, nor outcry, nor pain anymore. The former things have passed away."

God has promised all of these things for us, and he does not lie. God gave us his Son, and he died for us. Believe and trust in Jehovah God, follow Jesus's teachings, and we will live forever on a renewed parodies earth and be eternally happy.

ABOUT THE STORY

Crystal was conceived in Arizona and born in Detroit. Since her mother gave her up for adoption, she feels it has presented many problems. She grew up not knowing much about her biological background. Crystal is Native American, from the Apache tribe. She grew up thinking she was German. Later in life, she found out about her Indian history from the German people that adopted her. Crystal became a go-go dancer and worked all over the country for thirty years. Also, she has been married nine times. Crystal has sung in operas and was in the movie PORKY'S; she has been into her native art, making clothing. And also she is a beekeeper. Now she is a Baptized Jehovah Witness and was going out door to door, preaching God's word just like Jesus did.

www.ingramcontent.com/pod-product-compliance
Lightning Source LLC
Chambersburg PA
CBHW021423070526
44577CB00001B/37